Computational Conflicts

Springer-Verlag Berlin Heidelberg GmbH

Heinz Jürgen Müller • Rose Dieng (Eds.)

Computational Conflicts

Conflict Modeling for Distributed Intelligent Systems
With contributions by numerous experts

With 70 Figures

 Springer

Editors

Dr. Heinz Jürgen Müller

Technologiezentrum Darmstadt FE14k
Deutsche Telekom AG
64307 Darmstadt, Germany
E-mail: muellerj@tzd.telekom.de

Dr. Rose Dieng

INRIA – Sophia Antipolis
2004, route des Lucioles
06902 Sophia Antipolis Cedex, France
E-mail: Rose.Dieng@sophia.inria.fr

Library of Congress Cataloging-in-Publication Data applied for

Die Deutsche Bibliothek - CIP-Einheitsaufnahme

Müller, Heinz Jürgen:
Computational conflicts: conflict modeling for distributed intelligent systems;
with contributions by numerous experts/Heinz Jürgen Müller; Rose
Dieng. - Berlin; Heidelberg; New York; Barcelona; Hong Kong;
London; Milan; Paris; Singapore; Tokyo: Springer, 2000
ISBN 978-3-540-66799-5   ISBN 978-3-642-56980-7 (eBook)
DOI 10.1007/978-3-642-56980-7

© Springer-Verlag Berlin Heidelberg 2000
Originally published by Springer-Verlag Berlin Heidelberg New York in 2000

The use of general descriptive names, trademarks, etc. in this publication does not imply, even in
the absence of a specific statement, that such names are exempt from the relevant protective laws
and regulations and therefore free for general use.

Typesetting: Camera ready pages by the editors
Cover Design: design & production, Heidelberg
Printed on acid-free paper   SPIN 10752594   33/3142SR – 5 4 3 2 1 0

Preface

One aim of Artificial Intelligence is to model the world (facts, relationships, actors, action, behaviour etc.) in computers in order to build systems to enhance people's living. Since conflicts are part of our world the question is how to model them and how to model human behaviour in the context of conflicts. This is what the book is about and our aim is to convince our readers that it is worth attacking real world modelling problems through thinking in terms of conflicts, their management, their resolution strategies or their avoidance.

Research from several disciplines contribute in a deeper understanding and management of conflicts among human agents or among artificial agents: Cognitive Psychology, Philosophy, Social Sciences, Organization Sciences, CSCW, Distributed Artificial Intelligence (in particular, Multi-agent systems), Software Engineering (in particular Requirement Engineering), Concurrent Engineering, Design, Knowledge Representation, Knowledge Engineering, Knowledge Management, Knowledge-Based Systems, Game Theory...

Such multidisciplinary research helps to understand the different facets of conflicts, to build a formal theory of conflicts for reasoning about them, to develop applications relying on interacting computational agents that may be in conflict, to offer generic strategies for solving or managing such conflicts. Therefore, this book gives an overview of different viewpoints from several disciplines, and aims at answering to several questions:

- What is a conflict? What is the function of conflicts, both at the intra-individual level and at the inter-individual level ?
- What are the basic ingredients of conflicts? How do conflicts emerge, what are their grounds?
- How can conflicts be modelled? What are the adequate formalisms to modelthem?
- What is the influence of conflicts on multi-agent applications?

Editing a book is a complex activity and we are happy to say that though there is a huge potential for conflicts there were no conflicting situations during the editing process. This fact is due to the patience of the numerous authors of this book, who worked hard to write excellent chapters. We deeply thank all the authors for their high-quality contributions. Moreover we are grateful for the assistance of Christian Schmitt who was responsible for producing the corporate look of the book which was a tough task. His work was supported by Bruno Beaufils. His deep knowledge of LaTeX helped us a lot to get things work.

H. Jürgen Müller   Darmstadt/Sophia-Antipolis, February 2000
Rose Dieng

Table of Contents

CHAPTER 1

On Conflicts in General and their Use in AI in Particular

H. Jürgen Müller[1], Rose Dieng[2]

[1] Deutsche Telekom AG

[2] INRIA Sophia-Antipolis

Conflicting situations are not only a driving force in nature, they are also the entry points for many investigations in AI. Especially conflict resolution techniques and conflict management approaches are studied in AI subfields like Expert Systems, Planning, Design, Knowledge Acquisition, Knowledge Representation, Natural Language Processing, Game-theory, Computer Simulation Study of Social Dynamics and intensively in Distributed AI, formal models of rational action, CSCW, Concurrent Engineering and HCI. Though the research on argumentation, resolution and management of conflicts grows, the essential question about what a conflict is, remains misty.

As an introduction to the book at hand this chapter will give an initial overview of definitions and the use of the term conflict in AI and associated disciplines as well as formal modelling efforts. It will close with a summary of the following chapters.

1. Introduction

If two or more parties are doing something together, there is a high potential of conflicts. This statement is common sense knowledge, and we all know, that the statement is true even if we instantiate "two or more parties" by "a couple in love". Hence, conflicts were the matter of studies in all scientific disciplines dealing with people and groups. Searching for conflicts in literature data bases results in waste of books and papers from Psychology, Sociology, Philosophy, Political Sciences, Economics etc. There is a whole Journal of Conflict Resolution, an Institute of Conflict Analysis and Resolution, and a Center for Security Studies and Conflict Research.

Consequently, the term also became a part of the interdisciplinary studies in Artificial Intelligence (AI) in general and in the fields of Computer Supported Cooperative Work (CSCW) and Distributed Artificial Intelligence (DAI) in particular. In AI the term conflict is mainly used in the context of knowledge representation and in expert systems, especially expert systems for diagnosis.

In CSCW and DAI the research is closer connected to conflicts, because it deals explicitly with interacting parties. While CSCW became aware of the importance of the basic notion of conflict (cf. (Easterbrook(Ed.) 1993) as an excellent sampler), the DAI community focused on the pragmatic use of conflict and the procedures that have to be done when a conflict is detected, i.e. conflict resolution or conflict management. Though we could not hope for a general accepted definition of what a conflict is, it seems to be necessary to clarify the term conflict in the context of interacting computational agents, i.e. agents in multi-agent systems. We should take that task

- to get a better understanding of what an agent-conflict is and what it is not.
- to use that understanding for an application independent development of resolution and management strategies for conflicts
- to build a formal theory of conflicts for reasoning about the corresponding outcomes
- to specify multi-agent applications in a more precise way.

Hence we would like to answer the following questions:

- What is a conflict?
  e.g.: What is the function/role of conflicts, both at the intra-individual and at the inter-individual level?
- What are the basic ingredients of conflict?
  e.g.: How are conflicts possible, why do they emerge, what are their grounds (e.g., at the intra-individual level, bounded rationality, contrary-to-duty obligations, etc.)?
- How can conflicts be modelled?
  e.g.: What are adequate (mathematical) formalisms to model conflicts?
- How can conflicts be handled by machines?
  e.g.: What type of implications/consequences the existence of conflicts should have with regard to the agent modelling and architecture?

2. Fundamentals

Conflics are ubiquitous and hence there is a great variety of definitions and classifications. Though our goal is a definition of conflict for computational agents operating in a multi-agent world, it is worth to have a look at the general meaning of conflict. The usual procedure is to look in a lexicon for a first introduction. Then an overview will be given that is based on socio-psychological literature and eventually the use of the term conflict will be examined.

2.1 Lexical Sources

The Encyclopedia Britannica[1] offers the following definition:

> *conflict*, in psychology, the arousal of two or more strong motives that cannot be solved together.....Psychologically, a conflict exists when the reduction of one motivating stimulus involves an increase in another, so that a new adjustment is demanded.

Besides the definition that conflict means fight, battle or an opposing role in a drama the following characterization can be found:

> a: competitive or opposing action of incompatibles: antagonistic state or action (as of divergent ideas, interests, or persons)
> b: mental struggle resulting from incompatible or opposing needs, drives, wishes, or external or internal demands

This is essentially the same as in Meyers Lexikon[2] with the addition, that a conflict is usually recognized by the more or less heavy dispute.

> *Konflikt* [lat.], der Widerstreit unterschiedl., konträrer Positionen zw. verschiedenen Menschen, Gruppen und Staaten o.ä., der sich als Interessen-K. oder Wert-K. meist in einer (mehr oder weniger heftigen) Auseinandersetzung äussert; im Hinblick auf den einzelnen Menschen auch innerer Widerstreit von Begehrlichkeiten, Motiven, Wünschen, eth. Werten.

So let's stop here for a moment to analyse the quotations: The first one is the most abstract describing the connection of certain changing motives and motivating stimulus that change to the invocation of a conflict. So this is a definition by if-then causal relations. The others divide their definition into two cases. First, conflict between two or more parties and second, conflict within one person. They both give examples for the triggers of conflict: antagonism and struggle because of opposing and divergent ideas, interests, needs, motives, wishes and (ethic) values. The differentiation of conflicts with respect to a single unit and a multiple unit is of certain importance, as we will see later. Technically, in the case that multi is equal to two, this conflict is also called "dyadic conflict" (Thomas 1976), others speak of interindividual conflicts in contrast to intraindividual conflicts (Coombs and Avrunin 1988). Just to be complete on that matter, the Encyclopedia Britannica mentioned the intraindividual aspect too, as a special conflict in the definition of

> *cognitive dissonance*, the mental conflict that occurs when beliefs or assumptions are contradicted by new information.

---

[1] http://www-lj.eb.com for Britannica Online
[2] http://hgiicm.tu-graz.ac.at

2.2 Socio-psychological Sources

In Psychology and social sciences the term conflict is one of the most intensively studied subjects. However, as mentioned before and as to be read in almost all papers about conflict, there is no clear definition of what conflict is. Most works try to give a general definition, but then often go into classifications, structures, and types of conflicts, because the given definition seems to be too general to them. Nevertheless, as with the lexica, the different definitions might give us an orientation.

Thomas (Thomas 1976) mentioned that in a psychological context, conflict means:

> ... incompatible response tendencies within an individual.

His working definition for dyadic conflict and the basis for his models is the following:

> Dyadic conflict will be considered to be a *process* which includes the perception, emotions, behaviours, and outcomes of the two parties. Specifically, in order to differentiate conflict processes from other processes, I shall say that conflict is the process which begins when one party perceives that the other has frustrated, or is about to frustrate, some concern of his.

So first of all Thomas differentiates between inter- and intrapersonal conflicts and second he defines conflict as a process rather than a situation or state. The main contribution of his work is the development of two conflict models. The *Process Model* focuses on the sequences of the events which lead to a conflict and the *Structural Model* deals with the conditions leading to a conflict. That is interesting, because it means, that there might be disparities between two parties, which are not conflicts per se. Only with regard to a certain process the disparities evolve to a conflict. But, beside the dynamic case there is also a static one which lies in the structure of the opposing parties. The last point seems to be important for our underlying agent model.

More than ten years later a standard work for the "conflict science" was presented. Coombs and Avrunin (Coombs and Avrunin 1988) tried to structure the jungle of conflict approaches and to develop a mathematical theory for conflicts. They also stressed the phrase of "the opposition of response (behavioral) tendencies, which may be within an individual or in different individuals". Their perspective is defined by the key phrase:

> The essence of social conflict is interaction.

which is refined through the definition of Schellenberg (ref. (Coombs and Avrunin 1988) p.3) stating that a conflict is

> ... a conflict of interest between individuals, motivated by self-interest and bounded by moral and ethical limits.

On this general basis they define three types of conflict:

- Type I is a conflict within an individual because he or she is torn between incompatible goals.
- Type II is conflict between individuals because they want different things and must settle for the same thing.
- Type III is conflict between individuals because they want the same thing and must settle for different things.

The mathematical setting for modelling the three types of conflict is based on Single Peak Functions expressing the preferences and options in the choices the parties (resp. the individual) have.

The broadest, but most pleasing definition was given by Putnam and Poole (Putnam and Poole 1987):

> Conflict is the interaction of interdependent people who perceive oppositions of goals, aims, and values, and who see the other party as potentially interfering with the realization of these goals.

Though the definition is not very concrete, it is pleasing because it describes the main characteristics of conflicts, namely interaction between parties, their interdependence, and their incompatible goals, which will be essential to conflict situations in multi-agent worlds.

Deutsch defines conflict as incompatible activities (Deutsch 1973):

> one person's actions interfere, obstruct or in some way get in the way of another's action.

He distinguishes three alternative goal interdependencies : cooperation, competition and independence.

(Tjosvold 1997) notices that conflict has traditionally been defined as opposing interests involving scarce resources and goal divergence and frustration. When people have both competitive and cooperative interests, the competitive elements may produce the conflict while the cooperative elements incite to bargain to reach an agreement. According to Tjosvold,

> Conflict as opposing interests confounds conflict with competition defined as incompatible goals.

Therefore Tjosvold refers to Deutsch's previous definition of conflict as incompatible activities (Deutsch 1973):

> one person's actions interfere, obstruct or in some way get in the way of another's action.

Tjosvold then studies the effects of conflict in competitive and cooperative contexts.

Let us recall Webster's definition:

A process in which one or both sides consciously interfere in the goal achievement efforts of the other side.

The following causes of conflicts can be distinguished: individual differences, misunderstanding circumstances, conflicting priorities, unrealistic goals. Approaches to conflict resolution are : accommodation, avoidance, collaboration, compromise, force, consensus.

2.3 Conflicts in (D)AI

Quite recently the conflict theme was taken by the people in the field of Computer Supported Cooperative Work (CSCW) and Steve Easterbrook came up with a respectable selection of related works commencing with an excellent survey of empirical studies of conflicts (Easterbrook(Ed.) 1993). He basically agreed with the definition of Putnam and Pool and he clustered assertions about conflict into six categories:

1. **occurrence**, the factors that affect whether conflict will arise
2. **causes**, the specific causes of conflict
3. **utility**, the role that conflict may play in group interactions
4. **development**, the processes involved in an individual conflict episode
5. **management**, approaches to handling conflict, including resolution techniques
6. **results** , the outcomes and long-term effects of conflict

Along these categories he then gave a "A-Z" discussion of the topic.

DAI literature mainly concentrates on the fifth category. This is a consequence of the application-oriented view of most of the projects. In order to model a multi-agent world or to realize a distributed problem solving behavior for a given application, the DAI-engineers have to model the *interaction* of agents, which are operating *interdependent* together but they have their *local goals* to achieve. Hence if subgoals are contrary, the entry definition of Putnam and Poole are matched exactly. And since there should be a solution to the application driven problems, the DAI-designers have either to come up with resolution techniques in such cases or they have to manage these situations by other conflict handling procedures.

Conflicts in Cooperative Design The main application field of DAI where conflict play a major role is the field of Cooperative Design. The idea is to model the design process of artifacts as a cooperative activity of groups of interacting design agents. Mark Klein is one of the main promoters of this idea stating that: "A critical component of a model of cooperative design is a theory of how conflicts among the different design agents can be resolved" (Klein and Baskin 1990). Further he demands to raise conflict resolution to a "First-Class" formalism. Instead of giving a definition of conflicts he differentiates between competition versus cooperative conflict situations and between conflicts on the domain level and the control level. The differentiation is strongly aimed at the corresponding conflict resolution strategy. While in the competitive case the agents have to be forced to solve the conflict in the cooperative case the resolution could be reached by negotiation. The domain level conflict concentrates on the object to be designed, while the control level conflict is a conflict on the design process level. While this classification helps little in the formal definition of conflict, it turns out by some of the examples, that the main conflict types are *preference violation, esthetic versus practical arguments, and costs versus security.* A remarkable point is his work with Lu (Klein and Lu 1989) where they worked out a whole hierarchy of conflicts with respect to the design domain. As in the first mentioned paper the conflicts are centered to the possible resolution strategies in the sense of 'what could we do if a conflict arise and one side is flexible' or '... if the conflict is based on a shallow model'. However, a set of conflict resolution strategies is given and with each node in the conflict hierarchy there is an associated subset of it.

Though the aim of Sycara and Lewis was to introduce negotiation as the major conflict resolution strategy for Concurrent Product Design (Sycara and Lewis 1991) they fix four classes of conflicts:*validation criteria (evaluation) conflicts, methodological conflicts, goal conflicts and constraint violations.*

Just to round up the "design&conflict" part the conflicts in the monolithic design process should be addressed by the work of Brazier et al. (Brazier, VanLangen, and Treur 1995) on conflict management in design. They recognized conflicts on the object description level, the requirement qualification, and the process coordination level. They refine the conflicts along these different levels, keeping the application as the guideline and supporting their arguments with a lot of examples. The remarkable part is the representational point. The knowledge is represented with a rule system and so are the conflicts. In this sense, conflicts have the status of meta-knowledge. By analysing the rule set of the knowledge base searching for inconsistencies, rules for conflicts are generated and managed.

Software engineering As noticed in (Easterbrook 1991), during software development, conflicts can occur among the group of developers or between the different stakeholders (i.e. clients, erc.) involved in it. Organizational conflicts can occur during the introduction of a new software in the organization (cf. its integration in the existing human, software and hardware environment of the organization). Easterbrook uses a general definition of conflict, i.e.

> any interference in one party's activities, needs or goals, caused by the activities of another party.

In his model allowing to describe several viewpoints, he considers that a difference between viewpoints is not important, unless it leads to interference between the parties:

> a conflict is simply a difference between viewpoints, that matters.

Deutsch distinguished real and apparent conflicts (for example due to mis-understandings of the parties) (Deutsch 1973). In software design, conflicts can be characterized as disagreements among the requirements originators and such disagreements may lead to inconsistencies in the specification (but not necessarily) (Easterbrook 1991). Whereas typical software engineering methodologies rather try to maintain consistency and thus avoid conflicts, the interest to integrate different, sometimes competing perspectives on the software development process is more and more recognized. (Finkelstein, Goedicke, Kramer, and Niskier 1989; Finkelstein, Kramer, Nuseibeh, Finkel-stein, and Goedicke 1992), formalize this concept of perspective thanks to *viewpoints.*(Finkelstein and Fuks 1989) proposes a formal model of dialogue among agents sharing knowledge; this model allows to detect conflicts based on misunderstandings and incomplete knowledge. Easterbrook also considers that conflict avoidance is not a satisfactory approach for handling conflict-ing requirements. He cites the following possible sources of conflicts: typical group conflicts as in any application domain involving more than one person, conflicts between suggested solution components, conflicts between stated constraints, conflicts between perceived conflicts in resource usage, discrep-ancies between evaluations of priority. Considering that explicit management of conflicts explicitly expressed can lead to higher quality solutions, he offers a model of computer-supported negotiation, with three phases :

1. an exploratory phase with conflict decomposition, elicitation of issues underlying disagreements and of criteria for assessing satisfaction,
2. a generative phase for generating possible resolutions of such conflicts,
3. an evaluation phase according to the previously elicited criteria. The whole process is highly interactive.

(VanWelkenhuysen 1965) proposes an architecture for cooperative, customer-centered design, allowing to express and evaluate several viewpoints of a group of heterogeneous customers. Then "resolutions of inconsistencies among viewpoints are focused on the decision at hand rather than on the logical con-sistency of disparate knowledge".

Multi-Agent Conflicts The aim of Julia Galliers thesis was "the devel-opment of a theoretical framework for computer models of multi-agent di-alogue" to be used to negotiate and resolve conflicts between cooperative systems (Galliers 1989). Her definition for *multi-agent conflict* was:

> Conflict of goals and conflict of beliefs exist between one agent and another, when the agents' beliefs or goals with respect to the same proposition are believed by the one agent to be in opposition, and this agent also has a persistent goal to change the other's belief or goal. Alternatively, there may be a mutual belief about the difference in belief or goal between the participating agents, in which case, conflict exists if either or both also has a persistent goal to change the other's belief or goal.

So this is clearly a definition in the context of dialogs, which are used to persuade another's mental state or goal. Yet, it describes one category and moreover it brings into the discussion the point that in a conflict there is a power from outside the agent, which forces him to change its status quo. It's considered as an approach to influence the agent. Galliers broke down her informal definition into formal, logical definitions based on belief and goal predicates. We will go into these details later.

Aspects of Conflicts in AI Conflicts play also a role in other AI sub-fields like planning, knowledge acquisition, knowledge representation, automated reasoning or expert systems, although sometimes in disguise with other names. In automated reasoning the corresponding term is *inconsistency, contradictory knowledge* or *incompatible beliefs* is often used in KA and KR, and *viewpoints* is the expert systems term also to be found in KA literature.

In his theory of diagnosis Reiter used the term conflict to define the possible set of faulty components (Reiter 1987). Given the set of formulas for the system description, a set of observations (e.g. input/output behaviour), and the set of suppositions that a subset S of components of the system are not mal functioning (i.e. using the abnormal predicate AB) then S is a conflict set if the conjunction of the three sets is inconsistent. Provided that the system description together with the observations is consistent, the conflict is detected by the refutation of at least one not(AB(comp)) literal. On an abstract level one might define a conflict in technical systems by the discrepancy of what is and what should be (see also conflicts in CommonKADS below).

A rather technical definition was given by Rochowiak et al. (Rochowiak, Rogers, and Messimer 1994). Their task was to identify conflicts during the planning and decision making processes. They state that: "A conflict occurs when the parameter values and criteria do not produce an acceptable level of satisfaction". In some sense this is the technical premise for the definition of Shaw and Gaines (Shaw and Gaines 1994) who defined: "Conflicts are modeled abstractly as any failure of coordination, and hence conflicts may be instantiated through a diversity of phenomena such as inconsistent actions, inconsistent models at different levels, inconsistent terminology in discourse, and so on". So a conflict is a consequence of a failed coordination attempt. This is a strange view since usually coordination, e.g. by negotiation, is used to resolve conflicts. Another but more precise notion of conflict in planning is given by Yang (Yang 1992). In his formal theory for conflict resolution in planning, he differentiates between three kinds of operators: the operator *Establisher* which makes the precondition of other operators valid, the operator *Clobberer* which falsifies the formerly established conditions, and the operator *White Knight* which re-establishes to the conditions falsified by a Clobberer. Now a conflict in a plan is each constellation where there is an Establisher, neutralised by a Clobberer and there is no White Knight that defeats the Clobberer. Though the idea is developped for single agent planning it is general enough to be applied to inter-agent conflict too.

Knowledge engineering As a knowledge-based system is a specific kind of software, the previous analysis on conflict management during software development are still valid. But the specificity of knowledge-based system, i.e. representing human expertise, may lead to other conflicts due to the presence of multiple sources of expertise.

In the lifecycle of a knowledge-based system, conflicts could be detected at each phase: in knowledge elicitation, knowledge modelling, divergences may occur among the knowledge engineers or among the experts; during the system design and implementation, there may be conflicts among the developpers and the stakeholders (i.e. customers, potential end-users etc.) and during the system integration in the organization, conflicts may also occur about the use of the system by the end-users.

Dieng grouped conflicts among experts into three classes in general: terminology conflicts, reasoning method conflicts and reasoning result conflicts (Dieng 1995). She focused on a multiple expert approach for knowledge engineering in the framework of the KADS-I method. In this case, conflicts might occur in the domain layer, the inference layer and the task layer in various forms. To each problem class offered in the library of KADS-I interpretation models, she associates a set of possible conflicts (cf (Dieng 1995) for an overview). When the experts' knowledge is represented through knowledge graphs, comparison of knowledge graphs can help some recognize expertise conflicts (Dieng 1995).

Gaines and Shaw distinguish the following terminological situations between experts (Gaines and Shaw 1989): - consensus: the experts use the same terminology to describe the same concepts, - correspondence: the experts use different terminology to describe the same concepts, - conflict: the experts use the same terminology to describe different concepts (so it is a very specific definition of conflict). - contrast: the experts use different terminology to describe different concepts. The conceptual systems of different experts are compared thanks to the rating grids comparison, in order to recognize such terminological situations (Shaw and Gaines 1989).

The creation of consensual ontologies in a given community of experts can rely on cooperative resolution of conflicts among such experts in order to determine their shared knowledge. More and more tools aim at supporting such a collaboration bewteen experts for building a consensual ontology from their "personal" ontologies. For example, APECKS aims at "enabling the experts to address the sources of their disagreements and to argue with a productive end" (Tennison and Shadboldt 1998). APECKS may also "help knowledge engineers using ontology servers, to discuss their differences more thoroughly, leading to a better understanding of the criteria on which ontology design was based". Euzenat (Euzenat 1996) proposes a protocol for building consensual knowledge bases from several experts. In (Dieng and Hug 1998a), the authors describe techniques for comparing knowledge of several experts for building a common ontology and in (Dieng and Hug 1998b) they present several strategies of integration of knowledge of several experts : the tool Multikat supports this integration when this knowledge is represented through conceptual graphs formalism.

Another kind of conflict is processed in (Eggen, Lundteigen, and Mehus 1990) in the framework of integration of new knowledge in an existing knowledge base: potential inconsistencies of the new knowledge (represented through frames or through rules) w.r.t the existing knowledge base are solved through an interactive process between the KEW system and the user. This work is an alternative to the automatic approach studied in the framework of knowledge base revision (Sombé 1992)..

VanWelkenhuysen and Mizoguchi discussed in (VanWelkenhuysen and Mizoguchi 1995) conflicts that occur even in the case where the experts have the same domain, the same terminology and the same task to work on. These conflicts then could be fixed because the experts either work at different workplaces or their task should be fulfilled at different levels (at a different time) in the product life cycle. This research gives rise to the fact that defining conflicts in terms of residue classes is critical, because of the diversity of possible situations. Further it shows that the whole context of an agent plays a role when a conflict occurs. In the recent CommonKADS literature the term conflict is defined within the problem identification phase. (Breuker 1994) mentioned that conflict is a "spontaneous" problem describing the difference between what is the case and what should be the case, i.e. the discrepancy of a current state and a norm state. Where norm state might be an expectation predicted on the basis of the knowledge about the world or by a desire how certain states of the world ought to be.

3. Theoretical Frameworks for Conflict

In the following some formal frameworks will be discussed which are used to define conflicts or which were necessary to describe a certain model of conflict. In general the theories are either pure Mathematics, e.g. Game Theory, or variations of Predicate Logic.

3.1 Discrete Mathematics

In his work "On conflicts" (Pawlak 1984), Pawlak gave a formal description of conflict situations between objects.

Let X be a finite set with elements $x \in X$ called objects.

These objects might be interpreted as humans, groups, organizations or as agents. With each pair of objects we associate an attribute either allied (+1), antagonistic (-1) or neutral (0). Formally

Let $\phi : X \times X \to \{-1, 0, +1\}$, s.t. $\forall x, y \in X$ holds:
a) $\phi(x,x)=+1$ and
b) $\phi(x,y)=\phi(y,x)$

Hence the *configuration* $C=(X,\phi)$ defines three disjoint sets R^+, R^0, R^- on all pairs of elements in X corresponding to their ϕ-values.

If $R^- \neq \emptyset$, the C is a *conflict* configuration.

It can be easily shown that R^+ is reflexive and symmetric and if it is also transitive, then it defines an equivalence relation on X and the corresponding equivalence classes could be interpreted as the *coalitions* of C. C is then called regular.

In analogy it can be shown that R^- is irreflexive and symmetric. Because of the irreflexibility the set could never be transitive. However, there might be the rule that if x is antagonistic with y and y is antagonistic with z the x and z are allied. In this case we call R^- regular, too. In the regular case it is possible to conclude that if x and y are antagonistic while y and z are allied, the x and z have to be antagonistic.

More formally we have:

Definition:
$$R_C^+ (x,y) \leftrightarrow \phi(x,y)=+1$$
$$R_C^0 (x,y) \leftrightarrow \phi(x,y)=0$$
$$R_C^- (x,y) \leftrightarrow \phi(x,y)=-1$$

Axioms:
$$R_C^+ (x,x)$$
$$R_C^+ (x,y) \to R_C^+ (y,x)$$
$$\neg R_C^- (x,x)$$
$$R_C^- (x,y) \to R_C^- (y,x)$$

Hypothesis:
$$R_C^+ (x,y) \wedge R_C^+ (y,z) \to R_C^+ (x,z)$$
$$R_C^- (x,y) \wedge R_C^- (y,z) \to R_C^+ (x,z)$$

Consequences:
$$R_C^- (x,y) \wedge R_C^+ (y,z) \to R_C^- (x,z)$$
$$R_C^+ (x,y) \wedge R_C^- (y,z) \to R_C^- (x,z)$$

Up to this point we have a kind of meta-model for describing the coalition/conflict network in a society of agents. This might be useful for example in the reasoning process during negotiation. However, it describes a status not the process which leads to conflict. For that, we need to have a more elaborated model, which will be developed in the following.

A configuration $C=(X,\phi)$ is extended to a *situation* by associating a non-negative real number to each object of X.

Let $\mu : X \to \Re$ be a total function on X with $\mu(x) \geq 0$, then $S=(X,\phi,\mu)$ is a situation of X.

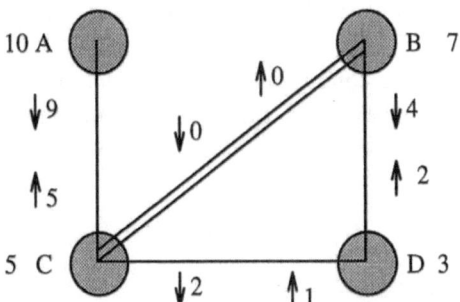

Fig. 3.1. A Situation with strength and strategy values

A situation tells us the relationships between the objects and, by μ, the strength of the objects. Since we like to know how conflict will arise in a certain situation we need an operator which transforms a situation into another. A *strategy* might serve for such an operator. In the first instance a strategy represents the distribution of strength against enemies and in the second instance the strategy is applied to a situation by settling accounts of the strength. Figure 3.1 shows a situation with strength and strategy values.

Let $\lambda : X \times X \to \Re$ be a function, s.t.:

a) $\lambda(x,y) \geq 0, \forall x,y \in X$
b) $\lambda(x,y) = 0$, if $y=x$ or R_C^+ (x,y) or R_C^0 (x,y)
c) if $\lambda(x,y) \neq 0$, then R_C^- (x,y)
d) $\sum_{y \in X} \lambda(x,y) \leq \mu(x) \; \forall x \in X$

Note that the conditions are minimal conditions for a strategy, i.e. for a specific strategy we have to precise the function. E.g. defining a null strategy by setting $\lambda(x,y) = 0 \; \forall x,y \in X$ or an equal distribution of strength based on the number of enemies.

Now, if the strategy is fixed, that is the objects forces are divided w.r.t. the enemies, then the strategy can be applied by transforming the current situation.

Let $S=(X,\phi,\mu)$ be a situation and let λ be a strategy for S, then the situation $S_\lambda=(X_\lambda,\phi_\lambda,\mu_\lambda)$ is derived by realization of λ, such that:

a) $\mu_\lambda(x) = \mu(x) = \sum_{y \in X} \lambda$ (x,y)
b) $X_\lambda = \{x \in X \; || \; \mu_\lambda(x) \; 0\}$
c) $\phi_\lambda = \phi_{|X_\lambda \times X_\lambda}$

Note that for every situation S there is a strategy λ, s.t. S_λ is conflictless. The other way around is not true. Yet, if S_λ is conflictless we call λ a *maximal strategy* in S.

So now we got the first step toward generating conflict situations. In recognizing that a conflictless situation could never been transformed into a conflict situation with the current framework, it is necessary to introduce another concept. In some sense there must be a reason for a possible conflict, a *capture*. The idea is that the capture increases the strength of an object if it is a winner.

Let $S=(X,\phi,\mu)$ be a conflictless situation, let λ be a strategy for S, and let $\wp$ be a non-negative real number (the capture), then the situation $S_\lambda^\wp=(X_\lambda^\wp,\phi_\lambda^\wp,\mu_\lambda^\wp)$ is derived by realization of λ relative to capture $\wp$, such that:

a) $X_\lambda^\wp = X$

b) $\phi_\lambda^\wp = \phi$

c) $\mu_\lambda^\wp(x) = \mu(x) + \dfrac{\mu(x)}{\sum_{x \in X} \mu(x)} * \wp$

If S would be a conflict situation and λ a maximal strategy, then:

a) $X_\lambda^\wp = X_\lambda$

b) $\phi_\lambda^\wp = \phi_{|X_\lambda^\wp \times X_\lambda^\wp}$

c) $\mu_\lambda^\wp(x) = \begin{cases} \mu(x) & \text{if x is not involved in a conflict} \\ \mu_\lambda(x) + \dfrac{\mu_\lambda(x)}{\sum_{y \in X_\lambda^+} \mu(y)} * \wp & \text{if } x \in X_\lambda^+ \text{ the set of winners} \end{cases}$

With this definition the capture is distributed in proportion to the strength of each object (in the non-conflict case) and the winners respectively in the conflict case.

An object can change the situation by updating its relations to other objects via ϕ. An object would do so if its part of the capture would get bigger. Formally:

A situation $S=(X,\phi,\mu)$ is *better* for $x \in X$ w.r.t. a capture $\wp$ than a situation $S'=(X,\phi',\mu)$, if $\forall\lambda'$ maximal for S $'\exists\lambda$ maximal for S, such that $\mu_\lambda^\wp(x) > \mu_{\lambda'}^\wp(x)$.

A situation S is unstable if there is a situation S' and a caption $\wp$, such that S' is better than S for some $x \in X_S$.

Using this framework the main theorem of Pawlak is:

For every unstable conflictless situation $S=(X,\phi,\mu)$, there exists a conflict situation $S'=(X,\phi',\mu)$, such that S' is better than S for every $x \in X_\lambda^+$, w.r.t. every $\wp > \sum_{x \in X} \mu(x)$

3.2 Single Peaked Preference Functions

Coombs and Avrunin defined conflict as a situation in which a choice must be made in absence of dominance and based their three-typed model of conflict on the mathematical notion of single peaked preference functions (Coombs and Avrunin 1988). The idea is that the individual needs a notion of options and a corresponding utility or preference to make a decision. If there is no dominating preference a conflict must eventually occur. The options are vectors of elementary elements which have to be measurable and which are either increasingly desirable or increasingly undesirable. The preference function then gives us an ordering on the options, such that if an increasingly desirable element increases then the preference function increases and if an increasingly undesirable element increases, then the preference function decreases. Moreover, if we fix all elementary components but one, say x, and compute the corresponding preference functions along the values x, then if x is increasingly desirable, the preference functions should flatten for higher values, and if x is increasingly undesirable, then the preference function should be steep for high values. Coombs and Avrunin said that the preference function should be governed by the psychological principals that good things statiate and bad things escalate. This idea leads to the following formal definition:

A function $f:\Re^n \to \Re$ is a *proper preference function* for a set of options $S \subseteq \Re^n$ iff
a) all its first-order derivatives f_i exists
b) if the i-th elemental component is increasingly desirable , then
$$\forall j \forall x_i < y_i : x_j \le y_j \to f_i(x_1, ..., x_n) > f_i(y_1, ..., y_n) > 0$$
c)if the i-th elemental component is increasingly undesirable , then
$$\forall j \forall x_i < y_i : x_j \le y_j \to 0 > f_i(x_1, ..., x_n) > f_i(y_1, ..., y_n)$$

A proper preference function f is *single peaked* with respect to an ordering $\prec$ on the options, if there is no ordered triple $a \prec b \prec c$, such that $f(a) > f(b)$ and $f(c) > f(b)$. Figure 3.2 shows a single peak function.

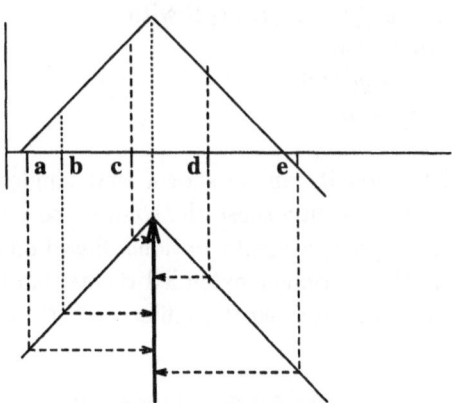

Fig. 3.2. A Single Peak Function

This means that in the corresponding curve there is no sink. Either the values increase up to the peak or (after the peak) they decrease monotonically. A real conflict occurs exactly on the peak. If an agent has to choose one of the options with current peak values, then it is in a conflict since each decision leads to a worse utility. Other conflicts (choices) could be resolved, because the preference function always shows the best choice. In general, in a case where each step leads to a worse situation, a set of possible options fulfils the pareto optimality condition. Or positively formulated, a set of options is pareto optimal if there is no dominating option, i.e. each option is better than another in some respect.

A set $S \subset \Re^n$ of options is *pareto optimal* if $\forall((x_1, ..., x_n)$, $(y_1, ..., y_n) \in S$, at least one of the following conditions hold:
a) $\exists i, i'$ indices of increasingly desirable components,
such that $x_i < y_i$ and $x_{i'} > y_{i'}$
b) $\exists j, j'$ indices of increasingly undesirable components,
such that $x_j < y_j$ and $x_{j'} > y_{j'}$
c) $\exists i, j$ indices of an increasingly desirable component and of an increasingly undesirable component respectively, such that
$x_i > y_i$ and $x_j > y_j$ or
$x_i < y_i$ and $x_j < y_j$

Note that the definition does not require a special ordering on the elementary components, i.e. desirable and undesirable components are mixed and hence it is hard to build a "nice" preference function. This could be solved if the options are ordered the same or reversed on every elemental component and that the relative increment on each desired component never increase in proportion to the decrements on each undesired component.

An *efficient set* is a subset $S \subset \Re^n$ ($n \geq 2$) together with a partition of $1, ..., n$ into nonempty subsets I_1, I_2 such that:
a) $\forall((x_1, ..., x_n), (y_1, ..., y_n) \in S$:
$(\exists i : x_i < y_i$ iff $\forall j : x_j < y_j)$ and
$(\exists i \in I_1 : x_i < y_i$ iff $\exists j \in I_2 : x_j < y_j)$
b) $\forall((x_1, ..., x_n), (y_1, ..., y_n), (z_1, ..., z_n) \in S$ with
$x_1 < y_1 < z_1 \exists c > 0$, such that
$\forall i \in I_1 : c(y_i - x_i) \geq z_i - y_i$ and
$\forall j \in I_2 : c(y_j - x_j) \geq z_j - y_j$

Based on this definition it can be shown that single peaked functions exists for any efficient set. So in a sense the solution to intra-agent conflicts lies in the proper ordering of the agents' options. Based on the mathematical framework of single peak functions a extended theory can then be developed to a formalism for handling inter-agent conflicts. (cf. (Coombs and Avrunin 1988))

3.3 Logic of Beliefs

Julia Galliers proposed in her thesis (Galliers 1989) an extension to Cohen and Levesque's logic of beliefs. The main assumption is that a conflict between two agents is either a goal conflict or a belief conflict represented in a proposition:

$(CONFLICT\ x\ y\ p) =$
$(B - CONFLICT\ x\ y\ p) \lor (G - Conflict\ x\ y\ p)$

Both types of conflict can be further classified as being subjective conflict or mutually known conflicts:

$(B - CONFLICT\ x\ y\ p) =$
$(B - CONF - I\ x\ y\ p) \lor (B - Confl - M\ x\ y\ p)$
$(G - CONFLICT\ x\ y\ p) =$
$(G - CONF - I\ x\ y\ p) \lor (G - Confl - M\ x\ y\ p)$

The subjective belief conflict is defined on the basis that it is assumed that the other agent beliefs an opposite proposition and that it should correct his belief.

$(B - CONFL - I\ x\ y\ p) =$
$(BEL\ x\ p) \land (BEL\ x\ (BEL\ y\ \neg p)) \land$
$(PR - GOAL\ x(BEL\ y\ p)\ q)$

The PR-GOAL states that x will give up its goal that y should belief p only if the goal is achieved or impossible to achieve or q becomes false. In analogy the subjective goal conflict is defined with respect to goals rather than beliefs:

$(G - CONFL - I\ x\ y\ p) =$
$(GOAL\ x\ \Diamond p) \land (GOAL\ x(GOAL\ y\ \Diamond \neg p)) \land$
$(PR - GOAL\ x(GOAL\ y\ \Diamond p)\ q)$

The mutually conflicts are the generalization of the subjective ones. So the agents know that they have opposite believes and they have the mutual goal to change the others belief:

$(B - CONFL - M\ x\ y\ p) =$
$(BMB\ x\ y((BEL\ x\ p) \land (BEL\ y\ \neg p))) \land$
$((PR - GOAL\ x(BEL\ y\ p)\ q) \lor (PR - GOAL\ y(BEL\ x\ \neg p)\ q)))$

The BMB predicate stands for "it is mutual believed that".

$(G - CONFL - Mxyp) =$
$(BMB\ x\ y((GOAL\ x\ \Diamond p) \land (GOAL\ y\ \Diamond \neg p)) \land$
$((PR - GOAL\ x(GOAL\ y\ \Diamond p)\ q)\ \lor$
$(PR - GOAL\ y(GOAL\ x\ \Diamond \neg p)\ q)))$

4. Plan of the book

In the previous sections we gave a brief overview on the use of the notion of conflict within AI and we tried to give an introduction to formal modelling approaches. In this last section we will give a brief overview to the chapters of the book. The chapters divide into 3 general parts:

1. Formal Conflict Models and their Use in Agent Communication
2. Conflicts in Concurrent Engineering and Design
3. From Conflicts to Cooperation via Negotiation and Reasoning.

Part I: Formal Conflict Models and their Use in Agent Communication

- a) *Conflict Ontology* by C. Castelfranchi, identifies various types of conflicts and gives a classification of the conflict types. The main emphasis is to work out the relationship between mental conflicts of one agent and social conflicts within a group of agents.
- b) *Modeling Conflict Resolution Dialogs* by F. de Rosis et al. uses a logic of belief in order to model conflicts between deliberative agents. The logic is used to model the conflict resolution process in terms of a dialog between the agents.
- c) *Managing Conflicts in Reflective Agents* by F. M. T. Brazier and J. Treur proposes a structure for reflective agents and exploits reflective reasoning for managing conflicts among such agents.
- d) *Difference: a key to enrich knowledge. Concepts and Model.* by L. Chaudron and C. Tessier presents formal tools for knowledge representation and cooperation and conflict management among cognitive agents.
- e) *Detecting Temporal Agent Conflicts* by L. Ekenberg and P. Johannesson presents a model for analysis of temporal conflicts among autonomous agents.

Part II: Conflicts in Concurrent Engineering and Design

- a) *Conflict Management in Concurrent Engineering* by N. Matta discusses several types of conflicts in Concurrent Engineering. The aim is to work out generic methods for conflict management, which then can be associated with concurrent engineering subtasks to support the general design process.
- b) *Modelling Conflicts Between Agents in a Design Context* by D.C. Brown uses fine-grained agents to represent design knowledge. By this model conflicts in the design process can be made explicit and sophisticated conflict resolution and management strategies can be applied.
- c) *Conflict Management as Part of an Integrated Exception Handling Approach* by M. Klein, views collaborative design as an instance of the more general coordination technology. Within the coordination technology the re-engineering of the work processes plays a central role. The redefinition of the processes is triggered by exceptions, which include various types of

conflicts. Hence, conflict management strategies are essentially exception handling methods.

Part III:From Conflicts to Cooperation via Negotiation and Reasoning

- a) *Handling Conflicts in Distributed Assessment Situations* by K. C. Ranze, H. J. Muller, O. Hollman and O. Herzog presents an agent-based approach to support a group of experts for finding a common evaluation for several assessment objects.
- b) *The Iterated Lift Dilemma: How to Establish Meta-Cooperation with your Opponent* by J.-P. Delahaye, P. Mathieu, and B. Beaufils uses a variation of the famous Prisoner's Dilemma to show how confronting situations may be resolved via probabilistic reasoning.

5. Conclusion

Conflict modelling opens the view for the essentials: In developing AI systems for real applications, the use of the concept of conflicts gives the designer a new perspective to the problem at hand. Interdependencies between parts of the solution can be precisely described and critical parts can be resolved.

Conflict handling is a general technology: Incorporating conflict management and conflict resolution strategies into a knowledge based system provides the system with a technology that makes the system robust against unforeseen situations. Since the techniques are general they'll work even in cases the designer has not considered.

Conflict models are third order design concepts for intelligent agents: Agents which are provided with conflict models and conflict handling strategies are more flexible when being thrown into a unknown multi agent world. The models are developed in the third design phase of an agent and they are built on top of the agent's communication and local planning abilities together with the multi agent planning modules. Hence, they are essentials to the most sophisticated behaviour of an agent.

Conflict models provide analytic tools for distributed activities: Distributed systems are difficult to evaluate. Formal models of conflicting situations can serve as a basis to calculate future states of the system and they can show the development of the system towards stable, conflict-free states.

Acknowledgements

The main parts of this chapter were prepared during a sabbatical stay of the first author at the ACACIA group, INRIA Sophia Antipolis. He would like to thank the whole group for the inspiring weeks and the stimulating discussions.

CHAPTER 2

Conflict Ontology

C. Castelfranchi

Institute of Psychology, Italian National Research Council, Rome

In this work a goal-based notion of conflict is presented. Various kinds of conflict, including meta-level conflict, are identified. Psychological conflicts are distinguished from "internal" ones, and Lewin's famous typology is reconsidered. Internal conflict and choice are disentangled. Social conflict, tendency to hostility and aggression are explained on the basis of competition relations. General principles and processes of both internal and social conflict resolution are presented, and a theory of "compromises" is outlined.

1. Conflict is a Form of Sociality

Conflict should be conceived of just as a form of sociality and interaction. Too frequently "sociality" is identified with "cooperation", or with "pro-social behavior". On the contrary, competition, conflict, and hostility are one of the sources (and a very important and autonomous source) of social relations and actions (Castelfranchi 1992; Conte and Castelfranchi 1995).

Conflictual behavior is not only interesting in social or evolutionary theory, but could be interesting also in DAI applications. In fact, cooperation is just one way for improving the performance of a bunch of systems acting in a common world. Competition and then selection of the best results can be another way to exploit diversity and society. In a sense, for example, the Contract Net model exploits also competition: on one side, it incorporates "cooperation" (the bidders are normally "benevolent", willing to help), but on the other side, it is based on competition and selection among several bidders. If we suppose that this competition could improve the performance or increase the offer of the concurrent bidders, we will have a stronger effect of competition on the quality and convinience of the solution.

Conflicts are important not only for conflict resolution or for improving (sometimes) groups and organizations' results (Galliers 1990). They are important *per se*. However, the study of conflict in AI and Cognitive Modelling is at its beginning. Both an ontology of conflicts and its formalization are needed; a cognitive model is needed of their place in the architecture of reactive or deliberative agents; and a formal model of conflicts in interactions.

All this cannot be accomplished ignoring what has been done in psychology, sociology, political science, etc. So, it is a long run work.

In this chapter I just attempt to give some contribution to a core aspect of conflict theory: *the relationship between intra-agent (mental) conflicts and inter-agent (social) conflicts.*

I try to clarify (in a pre-formal way) some basic notions, to establish some general principles, and to make some predictions about these relationships, for example, explaining how the solution of inter-agent conflicts can be based on the creation and solution of a mental conflict.

2. Basic Notions

I assume that:

2.1 *Conflicts exist only in relation to goals, then with true agents (goal-oriented systems).* The notion of conflict presupposes the notion and the existence of goals.

There are no real "conflicts" (but just oppositions, contrasts, etc.) *between mere forces* (when we use "conflict" in such cases, we are just animating physical forces).

When there is a conflict, it is a conflict between two goals.

By "goal" I mean a mental representation of a world state or process that is *candidate for*:

- *controlling* and *guiding* the action thanks to repeated tests of the action's expected or actual results against the representation itself (so it is a *potential* intention);

    - being object of *decisions* (including the decision to do nothing);

    - determining the action search and selection;

    - qualifying its success (and thereby the reward) or failure;

    - determining what is *positive* or *negative* for an agent, what is expected or avoided by it; what is its *utility*.

Thus "goal" is not only something one actively tries to bring about (intention), but for example also something that one is anxiously waiting for and that will hopefully be realized by natural events or by another agent (Castelfranchi 1997). And also something that one is simply taking into account as a possible objective to be pursued but that might be non-preferred and abandoned.

"Goal" is the general class of motivational attitudes and representations. There are several types of goal either according to the level of processing (from vague wishes to executive intentional actions) (Castelfranchi 1996; Bell 1995), or the hierarchical structure (end-goals vs. instrumental goals or means), or other specific cognitive and social conditions: interests, duties, obligations, positive expectations, hopes, aspirations, plans, etc. are or imply goals. There may be conflicts between all these kinds of goal: between hopes and duties, between needs and plans, between interests and values, etc.; some choice may be required among them, and there will be differences of value, and hierarchies, etc. These common features are one of the reasons for a general theory and a general notion of "goal".

Some of these notions start to be formalized in AI, in particular within the BDI approach (Cohen and Levesque 1990; Bell 1995; Rao and Georgeff 1991; van Linder,van der Hoek and Meyer 1995; Conte and Castelfranchi 1995), and this give us the possibility of a bit more precise analysis of conflicts.[1]

2.2 Even when addressing *"epistemic" conflict* (a conflict between two beliefs, inferences, opinions, etc.) I am always implying that *the conflict is in fact between the goal/decision of believing p and the goal of Not believing p* (or believing Not p); and there is such a conflict between the belief that p and the belief that Not p, only *because of a meta-goal of having coherent/consistent beliefs* within a given context or between some contexts!

Anyway, in this chapter I will mainly address Goal conflict.

3. Intrinsic (Analytic) vs Extrinsic; Direct vs Indirect; Explicit vs Implicit

There are several kinds of conflict: intrinsic (analytic) vs extrinsic; direct vs indirect; explicit vs implicit. We use "implicit" and "explicit" in Levesque's sense (Levesque 1984), applying the notion both to beliefs and goals.

Conflicts are "intrinsic" or "analytical" when the two propositions (that are object of the goals or beliefs) are logically inconsistent.

I call *direct* and *explicit* conflict, a conflict between two goals or beliefs that are explicit and whose object-propositions are directly contradictory:
Let me use the following (simplistic) notation just for the sake of brevity.

---

1 As I said, when I use in the text the term "goal" it can be taken as referring to a broad family of motivational mental attitudes, however, the predicate Goal in the formula can be seen as more specific and well defined: it represents a specific sub-type of this class as it is used - with non identical formal definitions- in current BDI logics (for ex. in Cohen and Levesque, 1990; Bell, 1995; Rao and Georgeff, 1991; van der Linder, van der Hoek, Meyer, 1995). What I claim about conflicts is general -it may be applied to notions like needs or interests or aspirations (that have not yet been formalized)- but it holds also for the already formalized notions of Desires, Goals, and Intentions.

(Goal/Bel x p) 3 (Goal/Bel x (Not p)) [2]

A *direct* and *implicit* conflict is a conflict between two goals or beliefs that are directly contradictory and at least one of them is implicit.

An *indirect* and *explicit* conflict is a conflict between two goals or beliefs that are explicit and indirectly contradictory. Two beliefs are indirectly contradictory when there is a "crucial belief" that asserts that the one implies [3] the opposite of the other:

(Goal/Bel x p) 3 (Goal/Bel x q) [3]

(Bel x (p 2 Not q))   *<crucial belief>*

A *indirect* and *implicit* conflict is a conflict between two goals or beliefs that are indirectly contradictory and at least one of them or the "crucial belief" is implicit.

Implicit goals or beliefs are just "potential": they cannot have effects on the mind (for example conflicting with other goals or beliefs) until they are explicit. *Implicit goals or beliefs create only "potential" conflicts.*

It is possible that the instantiation/specification of two goals that are not in conflict generates two conflicting goals.

Contradiction (direct or indirect) between the object-propositions, and explicitness are just two necessary conditions for belief or goal conflicts, but they are not sufficient at least for internal conflicts (see later). For additional conditions see 5. and 7.

As I said, when the two object propositions are logically inconsistent, conflicts are "intrinsic" or "analytical". But conflicts can also be due to accidental, practical reasons. In this case, the two propositions p and q that are objects respectively of *goal G1 and goal G2 are not logically contradictory*. However, the chosen plan or action for G1 requires the use of certain resources while the chosen plan or action for *G2 requires the use of the same resources*, and these *resources are "scanty"* i.e. if one uses them for G1 s/he cannot use them also for G2, and viceversa. Goals

---

2 Conflict holds only between propositional attitudes of the same kind: (Bel x p) 3 (Goal x (Not p)) is not a conflict: it is a mismatch and it may be a frustration (Miceli and Castelfranchi, 1997). For the sake of brevity I wrote (Goal/Bel x p) 3 (Goal/Bel x q): this means (Goal x p) 3 (Goal x q), or (Bel x p) 3 (Bel x q); but not (Goal x p) 3 (Bel x q), or (Bel x p) 3 (Goal x q).

3 One might generalise this notion meaning by "implies" that one proposition may be derived from the other -through some inference rule- without remaining limited by the material implication that I use in the formula.

are incompatible because of their respective means (plans, actions), which are incompatible because of the required resources.

Any extrinsic -non analytical- goal conflict is resource based. Any resource-based (extrinsic) goal conflict can be reduced to an analytical conflict: in the sense that an analytical conflict will be derived in the decision process starting from a *resource-based conflict.*

In fact, given the practical incompatibility between G1 and G2, from G1 one derives the goal of not pursuing G2 (and viceversa). Now, between G1 and the (Goal x (Not (G1))) there is an intrinsic reflection conflict (see 4.1.).

4. Reflection and Conflicts

It is possible to have conflicts between different reflection layers. Let just stress the two basic cases:

Reflection Conflict:

(Goal/Bel x p) 3

(Goal/Bel x (Not (Goal/Bel x p)))

(Goal/Bel x p) 3

(Goal/Bel x (Goal/Bel x (Not p))) [4]

Metacognitive-Conflict:

(Goal/Bel x (Goal/Bel x p)) 3

(Goal/Bel x (Not (Goal/Bel x p)))

In this perspective, the Beliefs/Epistemic Conflicts (2.2.) can be considered just as a sub-kind of Metacognitive-Conflicts.

At the social level, there are two kinds of "social conflict":

a) *Same-level conflict*:

(Goal x p) 3 (Goal y (Not p))

b) Impinging Conflict (or Influence Conflict):

---

4 Of course these kinds of conflict between beliefs depend on the kind and level of "introspection" one assumes in the agent.

(Goal x (Goal y p)) 3 (Goal y (Not p))

Frequently *Same-level conflicts* evolve in *Influence conflicts* (see 8. and 10.): agents try to change the minds of the other agents. [5]

5. Internal, Social, and Psychological Conflicts

Conflicting goals (as well as conflicting beliefs) can belong to either one and the same agent, or to two different agents.

Let's call "Internal or Intra-agent conflict" the first case: a conflict between two goals (or beliefs) of the same agent.

Let's call "External or Inter-agent conflict" a conflict between the goals (or beliefs) of two agents.

A special kind of "Internal conflict" is the "psychological conflict".
Psychological conflict occurs among active goals; it requires quite important goals (high value, with important consequences and concerns); it implies the necessity to choose in order to act; it implies a difficult choice due to a quite balanced comparison between the goals' values, and some level of anxiety.
I don't like to call "psychological" all the "Internal conflicts", not only to better characterise what conflicts are in Psychology, but also because I need a concept that can be applied also to "abstract agents" (Rao, Georgeff and Sonenberg 1992) like: groups, organizations, states, etc. in which "Social conflicts" among members can implement/generate an "internal conflict" at the level of the abstract agent.

If there is an "Internal conflict" in an abstract agent there should be either an internal conflict in at least one of its members or an Inter-agent conflict between some of its members.

6. Psychological Conflicts: "Attraction" and "Rejection"

Psychology characterises four kinds of conflicts according to their behavioural and phenomenological differences. This typology can be generalized to all conflicts.
Lewin (Lewin 1935) distinguishes between tendencies to attain some objective (appetitive tendencies or attraction forces) and tendencies to avoid undesired

---

5 I presuppose a meta-goal of consistency or a meta-goal of arriving to a decision in order to adopt a given belief as the basis for the action.

events or situation (aversive tendencies or rejection). He and his followers characterized four kinds of conflict (see Figure 6.1):

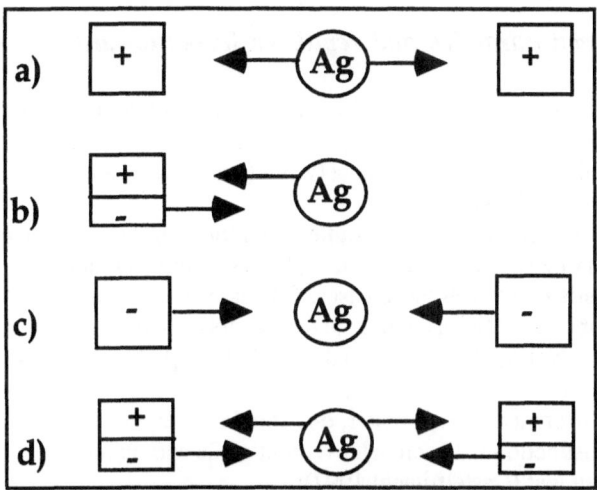

Fig. 6.1 Lewin's typology

a) conflict between two attractive forces

The agent has to choose between two positive, attractive objectives. This is a mild conflict. Of course the greater the value of the two attractors, the strongest the conflict. Equal "forces" should predict impossibility to choose.

(Goal x p) 3 (Goal x q) 3 (Bel x (p V q)))

In a sense this conflict is impossible, if we consider that the preference for an objective implies renouncing the other, that could be consider as a negative feature (type d).

b) conflict between an attractive force and a repulsive force

There is an "ambivalence" of the objective: it has positive attractive features and negative ones, for example it is quite costly or risky.

(Goal x p) 3 (Goal x (Not q)) 3 (Bel x (p 2 q))

c) conflict between two repulsive forces

This is psychologically the worst and more painful conflict situation. In any of the given alternatives the agent loses something (receives some damage). If possible the agent will try to avoid or escape from this situation, to avoid to make such a choice.

(Goal x (Not p)) 3 (Goal x (Not q)) 3 (Bel x (p V q))

d) conflict between attractive and repulsive forces towards the same object

This kind of conflict was introduced by Hovland and Sears (Hovland and Sears 1938) to complete Lewin's typology. In fact, it is just a more realistic combination of basic cases. Normally we have to choose between (ambivalent) alternatives that present both advantages and disadvantages.

To be rejected by z is psychologically quite different from being attracted in the opposite direction of z (behaviourally is not), but our simplistic notation is not able to really differentiate between these cases. Logically these cases are equivalent: since one can substitute (Not q) with r -and viceversa- there is no real difference between (Goal x (Not q)) 3 q, and (Goal x q) 3 (Not q). A more expressive representation is needed.

To express those differences a little better, one should have:

a) a good formal distinction between achievement goals and maintenance goals in an evolving environment (Castelfranchi 1997);

b) a good representation of the distinction between losses and missed gains (Miceli and Castelfranchi 1997). In fact, mere goal frustration - (Goal x p) 3 (Bel x (Not p))- is not enough.

d) conflict between attractive and repulsive forces towards the same object

7. Choice, Goal Conflict, and Goal Processing

7.1 Neither conflicts necessarily require choices, nor choices necessarily presuppose conflicts. In fact:

a) *there are choices that are not due to conflict.* For example, the choice among different equivalent means (plans, strategies) -that could also be non incompatible- for exactly the same goals (ex. to take a bath or to take a shower, to be clean). In this case there is no real "conflict". Not only psychologically there is no conflict (because the two alternatives are not useful per se but only relative to a given goal, and are equivalent: then nothing is lost in one case or in the other). Also formally there is no conflict because there could be no contradiction and incompatibility: the two plans might just be redundant.

b) *there are conflicts that can persist, without forcing to any choice.* Choice is needed only for *commitment.* An agent cannot -rationally (and consciously)- commit herself to two contradictory goals or beliefs [6]. But there are stages of the

---

6 A better model, especially for beliefs, would require "degrees" or "weights" of commitment (see also 7.3.)

belief and of the goal processing that are preliminary to any commitment (Castel-franchi 1996). So, for example, Desires do not require to be either realistic or coherent, while Intentions do (Cohen and Levesque 1990). The same holds for mere Hypotheses with respect to true beliefs (Assumptions). Thus, for example, given a conflict between two incompatible Desires, no choice and no conflict resolution is required. On the contrary if two conflicting Desires have to pass into the condition of Intention to be executed, one has to solve the conflict and to choose. In the post-decisional stage, among current active Intentions there cannot be conflicts. Thus conflict depends on the level of processing the two goals are involved in.

7.2 Conflict processing

This introduces a sort of *conflict dynamics* or *processing*.

a) a goal conflict can occur only at the same level/stage of processing of the goals involved. It has to be stressed that conflict is not only relative to contexts, etc., (in a static perspective) but (in a dynamic perspective) it is relative to the level of processing.

There is no more conflict if there is at one level (say "Desires") the goal that Not p, and at another level (say "Intentions") the goal that p.

b) the conflict creates a *"problem" to be solved* (for example by a choice) only if the goals are at *a level of processing in which the agent is required to be coherent and to commit herself* to a given goal.

7.3 Epistemic Internal Conflicts

In order for two beliefs [(Bel x p) and (Bel x q)] to be in Internal conflict, their (direct or indirect) inconsistency is only a necessary condition. Other conditions are needed:

a) the two beliefs should belong to the same context of belief.

If two beliefs belong to two different contexts they might not be in conflict (for example, in my dream or in a novel Paul is dead, but in the "reality" he is alive).

b) the context of the two belief should be a context which does not allow or tolerate inconsistency (dreams, surrealism, and mere hypotheses, for example allow contradictory beliefs).

c) the beliefs should hold at the same time (there is no conflict in believing at 5 pm that Paul will come, and at 6 pm that he will not; there is just a change of mind).

d) the beliefs should be about the same time: the time of p and the time of q should coincide (there is no conflict in believing that at 5 pm Paul was at home, and that at 6 pm he wasn't).

e) if there is some "force", "weight", "degree", or probability of believing, the sum of the force of B1 and B2 should not exceed a given limit, for example if the estimated probability of p is 45%, the estimated probability of q cannot exceed 55% (if probability -or weights- are compatible the beliefs are too).

8. From Competition to Social Conflict, Aggression, and Fighting

In the case of "External or Inter-agent conflict" (a conflict between the goals of two agents), one might say that between the two agents there is a "Social conflict". In my view, it is necessary to distinguish between the mere objective incompatibility between the goals of two agents, and a full social conflict between them. The situation of mere external conflict between the goals can be called "competition" or "objective conflict" between the agents. The agents could also be unaware of this situation. A full "social conflict" should be seen as the subjective awareness of this competitive situation.

Thus, there is "competition" (or objective conflict) between two agents when their goals are in conflict (incompatible).

(Competition x y p q) is defined as

$$(Goal \; x \; p) \; 3 \; (Goal \; y \; q) \; 3 \; (p \; V \; q)$$

The agents could even be unaware of this situation. There is a full *social conflict* when there is the subjective awareness of the competitive situation.

Awareness of course may be unilateral, bilateral, and mutual.

Bilateral awareness is like:

(Know x (Competition x y p q)) 3 (Know y (Competition x y p q))

There may be also merely subjective social conflicts where an agent wrongly believes to be involved in some Competition situation, because of some wrong belief about the goal or plan of the other, or about their inconsistency or practical incompatibility with her own goal or plan (de Rosis et al. 1996).

Subjective goal conflict (the awareness or the belief of incompatible goals) leads to *Hostility* or *Aggression*, then to a higher level of conflict: fight.

Hostility is just a consequence of competition and conflict. It is the exact opposite of Adoption (help): in Adoption an agent adopts the goal of another agent, because she believes that it is his goal, and in order to make the other agent fulfil it (Castelfranchi 1997). In *Hostility* an agent has the goal that the other agent does not fulfil or achieve some of his goals. Generalized hostility is the opposite of "benevolence".

Hostility is a quite unavoidable consequence of social conflict: if agent x believes that there is a conflict with the goal of agent y, she will have the goal that y does not fulfil his goal.

(Bel x ((p 2 (Not q)) 3 (Goal x q) 3 (Goal y p)) ==> (Goal x ((Not (Goal y p));

or (Not (Obtain y p)))

In this case Hostility is not generalized to any other goal of y, but just to those that are in conflict with x's goals.

Thus, each hostile agent has the goal that the other does not achieve his goal. When each of them actively pursues this goal, trying to prevent the other from achieving his goal, or to damage the other (*aggressive actions*, (Conte and Castel-franchi 1995)), there is a new level of conflict: *fight*:

y has the goal to prevent or hamper the aggressive action/goal of x: she has the goal that the aggressive goal of x fails <*defensive move*>; and so on.

Social conflicts are likely to generate new social conflicts, also in another way. In fact,

if
(Goal x p) 3   (Goal y (Not p))   *first level conflict*

(Bel x (q 2 p)) 3   (Bel y (q 2 p))   *belief agreement*

then
(Goal x q) 3   (Goal y (Not q))   *new conflict*

9. Epistemic Social Conflicts and Social Conflicts

9.1 Epistemic Conflicts can generate Goal-Conflicts (even among people with an identical Goal, for ex. among cooperating people):

(Goal x p) 3 (Goal y p)   *goal agreement*

(Bel x (q 2 p)) 3 (Bel y (q 2 (Not p)))   *belief conflict* [7]

(Goal x q) 3 (Goal y (Not q))   *conflict*

9.2 Epistemic Conflicts can generate cooperation, goal-agreement, among people with conflicting Goals, for ex. between enemies:

---

7 An epistemic social conflict is a conflict between x's decision/commitment of believing p and y's decision/commitment of believing Not p, when they or their group need, want or like that they agree or arrive to a coherent collective belief. In this case either there is the meta-goal that either x or y does not believe what he does, or there is the goal of choosing among the two incompatible beliefs.

if

(Goal x p) 3   (Goal y (Not p))   *goal conflict*

(Bel x (q 2 p)) 3   (Bel y (q 2 Not p))   *belief conflict*

(Goal x q) 3   (Goal y q)   *goal agreement*

In this form of cooperation one of the two agents is wrong and is acting in a self-defeating way.

9.3 In general, Goal-Conflicts cannot generate Epistemic Conflicts. People do not generate opposite beliefs just because they are in goal-conflict. The reason is that *the relation between beliefs and goals is a-symmetric*: while the goals depend on and derive (also) from beliefs, beliefs derive from and depend only on other beliefs (Castelfranchi 1995; 1996). [8]

To summarize: *goal social conflicts do not presuppose or imply epistemic social conflicts*: as we saw, agents can be in a social conflict also being in perfect belief agreement: they know the same things but they want different things. On the other side, two agents in an epistemic social conflict aren't necessarily in a social conflict. However, an epistemic conflict can generate a goal conflict.

10. How to Eliminate a Conflict

10.1 *Internal Conflict*

To eliminate/solve an Internal Conflict there are only three possibilities:

a) to choose among the goals by "promoting" one of them to the next level of goal-processing (see 7.);

b) to kill off at least one of the two "competitor" goals;

c) to eliminate the "critical belief" if it is an "indirect conflict". [9]

---

8 I don't consider here the "psychological" counterexample to this statement, i.e. self-deception and wishful-thinking (where agents change/adopt beliefs in accordance with their goals: pleasant/unpleasant beliefs). (Goal x p) ==> (Goal x (Bel x p)) ==> (Bel x p) [*wishful-thinking*]

9 In *Psychological Conflicts* there is another group of "solutions" which is merely "subjective": just remove the stress and anxiety related to the perception of an internal conflict:

For the Internal Conflict of an abstract collective agent, there is another possibility: see 10.2.1.

10.2 *Social Conflict*

Only agents in a "common world" -i.e. that could "interfere" with each other- may be in conflict (Castelfranchi 1997; Conte and Castelfranchi 1995).

To eliminate/solve a Social Conflict there are three possibilities:

a) to kill off at least one of the two agents from that world
This case covers both:
- the "expulsion" of an agent from a "common word"; and
- the physical suppression of that agent.

Killing and war are very diffuse and old approaches to conflict resolution. However, in general war is not really suppression of the enemy, it is just a very hard and coercive form of "persuasion" (case c). As von Clausewitz said "war is just the continuation of politics with other means". [10]

b) to eliminate the extrinsic incompatibility by giving more resources to the agents and/or by changing their beliefs relative to such an incompatibility.

c) the change of the mind of one of the agents
If one of the agents drops her goal there is no longer any social conflict. This goal dropping can be actively pursued by another agent, which could try to (overtly or hiddenly) kill of the other agent's goal.

This can be done in two different ways:

c1) by eliminating some support of or reason for the target goal: goals are dropped for lack of motivation (the end-goal their are instrumental to) or for lack of possible plans and means, or for invalidation of triggering or supporting beliefs, etc. (Castelfranchi 1995; Castelfranchi 1996; Cohen and Levesque 1990). So, for example in 9.1., if y drops (Bel y (q 2 (Not p))), which is her "critical belief", she will drop also (Goal y (Not q)) which is the conflicting goal.

c2) by conflict internalization
Let me better analyse this case which is in my view the most frequent and prototypical, and the basis of true negotiation.

---

d) *to remove the conflict from awareness* (attention, or accessible memories) or to eliminate the meta-belief that there is a conflict. This kind of "self-deceptive" solution is not interesting for our current AI purposes.

10 If the conflicting agents are members of an abstract collective agent and we want to eliminate the "internal conflict" at the systemic level, there is another possible move (similar to move (a) in the simple Interrnal Conflict):

d) *to choose among them by promoting one of them to the next level of goal-processing.*

10.2.1 The Bronze Law of Inter-Agent Conflict Resolution:

The general law of conflict resolution among agents is the following one, and can be described in two basic steps:

- •   1) the Inter-Agent conflict generates (is transformed into) an Intra-Agent conflict in at least one of the opponents (<u>Internalization process</u>);

- •   2) the internal (mental) resolution of the Intra-Agent conflict results into the resolution of the original Inter-Agent conflict.

In a more detailed analysis (among "cognitive" agents) one can identify 4 steps in the process of conflict resolution:

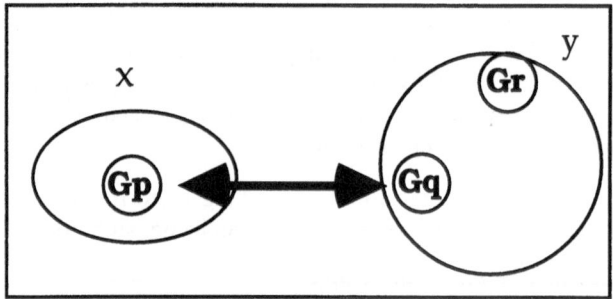

I - (conflict step)The Inter-Agent conflict between the goal p of agent x and the goal q of agent y, where (q 2 Not p) 3 (p 2 Not q).

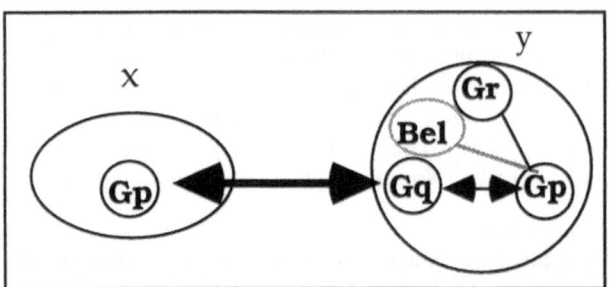

II - (influencing step) x tries to influence y by conveying a belief to her in order to change her goal .(Notice that y has also another goal r, which can be activated by the new belief).

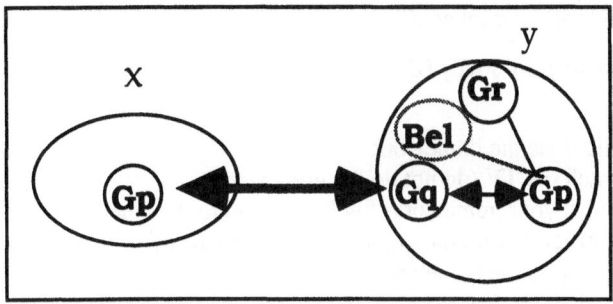

III - (internalization step) from the goal r and the belief, a new goal is generated that is in conflict with Gq: now there is an internal conflict in y.

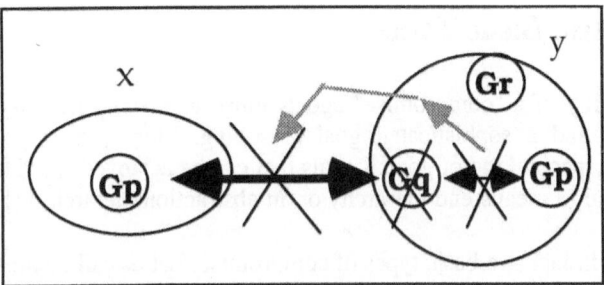

IV - (resolution step) the new conflicting goal of y prevails on (Goal y q); thus, y drops (Goal y q); then there is no more external Inter-Agent conflict between x and y.

A special (and specially interesting) case of this process occurs "via adoption"; that is, the influencing and interiorization occurs via the understanding (normally "communication") of x's goal about y's mind, and the adoption of x's goal by y.

In step (I) agent x believes that if y achieves her goal of doing a, he will not achieve its own goal; then x has the goal that y has the goal of not doing a.

(Bel x ((Do y a) 2 (Not p)) 3 (Goal x p) 3 (Goal y (Do y a)))

==>   (Goal x (Goal y (Not(Do y a))))

This is the belief that x conveys to y in step (II):

(Bel y (Goal x (Goal y (Not (Do y a)))))

Let us suppose (for the sake of simplicity) that y is "benevolent": on the basis of such a belief she will adopt x's goal:

(Goal y (Not (Do y a)))

At this point there is an internal conflict in y:

(Goal y (Not (Do y a))) 3 (Goal y (Do y a))

Example:
Mother's goal: child does the homework
Child's goal: to watch the TV (do not do the homework)
Mother: "if you finish your homework, I will take you to the cinema"
Child's internal conflict: "to do the homework in order to go to the cinema" or
"to watch the TV (do not do the homework)". [11]

In sum, y abandons her Goal q with a *unilateral* renunciation. But it is also possible, and more frequent, that a more fair and bilateral conflict resolution is allowed though a true *bilateral compromise*.

11. Compromises: Basic Types

To have the possibility of a "compromise" agents must necessarily have a complex goal structure and a sophisticated goal reasoning. More precisely, they should either have a special kind of goals - goals that can be achieved "partially" - or a hierarchy of goal (a means-end hierarchy or an abstraction hierarchy) (Kautz 1987).

There seem to be in fact two basic types of compromise. Let us call them: *Part-of Compromises* and *Substitution Compromises*.

11.1 *Part-of Compromises*

Some goals are of the Yes/No type: either you achieve them or you fail (for example, to pass the exam, to die, etc.). Some other goals on the contrary can be achieve in part:

- either gradually, since they have some quantitative dimension, some degree (for. example to gain a lot of money, to eat, etc.);

- or, in portion: the goal is in fact a compound goal, made of several goals, and one achieves some of these goals (for example, to go to the cinema and to a restaurant this evening).

In both cases one can realise a subset, a part of the original dimensional or compound goal. Let's call these goals "complex".

This kind of goals has two important although obvious properties: they can be "partially" conflicting and they can be "partially" dropped.

---

11 *Reverse conflict*: if both the opponents interiorize the conflict and solve it in favour of the new goal, we can have again conflict with reverse positions among the agents. It is a frequent situation among lovers ("you were right" "No I was wrong".....).

For a compromise of this kind to occur,

- both agents must have some "complex" goal and the conflict must be about these complex goals (i.e. some parts of the goal of one agent is incompatible with some parts of the goal of the other);

- both agents have to renounce to the complete achievement of their goal, and have to drop some conflicting part of the goal.

For ex. given a compound initial Goal of x $G1_x$ (p 3 q 3 r) and a compound initial goal of y $G1_y$ (s 3 t 3 v), where (the agents believe that) p V s and q V t, i.e. there is a conflict between $G1_x$ and $G1_y$, a *compromise* is a conflict resolution such that x renounces either p or q, while y renounces either s or t, so that eventually there is no conflict among their new goals (G2), and they do not achieve completely their original goals, i.e. the list/set of proposition of $G1_x$ is included in the list/set of propositions of $G2_x$, and the same holds for y's goals.

Thus, in our example there are two possible *compromises*:

$G2_x$ (p 3 r) 3 $G1_y$ (t 3 v)

$G2_x$ (q 3 r) 3 $G1_y$ (s 3 v)

while

$G2_x$ (p 3 q 3 r) 3 $G1_y$ (v)

is not a real compromise although it is a conflict resolution (there is no more conflict between the two goals).

In other words, the criterion guiding the Part-of Compromises is the idea that "something is better that nothing": x can either continue to pursue his global goal - either risking to fail or risking the costs of competition and fight -, or he can drop some part of his goal which is in conflict with the goal of y's (and the same for y).

A true (bilateral) compromise requires some form of cooperation (some common goal and agreement) and - more interestingly - some form of "social exchange": x renounces some (part) of his goals if and because y renounces some (part) of her goals; x adopts a goal/request of y's if and because y adopts a goal/request of x's. [12]

---

12 A compromise can succeed not only by reducing the number of the achieved part-goals i.e. the final goal is included in the original one; it can result in a new -non conflicting goal that has something more and new with respect to the original goal: something that has been activated, suggested or proposed (offered) by the other agent. Given a complex initial Goal of x $G1_x$ (p 3 q) and a complex initial goal of y $G1_y$ (s 3 t), where (the agents believe that) p V s, i.e. there is a conflict between $G1_x$ and $G1_y$, a *dynamic compromise* is a conflict resolution such that x does not renounce p, while y renounces s, so that eventually there is no conflict among their new goals (G2), and they do not achieve completely their original goals. But, y's renounciation to s is compensated by a new goal r of her that either is a consequence of realising p (that x

11.2 *Substitution Compromises*

There is a second type of compromise where both x and y entirely drop their original conflicting goals, but without a complete renounce and defeat. They just step-up, climb along the hierarchy of the conflicting goal to find at the upper layer a non conflicting solution. Either they find the solution by climbing the means-end hierarchy, or by climbing the abstraction hierarchy.

a) Alternative means (*replacement compromise*)

Conflicts about end-goals, motives (for ex. desires or needs) are different from conflicts relative to sub-goals, i.e. instrumental goals in a plans. In fact, in simple situations, abandoning an end implies not to achieve it, to renounce something important, not to be satisfied; while to drop a sub-goal can simply mean that we substitute it with another equivalent means: there is no renunciation, no dissatisfaction, since the means is not important *per se*, but only for the higher order goals it guarantees.

Thus, a conflict about the ends can be solved only through the complete or partial renounce of at least one of the conflicting agents. On the contrary, a conflict about the means can be solved without substantial renunciation by the two agents, if there are non incompatible plans for the two non incompatible ends. The problem is just to find some reasonable alternative plan for your goals; and to inform and/or convince the other about such a reasonable alternative.

b) Alternative instantiations (*compensation compromise*)

Suppose x cannot achieve his end-Goal p or execute his plan P; however he has an abstraction hierarchy where Goal p (for example *to dance*) is just a sub-case, an instance, a possible form of a more abstract goal (*to have a good time*), or the plan P (for example *to prepare fettuccini*) is just a specification of a more abstract plan (*to prepare pasta*). In this case x can climb up to a more abstract level and choose another way of instantiating that class of goals or plans.

The same holds in a conflict; x wants p: to go to the cinema (with y); while y would like q: to meet people by visiting friends (with x); the compromise consists in the fact that they do neither p nor q, but they choose a third alternative (r): to go to dance. This new goal satisfies both x's higher goal of having a good time and y's higher goal of meeting people.

Generally, if not always and necessarily, *Substitution compromises import some renunciation and then some Part-of compromise* (this is why they are not

---

induced y to take into account), or is the result of an additional action (and than *cost* of x) that represents what he lost. So the final situation is Goal of x $G1_x$ (p 3 q) plus a new cost (goal damage) and $G1_y$ (r 3 t).

only brilliant problem-solutions, but are really felt as "compromises"). This is due to the fact that two alternative means/sub-plans within the same plan or for the same goal, *cannot be really and completely equivalent* (producing *all* the same relevant results). Otherwise, how could we choose among them, and prefer one to the other? If we really choose on the basis of some preference, this means that the two alternative means/plans Pa (for ex. to fly) and Pb (to take a train) for the goal G1 (to go to Naples),

a) either, are not perfectly equivalent as for G1: they achieve G1 with different probabilities or in a different measure;

b) or, they are equivalent as for G1, but we can prefer one to the other because other independent ends are involved: G2 and G3 (for example, to save time, and to save money) and Pa and Pb are not equivalent relatively to these goals: for ex. Pa achieves also G2 while Pb achieves also G3, but G2 is more important than G3.

In the situation (b) -which is the usual one- *the choice among two alternative means (for G1) implies the choice between other ends* (G2 and G3); thus it implies some real "renunciation" to some of these ends.

However, even with these complications, it remains true that a conflict between end-goals (in particular "motivations") is different from the conflict between instrumental sub-goals. In fact, even if choosing among sub-goals one sacrifices some ends, these are just side-goals, they are not what was *motivating* her/his plan and action (we are not travelling for saving money or for saving time, but for reaching Naples). To sacrifice real motivations (the goal you are behaving for) is more difficult than scarificing side-goals. And also the argumentation for not achieving a motivation is different.

To conclude: agents with an articulated goal representation can solve their conflicts (both social or internal) in a more sophisticated way, by renouncing or substituting some part of their original global goal structure.

Conclusions

I hope I succeeded:
- in pointing out some of the basic aspects/notions of conflict theory to be formalized;
- in relating the notion of conflict to goals (and to their processing);
- in showing both the objective and subjective aspects of social conflict and some of their relationships;
- finally, in suggesting why and how cognition is relevant in solving social conflicts.

Acknowledgements

I wish to thank Amedeo Cesta, Rosaria Conte, Fiorella De Rosis, Rino Falcone for discussions on this topic. I'm in debt with Maria Miceli and Simon Parsons for their precious comments and criticisms on a preliminary version of this chapter .

This work has been supported by the European ESPRIT3 Working Group *"MODEL AGE"* and by the CNR special project on "Ontology for the Organisation and the Integration of Heterogeneous Knowledge".

CHAPTER 3

Modelling Conflict-Resolution Dialogues

Fiorella de Rosis[1], Floriana Grasso[2], Cristiano Castelfranchi[3], and Isabella Poggi[4]

[1] University of Bari

[2] University of Liverpool

[3] National Research Council, Roma

[4] University of Roma 3

In this chapter we discuss how conflicts between believable agent can be modelled, and how dialogues aimed at resolving these conflicts can be simulated on a machine. To support our analysis, we consider an example of doctor-to-patient interaction, in which several sources of conflict exist and where emotion and personality factors play a crucial role.

1. Introduction

In dialogue modelling research, human-computer or human-human dialogues are simulated by applying experience from human-human interaction analysis (Carletta, Isard, Isard, Kowtko, Doherty Sneddon, and Anderson 1997). This has led to several dialoguing agent architectures (among others, the Belief-Desire-Intention model in (Rao and Georgeff 1991)), where a cognitive model of interacting agents is built up, and a conversational strategy is assigned to each of the agents, in the form of either an algorithm or a set of decision rules. However, knowledge representation and treatment methods in these models usually privilege purely rational aspects of reasoning, whereas several studies have suggested that dialogue is strongly influenced by the relationships among participants, their role, their personality and their emotional status (Elliott and Ortony 1992).

The need for giving more weight to emotional and personality aspects is emerging as a new and promising research objective (Cañamero 1998; de Rosis 1999; Prevost and Churchill 1988), aimed at modelling *believable* agents. A believable behaviour would be shown by an agent which avoids answering questions which it is not able or willing to answer, is able to react to unexpected questions or attitudes of other agents, and assigns weights to its goals and beliefs according also to its emotional state, and not only to its knowledge (Reilly and Bates 1995).

Emotional and personality aspects of the mental state play a particularly relevant role when agents have to face a conflicting situation: *impatient, aggressive, polite, persistent, rude.*..people show radically different ways of managing conflicts with others.

In this work, we investigate how these aspects can be taken into account in the modelling of conflict-resolution dialogues. We start by examining (in Sect. 2. and 3.) the types of conflict that may exist between two interacting agents, and how conflict-resolution dialogues may be undertaken to try and solve them. To support our analysis, we consider, in Sect. 4., two examples of doctor-patient dialogues, in which several kinds and forms of conflict exist, which are solved only in part during the dialogues. We then analyse (in Sect. 5.) the reasoning process that the agents perform throughout such dialogues, and show how the sequencing of reasoning steps and the way each of them is performed are linked to personality factors. In Sect. 6., we briefly illustrate Xanthippe, a multiagent dialogue simulation system that was designed to test our theories, and we finally reflect (in Sect. 7.) on the interest and the limits of our approach.

2. Conflicts: Nature and Kinds

Two agents engage in a conflict-resolution dialogue (CRD) when at least one of them wishes to solve a conflict which has arisen with the other. A CRD is then initiated as soon as an agent believes that a conflict exists between its plan and the plan of another agent. The way the CRD is carried on depends, among other factors, on the nature of the conflict arisen.

2.1 Objective vs Subjective Conflicts

A first classification may be made with respect to the perception that the agent initiating the dialogue has of the conflict. The belief that a conflict exists can be right, and in this case there is also an *objective* conflict between the two agents, or mistaken, and in this case the conflict is merely *subjective*. CRDs aimed at solving merely subjective vs objective conflicts are different, at least from the moment when one of the agents suspects or realises that the conflict is only subjective:

– dialogues undertaken to solve conflicts based on erroneous beliefs are aimed at *clarifying misconceptions or misunderstandings*, on the grounds that eliminating these mistaken beliefs will eliminate the conflict itself;
– dialogues undertaken to solve an objective conflict are aimed at *changing the goal of the other agent*, with, typically, two distinct strategies:

1. inducing the other agent to drop part of his conflicting goals, in order to come to a *compromise* (in this case, both agents relaxe their goals and renounce to part of them) or
2. inducing the other agent to completely drop its conflicting goals (*unilateral renounce*).

In both cases, the interaction is not limited to the clarification of a misconception, but is a classical case of influencing, that is of attempting to change the goals and the intentions of the other, through argumentation and persuasion.

Of course, in real life CRDs, these two cases can coexist (we shall see some examples of this coexistence in Sect. 4.):

- agents can pass from a perspective to the other: they can start believing that there is an objective conflict, and then discover that it was just a problem of misunderstanding;
- the two agents may have different opinions about the objectivity of the conflict: one agent believes that there is just a misunderstanding, while the other believes that there is an objective conflict;
- the conflict might be in part (on certain goals) merely subjective and due to misconceptions, and in part (on other goals) objective.

A further distinction has to be made, to clarify the difference between subjective and objective conflicts:

a. *merely subjective* conflicts originate from some mistaken belief of one agent, concerning the two conflicting goals or their relations: the agent believes that there is a conflict, while such a conflict does not really exist, because the two goals are in fact not incompatible. This case has, in turn, two different sub-cases:

a.1. *false, apparent conflicts*, based on a misunderstanding about the other agent's goals:
   X believes that Y wants p, while Y, in fact, wants Not-p.
   In this case, the conflict does not exist at all objectively, but only subjectively (in X's mind), and is due to a mistaken belief of X about Y's goals.
   For example:
   Adam would like to go to the restaurant, tonight; he believes that Eve would not like it, while in fact she was just going to reserve a table at a nice restaurant in Trastevere.

a.2. *false indirect conflicts*, based on a misconception about the world:
   X wants q and believes that Y wants p and that p implies Not-q, while this implication is false.

In this case too the conflict does not exist objectively, but only sub-jectively (in X's mind), as it is due to a mistaken belief of X about the world[1].

For example:
Adam would like to go to the restaurant tonight, while Eve would like to go to the theatre. Adam would revise his belief that this is a conflict if Eve convinces him that the two plans are not incompatible (for instance, because the show starts late).

These kinds of conflict are very different from a real conflict:

b. *misconception based real conflict*:
X wants p because it (mistakenly) believes that q, while Y wants Not-p because it believes that Not-q.

In this case, the two agents do have opposite goals, but (at least) one of them is based on wrong beliefs, about the world or about the other; if this wrong belief is retracted, the goal will be abandoned and the conflict will be resolved.

For example:
Adam would not like to go to the theatre tonight, because he be-lieves that there is nothing interesting being played, at the moment; Eve attracts his attention to the new Dario Fo's play, that she would like to see, and maybe he will change his mind.

It is important, therefore, to understand that: (i) not all conflicts are due to misconceptions about the other (and about the conflict itself) or about the plans and the domain and (ii) misconceptions do not necessarily produce conflicts. Thus, only some CRDs are dialogues about a misconception and are aimed at clarifying it.

2.2 Conflicts about Ends vs Conflicts about Means

In principle, conflicts about end-goals, that is about motives (e.g. desires or needs) are different from conflicts about sub-goals, that is about instrumental goals in a plan. In simple situations, abandoning an end implies not achiev-ing it, and therefore renouncing to something important. On the contrary, dropping a mean, a sub-goal, may simply imply substituting it with another equivalent mean: in this case, there is no renunciation, no dissatisfaction, since the mean is not important *per se*, but only in view of the higher order goals it guarantees. Thus, a conflict about the ends can be solved only through a complete or partial renounce by at least one of the conflicting agents, while a

---

[1] In some logical systems, a.2 is a subcase of a.1, in the sense that if an agent has the goal that p, and believes that p implies q, then it has also the goal that q. A conflict of type a.2 would always imply, in these systems, also a conflict of type a.1 (but not vice-versa). The two types of conflicts have, in any case, different foundations.

conflict about the means can be solved without substantial renunciation by any of the two agents: the problem is just to find some reasonable alternative plan for the end-goals and to inform (and possibly to convince) the other of such an alternative.

Of course, this is an oversimplified picture. In fact, usually the alternative plans or sub-goals are not completely equipollent: if we really choose according to some preference, this means that in general two alternative means/plans P_a (e.g. "to fly") and P_b (e.g. "to take a train") to achieve a goal G_1 (e.g. "to go to Naples"):

1. either are not perfectly equivalent as for G_1: they achieve G_1 with different probabilities or in a different measure,
2. or are equivalent as for G_1, but one of them is "preferable" because other independent ends are involved (e.g., G_2 = "to save time", and G_3 = "to save money") and P_a and P_b are not equivalent with respect to these ends. For example: P_a achieves also G_2 while P_b achieves also G_3, therefore the choice depends on whether G_2 is more important than G_3.

In the latter situation -which is the most frequent- the choice among two alternative means (for G_1) implies the choice between other ends (G_2 and G_3); renouncing to a means, therefore, implies in fact renouncing to some of these ends.

Even with these complications, it remains true that a conflict between end-goals is different from a conflict between instrumental sub-goals. In fact, even if, by choosing among sub-goals, an agent gives up some ends, these are just side-goals, they are not those which were motivating the agent's plan and action (we are not travelling to save money or to save time, but in order to be in Naples). Sacrificing side-goals (even end-goals, which however do not motivate one's action) is less difficult than sacrificing real motivations, and also the types of argumentation to employ in the two cases are different.

2.3 The Compromise

For a possibility of a *compromise* to exist, agents must have goals of a special kind: goals that can be attained "partially". There are dichotomic goals (for example, to pass an exam, to die, etc.): either you achieve them or you fail. There are other goals that can be achieved only in part:

- either gradually, since they have some quantitative property (for example, to gain a lot of money, to eat, etc.),
- or partially, since they are complex goals which include several, less complex, goals: for example, to go to the theatre and to a restaurant are sub-goals of the more general goal of "enjoying oneself".

In both cases, one can achieve a subset, a part of the original -dimensional or complex- goal. Let us call these goals *composite*. These kinds of goal have two important, although obvious properties: they can be "partially conflicting" and they can be "partially dropped". For a compromise to be made, then:

- each of the two agents, A_i and A_j, must have a composite goal, G_i and G_j, and the conflict must be about G_i and G_j; this means that some parts of G_i are incompatible with some parts of G_j;
- both agents have to renounce to the complete achievement of their goal, and have to abandon some conflicting part of their goal.

3. Conflict-Resolution Dialogues: the Role of Personality

Human beings show a variety of behaviours, due to very diverse factors (knowledge, goals, preferences, etc.); adaptive systems try to embody these factors in a User Model, in order to customize their behaviour to them. In addition to more common factors related to the knowledge state of the user (the classic distinction between *expert* and *novice* is an example), new classes of factors are now being considered in the intelligent social systems community, which are often referred to as "personality traits": these factors are close to representing the "aims" of an agent and the ways to pursue them ((Carbonell 1980; Castelfranchi, de Rosis, Falcone, and Pizzutilo 1998)).

In conflict resolution conversations, as in any kind of conversation, personality traits can play various roles.

They can influence the choice of the **strategy** to employ in a conflicting situation; for instance a *fussy* agent will tend to argue about every single goal, without bothering with trying an alternative plan, and without considering that reaching an agreement on a minor goal can be time consuming and useless. On the contrary, an *accommodating* agent will always try to find different ways to achieve its own higher order goals in order to keep everybody's higher goals unchanged. Similarly, a *polemic* agent will argue even about not interfering goals; a *fair* agent will not use trick options (he will not lie), etc.

Personality factors also influence the **degree of attachment** an agent has towards its own goals. Many authors have addressed the problem of goal endorsement: (Carbonell 1980) makes a distinction between *cooperative* and *competitive* predisposition, and terms like *selfish*, *helpful* or *benevolent* have often been used to describe different attitudes with respect to goal endorsement (Cohen and Levesque 1990).

Finally, personality traits influence the agent's **reaction to the success or the failure** of one of its strategies: a *persistent* agent will try the same plan many times before abandoning it, an *ambitious* one will try every possible plan to achieve its goals, and so on.

If we assume that personality traits influence human communication, then also when conversing with a computer it has sense to consider these factors in the user model: there is by now agreement on the fact that a real "friendly" computer system has to be able to perceive the personality (and even the emotions, see (Picard 1996)) of its users to tailor its behaviour to them. But it should also be admitted that an "intelligent" system has, more or less implicitly, its own behaviour and idiosyncrasies, which can be allegedly seen as a "personality". It is time then to represent this model explicitly, by examining how it influences the algorithms behind system-user dialogues.

4. A Case Study in Doctor-Patient Dialogues

In this section we analyse two CRDs from the perspectives outlined so far. We have chosen two dialogues in a Doctor-Patient scenario, for several reasons. Doctor to patient interrelations are influenced by a number of underlying conflicts: the degree of information that patients should receive about their treatment (Berry, Michas, Forster, and Gillie 1997) and the level of autonomy they should have in contributing to establish the therapy (Savulescu and Momeyer 1997) are just two of a very large set of samples of potential conflicts. Dialogues in medical setting thus provide significant examples of the types of conflict that we classified in the previous Sections, and of how they are frequently only in part raised, and only in part solved, in the dialogue. The conversations shown in this Section include several of the conflicting situations mentioned before. Both dialogues have, as a trigger situation, a *purpose declaration* by one of the participants, which the other one realises to be in conflict with one of its goals. The conversations consist of a set of *turns*; in each turn, a participant can make a claim (with or without justifying it), ask a question, or make a proposal (if it takes the initiative). Alternatively, it can answer a question, acknowledge a claim, or declare agreement or disagreement to a proposal (if it replies to a stimulus from the other agent). The dialogues have the aim to identify, step by step, the reasons for the original conflict, and to solve it, if possible, or to conclude that it cannot be solved.

4.1 A Clarification Dialogue

The first example (in Fig. 4.1) shows a computer simulation of a dialogue between an intelligent explanation system and a user (de Rosis, Grasso, Berry, and Gillie 1995). Both the system and the user are simulated by the computer system. In the figure, the explanator-agent's turns are labelled with D, for Doctor, as this is the role this agent would play in a session with a real user, and the user-agent's turns with P, for Patient. The conversation is about a piece of text D has just generated to describe the drug therapy that P should undertake. P is not satisfied with the text produced, because it does not mention the side effects of the therapy, and this creates a conflict between the two. It has to be remarked that the choice of this particular conflict is not fortuitous: experimental studies have shown that this type of situation is very common in real life doctor/patient relationships (Berry, Michas, and de Rosis 1998).

Turn 0 P:	*I would like you to tell me about the side effects of these drugs, because I don't know them.*
Turn 1 D:	*I know: but I'm not sure that it is really necessary that you know them.*
Turn 2 P:	*However, I have to inform you that, if I know them and I know, at the same time, the way that they occur (whether they are frequent, serious and so on), my motivation towards the treatment will increase.*
Turn 3 D:	*I understand now. I thought you were an anxious person, who might have been demotivated from knowing these aspects of treatment.*
Turn 4 P:	*All right. I therefore would like you to tell me about side effects, and the way they might apply to my case.*
Turn 5 D:	*All right, I will do it.*
Turn 6 P:	*Thank you.*

Fig. 4.1. A clarification dialogue

The conflict triggering this CRD is clearly concerned with the doctor's communicative goal: "Informing about the side effects of the drug". This conflict turns out to be only subjective, and is due to a misconception of the doctor about the personality of the patient. The two agents have a cooperative attitude and are both interested in solving the conflict: each of them tries to convince the other to change its opinion but, at the same time, is prepared, if necessary, to change its mind; the main part of the dialogue aims therefore at discovering the reasons for the conflict.

Let us examine this conversation from the personality traits point of view.

– D initially hypothesised that P had an *anxious* personality: mentioning the side effects of the therapy could then have weakened P's will to undertake it. Therefore, D decided to omit them from the explanation of the therapy.
– On the other hand, P mistakenly hypothesises that D believed that P already knew the side effects of this drug. P therefore proposes to D to mention them, and justifies this proposal with the claim that in fact they are not already known (Turn 0).
– D communicates that P's hypothesis is not true, and that its goal was actually to avoid mentioning them at all (Turn 1).
– P tries to find another explanation for the conflict (D's hypothesis about P's personality) and manifests its real attitude towards performing the action (Turn 2).
– D acknowledges this communication, changes its belief about P's personality and changes its mind about the goal, by accepting P's proposal (Turn 3).

The dialogue, although attempting to represent a real life conflict, is artificious, and especially the behaviour of the doctor-agent is probably unrealistic. In the next section, a real dialogue is presented, to give a flavour of the complexity of the behaviour that believable agents should, instead, show.

Turn 0 P:	*I'd like a prescription for the pill, please.*
Turn 1 D:	*You'd like the pill? And... you are already aware of other methods... What are your reasons for the pill?*
Turn 2 P:	*Oh, the coil! I don't wanna use that!*
Turn 3 D:	*You don't feel like it.*
Turn 4 P:	*....and I think this is the only solution...*
Turn 5 D:	*Why wouldn't you have a coil fitted?*
Turn 6 P:	*I don't know why... ...My gynaecologist advised me against it.*
Turn 7 D:	*Your gynaecologist advised you against it... did he say why?*
Turn 8 P:	*He says it's something foreign to the body, after all...*
Turn 9 D:	*OK, it's all right that you take the pill now, ...it's the right time, ...especially as you're young.*

Fig. 4.2. A compromise-Finding Dialogue.

4.2 A Compromise-Finding Dialogue

The second dialogue (Fig. 4.2) is the English translation of part of a real conversation between a patient (P) and a gynaecologist (D) in an Italian public surgery, reported in (Petrillo 1994). The conflict, in this case, concerns the contraceptive to be selected as the most appropriate to the specific patient, but also some related, higher order goals. This is, therefore, an example of objective conflict.

P's unique goal is to take a "suitable" contraceptive, where suitable means, to her, to take the pill; she therefore needs a prescription for that.

D's goal is more complex: she wants to promote a correct use of contraceptives, which does imply prescribing a suitable contraceptive, but also being sure, at the same time, that the patient is convinced about the chosen method and that she is informed about contraceptive methods in general. The first subgoal can be in turn specified by one of two -alternative- subgoals: prescribing the pill or let the patient have a coil fitted. Although the doctor seems to prefer, in principle, the second one, she believes that a high consideration should be given to the patient's preferences.

There are, therefore, in this conversation, both objective and subjective conflicts between D and P. The objective conflicts are about the doctor providing a complete and well-balanced vision of contraceptive methods, tailored to the patient's needs and beliefs, and the patient providing information about the reasons behind her preference for the pill. In contrast, the subjective conflict concerns what the two participants to the dialogue want to select as a contraceptive.

These conflicts might be solved in several ways:

To solve the *objective conflicts*:

a.1) P might accept D's goals: she might inform the doctor about the reasons why she prefers the pill, and might leave to the doctor the opportunity of providing information about contraceptives in general;

a.2) or, D might accept P's goal to avoid talking about herself, and renounce to inform her about contraceptive methods.

To solve the *subjective conflict*:

b.1) P might revise her belief about the selection of the pill, and accept a coil-based contraception; in this case, the conflict, though only subjective, would cause P changing her plan anyway;

b.2) or D might clarify that she is not against the use of the pill, and prescribe it; the correction of the misconception would then make the subjectivity of conflict manifest.

When, as in this example, goals are complex and several alternative ways to solve the conflict exist, the personality of the two interacting agents plays a crucial role in establishing a selection criterion: agents will select which goal to abandon in case of conflict, and which goal to try and achieve (by means of argumentation, clarification and so on), also according to their personality, and therefore to the value they attach to these goals.

To come back to our example, at the beginning of the dialogue D tries to push P towards solution a.1, though in a "soft" way. However, P is very determined not to renounce to her goal, and also not to adopt D's higher order goal. D, therefore, moves towards solution a.2, by means of a *unilateral renounce*.

Throughout the dialogue, the suspect of a misconception (that the coil is dangerous) arises to D, and she tries to clarify it; however, P misinterprets D's attempt, identifies a (subjective) conflict (that the doctors wants to convince her to have a coil fitted) and consequently refuses the clarification attempt of D, by adopting a deceptive strategy (that her gynaecologist advised her against the coil).

Remarkably, D is the agent who guides the conflict-resolution dialogue (probably because of her role).

It should also be noticed that, to induce D to her unilateral renounce, P does not employ any kind of sophisticated argumentation: she only manifests that she is closed to any offer of compromise. In this example, the personalities of the two agents (as well as their role, and the type of structure in which the dialogue takes place) contributed to establish the form and level of solution for their conflict.

We shall turn back to this dialogue in Sect. 5.2, for a more detailed analysis of the two agent's forms of reasoning at each turn.

5. Forms of Reasoning in Conflict Resolution Dialogues

To simulate CRDs in a convenient way, the reasoning process that each participant performs at each turn before issuing a "communicative act" needs to be modelled. This model can be based on the application of *conversational rules*, like, for example, in (Schlegloff 1988). However, if the dialoguing agents are represented as BDI agents, it is probably more reasonable to represent the reasoning process in terms of sequential activation of several *forms of reasoning*, applied to the agent's mental state. Examples of representation of such a mental activity are the recursive *Propose-Evaluate-Modify* cycle for modelling collaborative planning in (Chu-Carroll and Carberry 1995), and the model of proposal/acceptance (or rejection) sequences in (Sidner 1994). We go one step further, to examine forms of reasoning employed in the main phases of this activity.

5.1 The Reasoning Cycle

In our model, the conversation can be seen as the result of applying recursively the following steps: (a) interpreting the communication received, (b) revising one's own mental state, (c) deciding how to react, (d) answering. The sequencing of these steps, and the way each of them is performed, are linked to personality traits and to extralogical factors, such as emotions and higher order motivations.

a. interpreting the communication received: *"what did the other agent say?"*
We shall not consider here the linguistic aspects of interpretation, and shall assume that any statement is always interpreted "correctly", and translated into a standard communicative act. We make a distinction between two types of communicative acts: *questions* and *proposals*, which activate distinct forms of reasoning and reaction. The argument of both types of speech act can be either a belief or a goal of one of the interacting agents.

b. revising one's own mental state: *"what do I believe, and what does the other agent -presumably- believe?"*

b.1. *after a proposal:* the agent receiving the proposal has to decide whether it conflicts or not with its own belief and goal structure (by reasoning on its own mental state), and whether to update its model accordingly. The same reasoning process can be made, as well, on the other agent's image. The decision on whether to reason only on itself or also on the other agent's mental state is traditionally regulated by the agent's attitude towards its partner, which is defined as *cooperative* or *non-cooperative*. In cooperative dialogues (which are the majority, in the literature: see, e.g., (Chu-Carroll and Carberry 1995)), the agent would accept any non-conflicting proposal without reasoning on the other agent's mental state, while such a form of reasoning would be activated only to discover weaknesses in the other agent's viewpoint, to be exploited in argumentation (Sycara 1991). We maintain that this dichotomy between cooperative and non-cooperative agents is not realistic, and that believable agents show various *levels of cooperativity* as to specific goals, even within the same dialogue (Castelfranchi 1992). Cooperativity levels depend not only on the context, and therefore on the agent's higher order goals, but also on the agent's personality. For example: an *altruistic* agent would behave in a "truly cooperative" way by systematically considering the other agent's viewpoint, to verify whether the received proposal really matches this agent's presumed interests. Our assumption implies that, after interpreting any proposal, an agent may decide whether to accept it by either reasoning only on its own mental state or also on the other agent's one.

b.2. *after a question:* in order to provide an appropriate answer, the agent has to verify the truth value of some of its beliefs or goals (in case of Yes/No questions), to instantiate one of its beliefs or goals (in case of Which questions), or to find out which data support one of its beliefs or goals (in case of Why questions). However, it may also ask itself why the other agent made such a question in the first place, especially if it has a "defensive" attitude ("what is it *really* asking me?") or a "highly cooperative" attitude ("how can I help?").

When the agent reasons on the other agent's viewpoint and finds out several candidate explanations for a question or a proposal, traditional, rationality based approaches suggest to select either the "most plausible", or the one which "most quickly resolves the conflict". This idea corresponds to a vision of "optimality in problem solving", which is prevalent in Artificial Intelligence.

We argue that this process is highly influenced by emotional or personality factors of *both* interacting agents, and that the optimality criterion has to be conditioned to the personality of the reasoning agent and to its hypotheses about the other agent's personality. For example: doctor's conclusions when hearing the sentence: "...*My gynaecologist advised me against it.*" (at Turn 7) would vary depending on whether D has reasons to believe that P is *trustful* towards her, or whether they had an old or a recent relationship. Another example: a *selfconfident* agent will tend to ascribe the reasons of a conflict to the other agent's errors rather than to errors of its own accord; the opposite will be for an *insecure* agent.

c. deciding how to react: *"what is really convenient, to me and to the other agent?"*

Once the agent has come to a full understanding of the other agent's message, its reaction will be conditioned by its own interests and beliefs. In deciding how to react, the agent will consider not only the subject of the message, but also whether other (higher order) goals exist, which deserve consideration. Let us suppose, for example, that the agent concluded in the previous step that the conflict may be due to a divergence about a specific belief. It has thus to decide whether to change its mind about that belief or try to convince the other agent to do it: this decision will depend on how *persistent* the agent is. Another example: an *aggressive* agent might be willing to hold on a conflict even after the original causes have been -partially or totally- clarified. An *acquiescent* agent might decide, on the contrary, to pass over the conflict even though it has not been solved. Personality traits, attitudes, roles and higher order goals are strictly interrelated issues.

Similar considerations can be applied in deciding whether no more conflicts exist, and the conversation can be terminated with a declaration of "agreement". In our example dialogue the doctor clearly agrees with the patient's contraceptive choice: therefore, she might well have just answered "OK", at Turn 2, and written down the prescription. On the contrary, she wants to verify whether the patient's decision is really informed and conscious, and carries on the dialogue accordingly. In a different context, agents might show a different attitude, corresponding to different higher order goals, and would therefore behave differently.

d. answering: *"what shall I say?"*
Several decisions may need to be made:

d.1. *when to argue and how to argue*: the agent may reply to a proposal by declaring to accept it, or by making a counterproposal, and arguing for it. In the simulation of purely rational dialogue, argumentation is typically a function of the strength of the arguments available. In a believable agents context, strong or highly plausible arguments are not necessarily employed in the replies.

In the example dialogue, the doctor never argues "by discredit of a contraceptive", but prefers "positive" arguments: even if she seems to think that the coil is preferable to the pill in the specific case, she never argues against the pill. If the doctor did, because of her role and authority, the patient might let her pursue her informative goals. The reason why she renounces to this is probably that her goal to avoid encouraging negative attitudes towards any contraceptive has higher priority.

d.2. *when to make a question*: in purely rational negotiation dialogues, information is requested only when the agent has not enough data to decide whether to accept the other agent's proposal. When believable agents are modelled, this decision is also conditioned to the agents' higher order goals. Some of these goals are linked to the context and to the interrelations between the agents, whereas others may come from previous phases of the dialogue, or may even be active *a priori*.

Taking these higher order goals into account is therefore essential to establish how to reply: as we have discussed before, this decision may presume different reasoning styles in the previous phases of the dialogue (only on one's own mental state, or also on the other's). Conversely, higher order goals may also lead to different decisions about asking: in our example dialogue, the doctor maybe wonders why the patient made a specific statement, guesses one or several reasons for that, but decides to abstain from asking about them, because of her higher order goals.

d.3 *which question to make*: in our example dialogue, the doctor makes either *open* (Turns 1 and 5) or *closed* (Turn 3) questions. The first question type is not necessarily preferred only when the doctor has not enough information to provide a list of possible replies. The decision can be influenced, as well, by higher order goals, such as "to encourage the patient to assume an active role", or "to manifest an enlistening attitude". In selecting a closed question, the doctor might, on the contrary, be willing "to show her competence", or "to manifest her intention to place the patient on a parity position", and so on.

d.4. *when to avoid a question, to answer in a doubtful or elusive way, or to lie:* when an agent is on the defensive (maybe because it is aware of the weakness of its argumentation ability), it will be induced to select "elusion", "reticence" or "deception" as an alternative to a sincere assertion (see, for example, the patient at Turn 6). Conversely, the intention "to avoid polemizing" may induce to answer in a "slightly doubtful" way or to pretend not to notice a lie (as the doctor at Turn 9).

5.2 The Reasoning Cycle in the Compromise-Finding Dialogue

In this section we try to apply ideas sketched out in Sect. 5.1 to the analysis of the reasoning behind the doctor and patient dialogue about contraceptives.

Turn 0 P: *I'd like a prescription for the pill, please.*
Turn 1 D:

1. By reasoning on her model, D checks whether she agrees with P's goal
   `Goal(P, Prescribe(D, P, pill))`.
   She discovers to share the same goal, for "positive reasons" (the patient's age); however, she has no specific reason to exclude the alternative goal either:
   `Goal(D, Prescribe(D, P, coil))`.
   She therefore adopts a "non directive", slightly doubtful answering strategy, by saying:
   You'd like the pill?

2. D then examines her own goals, and concludes:
   `Goal(D, Promote a correct use of contraceptives)`.
   She also verifies that this goal is conditioned to the following subgoals:
   `Goal(D, P receives the correct contraceptive)`,
   `Goal(D, P is convinced about the method)`,
   `Goal(D, P knows about contraceptives in general)`.
   The first two could be achieved by just prescribing the pill. However, D privileges the third one (maybe it has the priority) and, as she does not know whether
   `Know-About(P, Contraceptives)`,
   she asks:
   And... you are already aware of other methods...

3. To satisfy the second goal, D needs to understand the reasons of P: she then puts herself "from P's point of view", by reasoning on P's model and trying to guess why P holds such a goal (i.e., why she prefers to take the pill). However, rather than suggesting possibly unknown worries about other contraceptives, she just asks:
What are your reasons for the pill?

Turn 2 P:

1. P has a "defensive" attitude. She then tries to guess why
   > `Goal(D, Know-why(Goal(P, Prescribe(D, P, Pill))))`

   and she concludes that:
   > `Goal(D, not Prescribe(D, P, pill))`

   possibly because:
   > `Goal(D, Prescribe(D, P, coil))`.

   P, therefore, presumes that a conflict exists, with D, about which contraceptive to use. As we shall learn later on, this conflict is only apparent.

2. By reasoning on her model, P checks whether she may agree with the (presumed) "real" goal of D, and realizes that
   > `not Goal(P, Take(P, coil))`,

   therefore she just says so:
   Oh, the coil! I don't wanna use that!
   This is also an implicit reply to D's second remark ("yes, I do know that a coil is an alternative to the pill!").

Turn 3 D:

1. By reasoning on her model, D discovers that she does not share completely P's goal
   > `not Goal(P, Take(P, coil))`,

   but decides to avoid manifesting her disagreement.

2. To pursue her plan, she needs to know why P has such a strong view against the coil. She then reasons on P's model, and tries to guess which beliefs supported that goal. D selects one of the candidate reasons:
   > `Bel(D, Bel(P, PsychologicalArgumentsAgainstCoil))`

   and tries to suggest the answer:
   You don't feel like it.

Turn 4 P:

1. By reasoning on her model, P discovers that she agrees with D; however, she does not want to talk about this issue (this is a real, objective conflict!) and then gives an elusive answer, by turning back to her first request
   > `Goal(P, Prescribe(D, P, pill))`:
   ....and I think this is the only solution...

Turn 5 D:

1. D interprets the communication as an implicit admission that her guess was correct.
2. To achieve her goal about "Correct information on contraceptives", D decides to go deeper into the reasons of P's bias about the coil, in order to correct possible misconceptions. She then adopts the goal:

    Goal(D, Know-why (not Goal (P, Take (P, coil)))),

    which is pursued by asking:

    Why wouldn't you have a coil fitted?

Turn 6 P:

1. By reasoning on her model, P discovers that she does not want to talk about it; she therefore gives an "elusive" answer:

    I don't know why...

2. However, P immediately realises that such an answer is implausible and, maybe in order to discourage D from arguing in favour of the coil, she lies by "recurring to the authority":

    Goal(P, Bel(D, Source(Gynaec, ArgumentsAgainstCoil)))

    ...My gynaecologist advised me against it.

Turn 7 D:

1. By reasoning on her model, D wonders whether the communication is plausible: she doubts about it, but does not want to manifest her doubts; she therefore reformulates P's statement:

    Your gynaecologist advised you against it...

2. She then decides to ask for more information:

    did he say why?

Turn 8 P:

1. By reasoning on her model, P decides to carry on with the lie, by ascribing to her gynaecologist maybe a belief of her own:

    Bel (P, Bel (Gynaec, ForeignBody(coil)))

    He says it's something foreign to the body, after all...

Turn 9 D:

1. By reasoning on her model, D considers implausible this statement, but once again she decides not to disclose her disagreement.
2. Maybe D understands that P is elusive and lies, probably to hide her negative "fantasies" about the coil. She decides that there is no point in carrying on with this conflicting situation, a compromise is not possible, and she is forced to a unilateral renounce:
   - she concludes that P definitely does not want to use the coil, and abandons the goal of suggesting it, as opposed to prescribing the pill, as a way to achieve her first goal, of providing the best contraceptive;
   - she also concludes that it is difficult to convince P that the coil is not a bad contraceptive method, and therefore abandons her third goal, of providing information on contraceptives in general;

in doing so, she also renounces to reveal P's lie and to correct her misconceptions;
- she therefore privileges her second goal, of insuring that the patient is convinced about the chosen method, and, as she herself is convinced that the pill is a suitable -to P- contraceptive, she decides to reinforce positive arguments for it:

OK, it's all right that you take the pill now, ...it's the right time, ...especially as you're young.

5.3 Asymmetry of the Reasoning Process of the Two Participants

The reasoning cycle that we described in Sect. 5.1. is the "generic" reasoning that a "generic" agent would perform. However, interacting agents do not necessarily reason in the same way: in the majority of cases, their relationship is not symmetrical, as personality, emotion and role factors are not the same.

Our compromise-finding dialogue is a significant case of such an asymmetry: the doctor makes questions, the patient answers, and rarely takes the initiative. Moreover, as far as the reasoning process is concerned, the patient reasons prevalently on her own model, whereas, at almost every turn, the doctor puts herself from the patient's viewpoint.

Such a dialogue cannot, consequently, be simulated by a recursive model in which an agent's behaviour is supposed to be unique (like in the artificial clarification dialogue in Sect. 4.1): reasoning strategies will rather have to be tailored to the two agent's characteristics and to their personality traits.

6. Xanthippe: A Dialogue Simulation System

To test our hypothesis about reasoning in CRDs between believable agents, we designed a system, Xanthippe, which enables us to simulate these dialogues in different conditions. Agents are programmed, in the system, by an agent-definition language which draws ideas from AGENT-0 (Shoham 1993) and adapts them to our needs. The system is made up of two components:

- an *agent creation* component, that enables defining agents with a given "mental state", a set of "reasoning tasks" that they are able to perform (implemented as C++ and Lisp programs) and a set of "commitment rules", to decide on when these tasks have to be activated;
- a *dialogue simulation* component, that enables simulating the dialogue between those agents.

6.1 Agent Creation

Agents are designed so as to hold specific goals, beliefs and personality traits, and to follow conversational strategies which are not necessarily unique and are not uniformly cooperative or non-cooperative throughout the dialogue.

6.1.1 Mental State. The mental model of each agent is made up of three main components:

1. *agent's own mental state*: this is a belief-goal tree structure representing the conditions under which a goal is held and the way higher order goals can be achieved, given a set of "basic" beliefs and personality traits, and as a function of presumed personality traits of the other agent;
2. *image of the other agent's mental state*: this default image has the same components as the first one, although a not necessarily identical structure. We assume that every agent may accept that the other agent can reason in a different (from its own) way. This attitude towards the others depends, again, on the agent's personality: an *egocentric* agent would expect that all agents reason in the same way as it does;
3. *shared beliefs and goals*: a set of common sense beliefs and goals (for instance: concept definitions) which, in the agent's view, are common to all the agents with which it interacts.

6.1.2 Forms of Reasoning. Our agents are able to perform various reasoning tasks, each implemented by a specific *knowledge processing module*:

1. *does a proposal conflict with my beliefs or goals?*
   When an agent reasons on itself to verify whether to adopt a proposed goal or belief, it applies a goal-directed reasoning to its own mental state; if neither the candidate formula nor its negation can be derived from this knowledge base, the agent concludes with an "indifference" towards the proposal; otherwise, with an "agreement" or a "conflict".
2. *does a proposal really fit with the other agent's interests?*
   A similar type of reasoning is made on the other agent's mental state, to verify whether a received proposal matches that agent's presumed higher order goals.
3. *why does the other agent believe a communicated fact (or hold a communicated goal)?*
   When the agent investigates on the reasons of a communicated belief or goal, it makes an *abduction* on the other agent's mental state. An abduction applies a stepwise backward reasoning by checking, at each step, which of the -presumed- supporting beliefs and goals of the other agent conflict with its own components. When several candidates to explanation of the conflict exist, the selection of the most plausible of them is made by attaching to each hypothesis an endorsement value, which is a function of the emotional state and of the personality of the agent which is performing the abduction process.
4. *why do I believe a fact (or hold a goal)?*
   A backward reasoning on the agent's own mental state is made to answer know-why questions, in order to retrieve the basic beliefs which support the inquired fact.

5. *which is the answer to a Yes/No question?*
   This requires a simple goal-directed reasoning.
6. *should I change my mind, or try to convince the other agent to change its mind (in case of conflict)?*
   This task applies personality-dependent criteria to decide what to do when the agent discovers that a divergence of beliefs about a fact exists.
7. *which are the consequences of my change of mind?*
   When an agent reasons on the consequences of changing its mind, it makes a data-directed reasoning on its mental state, to revise its beliefs and goals, and to check, in particular, whether the original conflict is solved or still exists.

Other forms of reasoning, which have not yet been implemented in Xanthippe, are the following:

1. *do I hold other higher order goals?*
   This form of reasoning requires examining all "pending" goals, that is all higher order goals which have not yet been achieved.
2. *(in case of agreement) should I stop the dialogue or carry on and consider other goals?*
   In this case, the pending goals retrieved are ranked according to their priority, by applying context-based criteria, in order to establish whether to try to achieve them or to abandon them.
3. *should I argue or avoid polemizing?*
   Higher order goals are applied to select the strategy in this case.
4. *should I make an open question or a closed one?*
   Again, the decision is based on higher order goals.
5. *how should I reply to a communication of "change of belief" by the other agent?*
   Such a reply can be just an "acknowledgment", or a more complex reply, with the decision based once again on higher order goals.
6. *should I answer sincerely or be elusive, evasive or other?*
   When an agent decides how to react to a communication or an answer, it may decide to apply various types of "insincere" behaviour (it may lie, elude a question, be evasive and so on), again according to its personality, and therefore depending on the set of its higher order goals ((Castelfranchi, Falcone, and de Rosis 1998)).
7. *should I believe the communication received, or should I hypothesize an insincere assertion?*
   The possibility of insincere behaviour of some agents implies the need -for all agents- for a careful examination of the communication received, in order to discover whether a misleading behaviour can be hypothesized.

Some of the reasoning modules of Xanthippe apply ordered resolution in a forward or a backward way, with true-false or fill-in-the-blank question types.

Others are based on an abduction algorithm which sets its endorsement attachment criteria according to the personality of the reasoning agent. All modules exploit an *ATMS* (de Kleer 1986), both to insure that truth is maintained in both components of each agent's model and to speed up the various forms of reasoning.

6.1.3 Communication Capability. Agents communicate in a standard language which is similar to that proposed in (Sidner 1994). Communicative acts are generated at the end of each reasoning turn, as a function of the result of reasoning.

6.1.4 Reasoning Strategies. When an agent receives a communication from the other agent, it starts performing a reasoning process. The steps of this process are the result of *commitment rules* which establish the reasoning task to activate, as a function of the communication received, the agent's mental state (and therefore, also emotions and personality) and the results of previous reasoning steps. In the case of the compromise-finding dialogue in Sect. 4.2, for example, the commitment rules defined for the two interacting agents would simulate, for the patient, a "non cooperative" behaviour (in which the agent reasons only on itself) and, for the doctor, a more "cooperative" one, (in which the agent also reasons on the other's mental state). Similar rules can also help to establish which communicative act to produce at the end of the reasoning process.

6.2 Dialogue Simulation

Once both agents have been defined, the dialogue simulation may start: the user chooses an agent and inserts the communicative act constituting the first turn, in which the agents makes its purpose declaration. The system shifts the control to the other agent, which starts reasoning on the communication received. When a reasoning turn is completed, the communication act produced is displayed, after having been translated into a simplified natural language, to favour an easier understanding of the dialogue. The control is then passed to the other agent, and so on, until the conflict is solved, or it is agreed that it cannot be solved. Changes of mind occurring in the two agents at each reasoning step are also displayed in a separate window, to dynamically monitor how the agents' mental states evolve.

7. Conclusions

In this chapter we discussed how the design of conflict resolution dialogues among believable agents should take account of factors like personality traits and emotions, in addition to purely rational attitudes. We also sketched the design of a system, Xanthippe, able to simulate such dialogues.

The fist prototype of **Xanthippe** generated the clarification dialogue that is shown in Sect. 4.1, but does not yet allow us simulating completely the type of believable behaviour that is shown in Sect. 4.2. Agents, in **Xanthippe**, consider one goal at a time, and act according to the "sincere assertion" and the "confidence" hypotheses. To simulate the more plausible behaviours that we have exemplified, our dialoguing agents should be empowered with at least three new abilities:

1. *ability to consider several goals at the same time*, and to assign a priority to each them; as a consequence, ability to select, in each reasoning phase, which goal to pursue, which goal to abandon and so on, according also to some personality-based criteria. At present, this is not possible, mainly because reasoning is purely logical, and the strength of goals, beliefs and relationships among them is not represented. This prevents modelling the graduality of the persuasion process, the dynamic selection and abandoning of goals and the simultaneous activation and consideration of several goals at the same time, which are typical of believable agents;
2. *ability to reason about the other agent's communication*, by wondering the reasons behind a question and by considering the possibility of "insincerity";
3. *ability to consider the possibility to avoid answering* (also when the answer is known) or to answer insincerely if needed.

This research turns the dialogue simulation focus towards considering the personality and emotional factors which may intervene in situations of conflict: this analysis will enable bridging the gap between argumentation and negotiation dialogues, and unifying them into a unique, more flexible theory and modelling. Forms of insincere behaviour (such as lie, elusion, or others), which are especially relevant in case of conflict, will be introduced in a rather "natural" way in such models. Management of unexpected questions or attitudes (that we mentioned in the introductory section as one of the distinguishing capabilities of believable agents) will be introduced by enabling the agent to deal with messages that it cannot explain with its image of the other agent (due to an error in this image or to an incomplete knowledge). Effects of messages on the emotional status of the receiving agent will be simulated by revising dynamically these aspects of the user model within the process of revising the mental state. This new view therefore promises to further enrich the very interesting results that have been obtained so far in the field of dialogue simulation ((Sycara 1991; Chu-Carroll and Carberry 1995)).

Our modelling approach can be applied in several domains: conflicts between a computer system and its user may hold in any phase of interaction, due to a number of reasons (different views about which information the user really needs, how results should be presented, and so on). The possibility of conflicts among software agents has been contemplated by many authors, and we believe that the sincere assertion should probably be relaxed also in these contexts, to introduce some form of "defense", in the society of agents, against unfair attitudes of some individuals (Castelfranchi, Falcone, and de Rosis 1998).

CHAPTER 4

Managing Conflicts in Reflective Agents

Frances M.T. Brazier and Jan Treur

Vrije Universiteit Amsterdam - AI department

This chapter addresses management of conflicts in an agent by means of reflective reasoning. A structure for reflective agents is proposed within which reasoning about observation, assumption making and communication, an agent's own information state and reasoning processes, other agents' information states and reasoning processes, and combinations of these types of reflective reasoning, are explicitly modelled. The types of knowledge needed to detect, analyse and resolve conflicts that arise by meta-reasoning within the agent are discussed. The knowledge and interaction between agents required to model the wise men's puzzle are used to illustrate the approach.

1. Introduction

Although not all distributed intelligent systems are designed as multi-agent systems, many are. The metaphor of autonomous agents in interaction with each other and the external world, provides a conceptual basis for the design of distributed systems for which interaction is of primary importance. The intelligent systems themselves can often be described in terms of characteristics associated with the notion of weak agency (Wooldridge and Jennings 1995). The characteristics of this notion of agency, *autonomy*, *reactiveness*, *pro-activeness*, and *social ability*, provide a means to characterise the behaviour of an intelligent system. Pro-activeness and autonomy are related to a system's ability to reason about its own processes, goals and plans, and to control these processes. Reactivity and social ability are related to the ability to be able to communicate and co-operate with other systems and to interact with the external world. In this chapter such distributed intelligent systems are viewed to be multi-agent systems. Each individual system is viewed to be an autonomous agent.

Autonomous agents are often reflective agents: agents capable of reasoning, for example, not only about the behaviour of the external world, but also about their own behaviour, and other agents' behaviour. More specifically, reflective agents are able to reason about:

- their own information states
- their own assumptions
- the control of their own reasoning processes (e.g., which strategy to follow and when)
- their observations (e.g., which observations to perform and when)
- their actions (e.g., which actions to perform and when)
- their communication with others (e.g., which communication to perform, with which other agents)
- other agents' processes (their information states, assumptions, reasoning processes, observations, communication and actions in the external world)
- interaction between agents (e.g., the extent to which co-operation is successful)
- their own tasks

Reasoning about reasoning, *meta-reasoning*, is essential to most problem solving behaviour. Reasoning about reasoning includes reasoning about conflicts. Conflicts occur continually, at all levels within a reasoning process, not only due to unexpected events, but often as an explicit part of a reasoning solving process, on purpose, to learn from the management and evaluation of the conflict. When monitoring and guiding a reasoning process, for example, an agent needs to decide which choices to make and when (given conflicting options), which choices to re-consider, which to accept. Which diagnostic strategy to employ is, for example, a question with which human doctors are confronted, but also automated diagnostic systems. Often the choice of strategy depends on the availability, quality and cost of relevant information. For medical diagnosis the benefit and cost of the acquisition of additional information includes consideration of a patient's comfort, risk, estimated information value, and financial implications - often conflicting factors. Which choices are made depends on the strategy deployed, but often need to be adapted continually, depending on the information acquired and the state of an agent's knowledge.

Another example of a situation in which an agent needs to be able to continually reason about conflicts:

Centralised air traffic control has resulted in limited use of the total available space: a limited number of highways have been defined within which all aircraft are scheduled. Currently the concept of free flight is being explored: aircraft are free to fly the route they themselves determine with very limited interaction with other aircraft. New traffic rules are being devised to this purpose. One of the main aspects involved is that to be able to determine his/her own course, a pilot needs to be able to reason about the expected behaviour of other aircraft: a pilot needs to be able to reason about a specific situation from the perspective of another pilot given limited information such as the characteristics of the aircraft, its position, its destination. On the basis of this information the pilot can determine his/her own strategy to adapt his/her own course, if and when conflicts occur.

Reasoning about conflicts necessitates reasoning about
- uncertainty of facts and/or inferences
- inconsistency of facts and/or inferences
- availability and adequacy of information in a given situation types of interaction needed
- (default) assumptions and the current information state

Often such meta-reasoning is needed at different levels. The pilot, for example, needs to decide whether his/her own past experience with specific airlines should influence his/her decision with respect to the best course to take, given the analysis of the other aircraft's expected behaviour. If the other airline has, in the past, shown to be reliable, a pilot may decide to rely on his/her own initial analysis. If not, the pilot may decide to adjust his/her own course to minimise the chance of conflicting courses. The pilot's analysis is based on the pilot's own observations, but may also be influenced by additional information acquired from other sources. Modelling this type of reasoning requires non-trivial nesting of reasoning. An arbitrary number of meta-levels may be needed, depending on the intricacy of the reasoning process.

In the literature on reflection such as (Weyhrauch 1980; Maes and Nardi 1988; Attardi and Simi 1994) a restricted number of the types of reflective reasoning distinguished above, are modelled. Non-trivial combinations of different types of reflective reasoning, however, have not been studied extensively. In the literature on modelling in the context of multi-agent systems, most often the types of reflective reasoning agents are capable of performing is limited.

To model management of conflicts, an agent model is introduced in this chapter that models non-trivial combinations of reflective reasoning. This model has been used to model distributed air traffic control, as discussed above. A generic agent model is introduced in Section 2 and refined in Section 4 for a reflective agent capable of performing the types of reasoning about conflicts listed above, illustrated for the specification of the wise men's puzzle (introduced in Section 3). An analysis of conflict management within the example domain is presented in Section 5. The role of meta-reasoning and reflection in the context of conflict management is discussed in Section 6.

2. Reflective Reasoning in a Generic Agent Model

To design a generic structure for autonomous agents capable of reflective reasoning, the types of reasoning agents can be expected to perform, must be distinguished. In (Brazier, Jonker and Treur 1997) a compositional generic agent model (GAM) is introduced which distinguishes seven main processes, modelled by components (see Figure 1). The types of reflective reasoning performed in each of these components are briefly discussed in this section.

Reasoning about *the external world* (*MWI*) is a basic type of reasoning reflective agents are assumed to be capable of performing. A reflective agent needs to be able to reason about a specific situation, extending its own knowledge, by, for example, confirming or rejecting assumptions about the world made in previous reasoning processes.

As autonomous agents capable of interacting with the external world, reflective agents must also be capable of reasoning about *interaction with the external world (WIM)*: about, for example, the types of information that can be observed in the external material world, when and how, but also which actions are to be performed, when and how.

Autonomous reflective agents need to be capable of reasoning about their *own processes (OPC)*. Reflective agents need to be able to reason about their own characteristics, capabilities and goals, of their success or failure in achieving these goals, about assumptions which need to be or have been made and when, about information which has been sought and not yet found, about information which has not yet been explored, about strategic preferences, about control, and about all other aspects of their own reasoning and acting.

Reflective agents also need to be capable of reasoning about *other agents' processes (MAI)*. Reflective agents need to be able to reason about the information available to other agents, about their (reasoning) capabilities, their goals and success (or lack thereof), their strategic preferences, their assumptions, et cetera.

To interact with other agents, reflective agents must be capable of reasoning about *interaction between agents (AIM)*. Agents not only need to be able to reason about which information can be obtained by communication with which other agents, but also about how and when this communication has to be initiated.

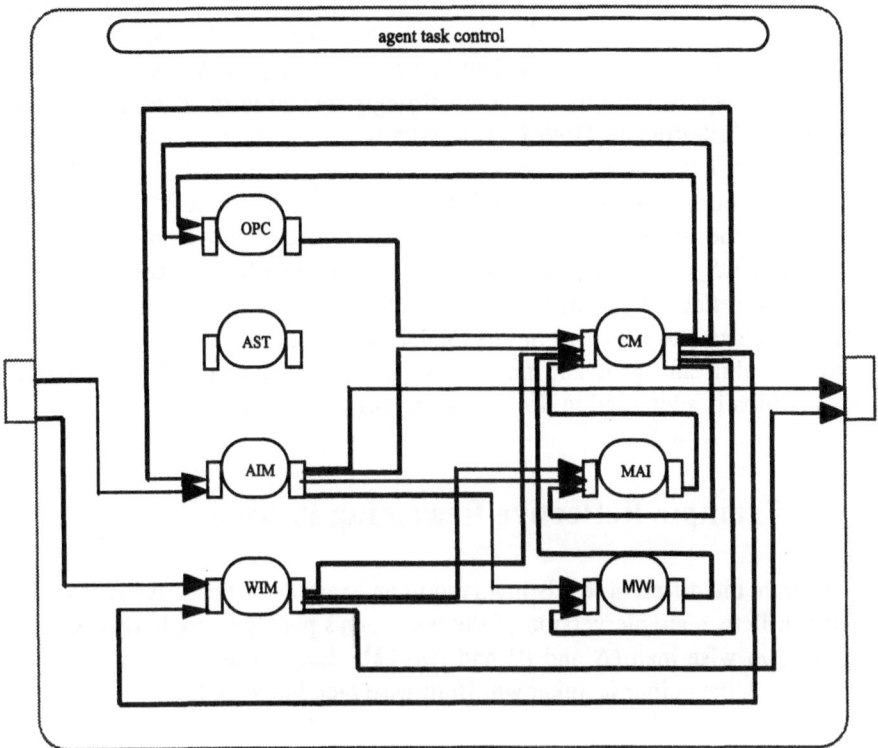

Fig 2.1. A Generic Agent Model

In situations in which *co-operation between agents* (CM) is required a reflective agent needs to be able to reason about the type of co-operation required, its success, its failure and appropriate actions to take.

Last, but not least, a reflective agent's *agent specific tasks* (AST) require reasoning, but also often include reasoning about the tasks the agent is to perform: about the way in which a task is to be approached, about assumptions which can be made, for example.

The seven types of reasoning distinguished above correspond to the seven generic components depicted in the generic agent model presented in Figure 2.1. These tasks are generic in the sense that all autonomous agents are assumed to be capable of performing these tasks. The corresponding components are most often composed. The number of levels of reasoning involved depend on the complexity of the tasks for which they are designed.

Within each of these components, an agent must be able to reason about conflicts. Conflicts within *own process control*, may be explicitly modelled as conflicts in beliefs, desires and intentions. A generic model for reasoning about beliefs, desires and intentions, in which such conflicts are explicitly modelled is proposed in (Brazier, Dunin-Keplicz, Treur and Verbrugge 1998). The concepts applied in this model are strongly related to the concepts distinguished by Castelfranchi (1998). Conflicts within *co-operation management* are addressed in the co-operation model applied in (Brazier, Jonker and Treur 1996); for a more detailed specification, see (Brazier, Jonker and Treur 1997). Conflicts in the *agent specific task* design are discussed in (Brazier, Langen and Treur 1995). This chapter focuses on a refinement of the generic agent model for a reflective agent, and how specific types of conflicts are deliberately introduced and managed in this model. Note that this chapter focuses on conflicts within an agent and not on the management of conflicts between agents (which is addressed in, for example, (Brown 1998)).

3. An Example Reflective Reasoning Process

To illustrate the different levels involved in an example of reflective reasoning about conflicts, a simple version of the wise men's puzzle is used. This puzzle requires two wise men (A and B) and two hats. Each wise man is wearing a hat, of which the colour is unknown. Both wise men know that:

– hats can be white or black
– there is at least one white hat
– they can observe the colour of each other's hat
– they both reason fully logically.

Assume, for example, that both men have a white hat and that wise man A is asked whether he knows the colour of his hat. Wise man A must answer that he is incapable of drawing a conclusion about the colour of his own hat. On the basis of this knowledge wise man B can then reason that its own hat is white. This reasoning process is depicted below in Figures 3.1 and 3.2. Wise man B not only reasons about his own state but also about A's reasoning processes. B reasons about the observations A could have made and the conclusions A would have drawn on the basis of these observations.

Fig 3.1 A reflective reasoning process: part 1

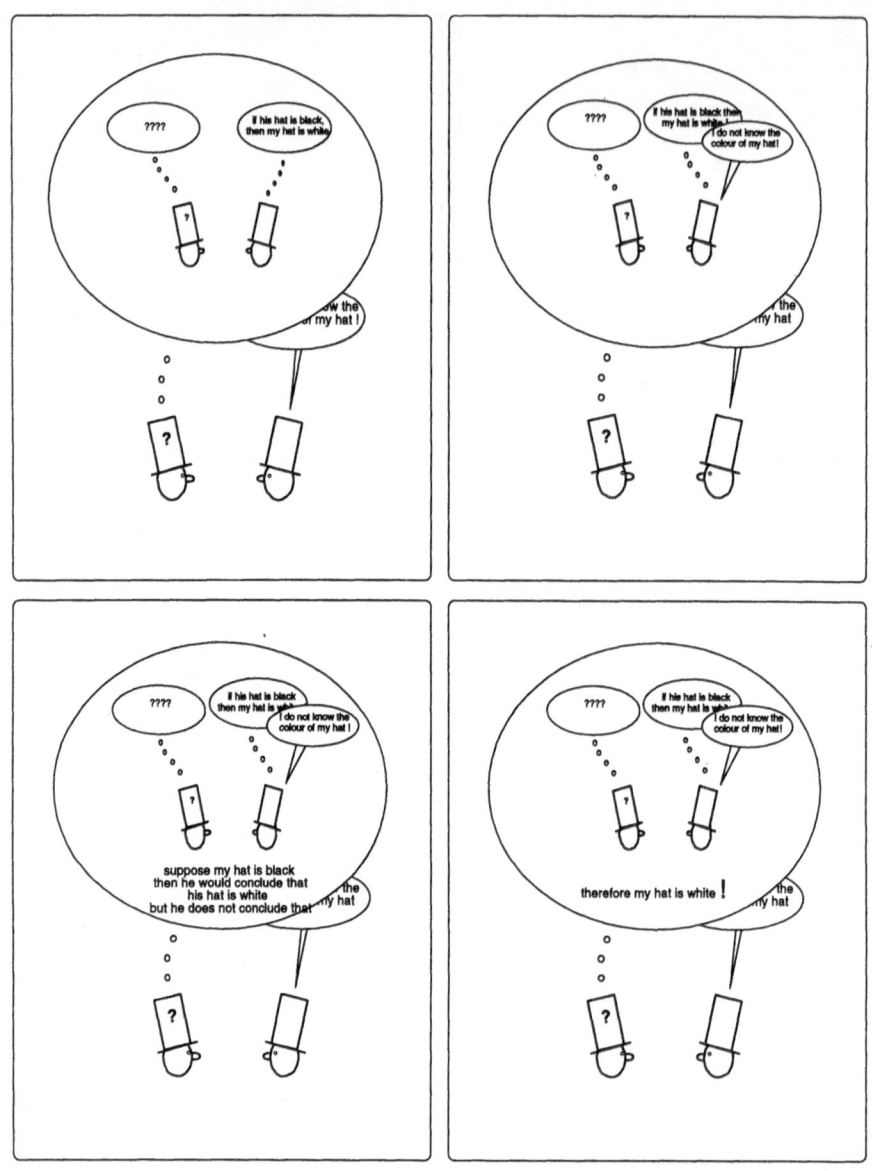

Fig 3.2 A reflective reasoning process: part 2

The generic agent model briefly presented in Section 2, is refined (special-ised and instantiated) to model an agent that is able to perform the reflective reasoning about conflicts needed to solve this puzzle. The resulting model can be used to model both wise men: wise man A as Agent A and wise man B as Agent B. For the purpose of explanation, however, the model is described from the perspective of Agent B: the concepts and specifications involved are illustrated from Agent B's point of view. Reflective elements in B's reasoning include reasoning about:

- observations (e.g., the decision to observe the colour of A's hat),
- A's reasoning (which conclusions should A have reached on the basis of specific information),
- B's own information state and B's assumptions (e.g., about the colour of B's own hat),
- control of B's reasoning and actions, and
- communication of B with A (which information can and should A provide and when).

Note that for convenience sake quotes to denote an object-meta naming relation have been omitted.

4. A Specific Compositional Model of a Reflective Agent

In this section the generic agent model is refined. For three of the generic agent components more specific compositions are introduced (see Figure 4.1). The most illustrative generic component of an autonomous agent in this example is the component devised to perform the agent's specific task of determining the colour of its own hat.

4.1 Processes at different levels of abstraction

The processes modelled within the agent model for a reflective agent are depicted in Figure 4.1. All but one of the processes distinguished for the generic agent, are applicable to the reflective agent in this example. Due to the simplicity of the example, co-operation management has not been included. As in the generic agent model the processes involved in controlling an agent (e.g., determining, monitoring and evaluating its own goals, plans) are the task of the component own process control.

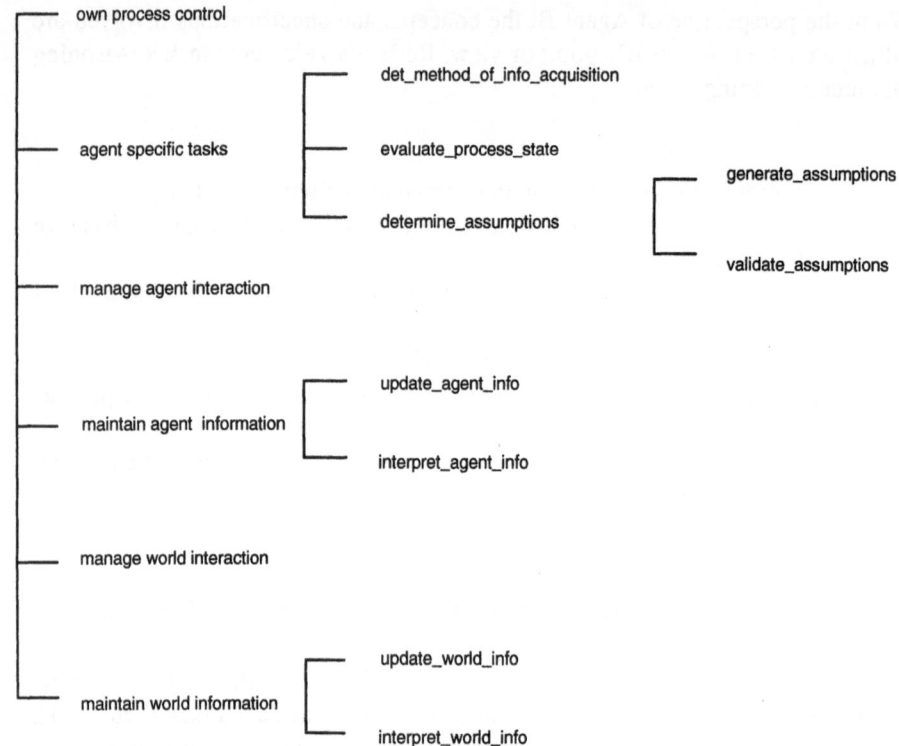

Fig 4.1 Process abstraction levels for the reflective agent

Maintaining knowledge of other agents' abilities and knowledge (the task of the component **maintain agent information**) involves two processes: interpreting available information on other agents (the task of the component **interpret agent info**), and keeping this information up to date (the task of the component **update agent info**). Comparably, the processes involved in maintaining information on the external (material) world (the task of the component **maintain world information**) are two-fold: interpreting available information on the external world (the task of the **component interpret world info**), and keeping this information up to date (the task of the component **update world info**).

The reflective agent's specific task in this example domain (the process performed by the component **determine hat colour**) is to determine the colour of the other agent's hat. This task involves three subtasks for which three components are distinguished: **determine method of information acquisition**, **evaluate process state** and **determine assumptions**.

The component **determine method of information acquisition** is responsible for the choice of one of three options: (1) observe the colour of agent A's hat hoping this will provide the information required, (2) communicate with agent A on A's conclusions concerning the colour of agent A's own hat and (3) make assumptions on the colour of his own hat and reason about the conclusions A should have drawn.

The component evaluate process state determines the results of having tried one of the methods: whether the method provided the colour of agent B's hat. To be able to reason about the results of the analysis process (the task of the component analyse process state) a separate component cwa analyse process state is needed.

The component determine assumptions determines which assumptions to make during reasoning. To this purpose determine assumptions first generates a possible assumption (the task of determine assumption's component generate assumptions). It then evaluates this assumption by reasoning about the consequences of the assumption (derived by the component interpret agent info in the component maintain agent info): the task of determine assumptions' second component, validate assumptions.

4.2 The processes at a lower level of abstraction

In this section the interface knowledge structures for each of the refinements of the top-level processes distinguished above, are presented together with the applicable (meta-)level of the knowledge structures with respect to the encompassing component (note that this is not the level within each of the componentís themselves), and task control knowledge.

Refinement of the agent specific task: determine hat colour

The component evaluate process state receives three types of information:
1. information on the agent's own observations (from the component own process control),
2. information on conclusions agent A has reached and communicated (from the component manage agent interaction), and
3. information on the best assumption (if the component determine assumption's component generate assumptions has been able to make a best assumption).

On the basis of this information the component analyse process state determines the state of the problem solving process (e.g., whether observations have been made, whether a definite conclusion on the colour of the hat can be drawn). The knowledge with which the state of the process is determined includes both knowledge on which positive conclusions can be based, and knowledge on which negative conclusions can be based. Positive conclusions on the state of the process can be drawn, given that information has been acquired from observation, communication and/or assumption determination. Negative conclusions are based on the lack of positive conclusions; they are drawn by a closed world assumption on the output atoms, explicitly specified at a higher (third) meta-level in the component cwa analyse process state.

The information on the state of the reasoning process is transferred from the component evaluate process state to the component determine method of information acquisition. The specifications for the knowledge structures used within the component evaluate process state are shown below for the components analyse process state and cwa analyse process state . The knowledge structures for the component evaluate process state, are comparable.

component analyse_process_state

input atoms:

known_to_me_based_on_obs(hat_colour(A, C:Colour))	(** meta-level 1 **)
communicated(A, concludes(A, hat_colour(A, C:Colour)))	(** meta-level 2 **)
communicated(A, cannot_reach_a_conclusion(A)))	(** meta-level 2 **)
best_assumption(observed(A, hat_colour(I,C:Colour)))	(** meta-level 2 **)

output atoms:

performed(observation)	(** meta-level 2 **)
performed(communication)	(** meta-level 2 **)
performed(assumption)	(** meta-level 2 **)
colour_known	(** meta-level 2 **)

knowledge base:

```
      if          known_to_me_based_on_own_obs(hat_colour(A, C:Colour))
      then        performed(observation) ;


      if          communicated(A, X:Comms)
      then        performed(communication) ;


      if          best_assumption(observed(A,hat_colour(I, C:Colour)))
      then        performed(assumption) ;


      if          best_assumption(observed(A,hat_colour(I, C:Colour)))
      then        known_to_me_based_on_comm(hat_colour(I, C:Colour)) ;


      if          known_to_me_based_on_own_obs(hat_colour(I, C:Colour))
      then        colour_known ;
```

if   known_to_me_based_on_comm(hat_colour(I, C:Colour))
then   colour_known

component cwa_analyse_process_state

input atoms:
known_true(X:INFO_ELEMENT)   (** meta-level 3 **)

output atoms:
to_assume(X:INFO_ELEMENT, false)   (** meta-level 3 **)

knowledge base:
    if   **not** known_true(X:INFO_ELEMENT)
    then   to_assume(X:INFO_ELEMENT, false) ;

Based on the status information provided by **evaluate process state** the component **determine method of information acquisition** determines which method to follow: observation, communication or assumption.

component determine_method_of_information_acquisition

input atoms:
performed(observation)   (** meta-level 2 **)
performed(communication)   (** meta-level 2 **)
performed(assumption)   (** meta-level 2 **)

output atoms:
method of acquisition(observation)   (** meta-level 2 **)
method of acquisition(communication)   (** meta-level 2 **)
method of acquisition(assumption)   (** meta-level 2 **)

knowledge base:

    possible_method_of_acquisition(observation);
    possible_method_of_acquisition(communication);
    possible_method_of_acquisition(assumption);

    prior_to(observation, communication)
    prior_to(communication, assumption)

    if   **not** performed(obs)
    then   selected_method_of_acquisition(obs) ;

```
if              possible_method_of_acquisition(X)
  and           possible_method_of_acquisition(Y)
  and           performed(X)
  and           not performed(Y)
  and           prior_to(X, Y)
then            selected_method_of_acquisition(Y) ;
```

The component **determine assumptions** receives explicit information on the agent's lack of knowledge of A's observations (the truth value false for the input atom known_to_me(observed(A, hat_colour(I, C:Colour)) from the input interface of the component **agent specific task: determine hat colour** (which it, in turn, has received from the component **own process control**). In addition, **determine assumptions** receives information on A's conclusions on its own hat colour (received from the component **manage agent interaction**), and information that the assumed observations of A on the agent B's own hat colour, are contradictory. Based on this input information the component **generate assumptions**, generates both possible assumptions (which are transferred to the component **validate assumptions** and **maintain agent information**) and best assumptions (which are transferred to the output interface of the component **determine assumptions**, and from there to the component **evaluate process state**).

component generate_assumptions

input atoms:
```
communicated(A, concludes(A, hat_colour(A, C: Colour)))   (** meta-level 2 **)
known_to_me(observed(A, hat_colour(I, C:Colour)))         (** meta-level 2 **)
contradictory(observed(A, hat_colour(I, C:Colour))        (** meta-level 2 **)
```

output atoms:
```
possible_assumption(observed(A, hat_colour(I, C:Colour)))  (** meta-level 2 **)
best_assumption(observed(A, hat_colour(I, C:Colour)))      (** meta-level 2 **)
```

knowledge base:
```
if              communicated(A, concludes(A, hat_colour(A, white)))
  and           not known_to_me(observed(A, hat_colour(I, white)))
then            possible_assumption(observed(A, hat_colour(I, white))) ;

if              communicated(A, cannot_reach_a_conclusion(A))
  and           not known_to_me(observed(A, hat_colour(I, black)))
then            possible_assumption(observed(A, hat_colour(I, black))) ;
```

if   contradictory(observed(A, hat_colour(I, black)))
then   best_assumption(observed(A, hat_colour(I, white))) ;

if   contradictory(observed(A, hat_colour(I, white)))
then   best_assumption(observed(A, hat_colour(I, black))) ;

Within the component maintain agent information a possible assumption with respect to observations on A's hat colour is transferred to the component interpret agent info, in which the conclusions A would draw on the basis of this assumption are derived. This information is transferred to the input interface of the component agent specific task: determine hat colour, which in turn, transfers this information to the input interface of the component determine assumptions. The component determine assumptions also receives information on A's communication with respect to its own conclusions with respect to its own hat colour from the component manage agent interaction. Both the information on the conclusions A would have drawn if A had observed specific assumed facts (the possible assumption) and the information on A's communicated conclusions with respect to its own hat colour are transferred to the component validate assumptions The component validate assumptions also receives information about the possible assumption directly from the component generate assumptions. The component validate assumptions determines whether these conclusions on the expected conclusions of A contradict the conclusions A actually has drawn (and communicated) on the colour of A's own hat. This information on the existence of a contradiction is transferred to the component generate assumptions.

component validate_assumptions

input atoms:
communicated(cannot_reach_a_conclusion(A))   (** meta-level 2 **)
communicated(A, concludes(A, hat_colour(A, C; colour)))   (** meta-level 2 **)
expected(concludes(A, hat_colour(A, C: colour)))   (** meta-level 2 **)
expected(cannot_reach_a_conclusion(A))   (** meta-level 2 **)
possible_assumption(observed(A, hat_colour(I, C:Colour))) (** meta-level 2 **)

output atom:
contradictory(observed(A, hat_colour(I, C: colour)))   (** meta-level 2 **)

knowledge base:
   if   communicated(cannot_reach_a_conclusion(A))
     and   expected(concludes(A, hat_colour(A, white)))
     and   possible_assumption(observed(A, hat_colour(I, black)))
   then   contradictory(observed(A, hat_colour(I, black))) ;

if	communicated(A, concludes(A, hat_colour(A, white)))
and	expected(cannot_reach_a_conclusion(A)))
and	possible_assumption(observed(A, hat_colour(I, white)))
then	contradictory(observed(A, hat_colour(I, white))) ;

Task control of determine hat colour

Activation of determine hat colour, in combination with activation of the links which can provide the information required by determine hat colour, is specified by agent B's task control. Task control of determine hat colour determines which internal components and links to activate. Activation of evaluate process state is done in combination with activation of the incoming links. If the final evaluation criterion depicting success of determination of colour of the hat, is reached then the task of determine hat colour is fulfilled. If, however, the evaluation criterion that specifies that one or more conclusions concerning previous performance have been reached, succeeds, task control specifies that the component determine method of information acquisition is to be activated, together with the related links. Based on the success or failure of the evaluation criteria, task control determines which component and links to activate next. If, for example, the evaluation criterion observations required, is successful, then determine hat colour sends a request to manage world interaction to make observations in the external world. If, for example, the evaluation criterion assumptions required is successful, then another component of determine hat colour, namely determine assumptions, is activated. The component determine assumptions, in turn, activates one of its components, based on its own task control knowledge.

Refinement of the component: maintain agent information

The component maintain agent information has two components: update current agent information, which stores information on other agents, and interpret agent info, which interprets the available agent information. The first component only stores and updates information, it does not reason. To interpret agent information the component interpret agent info has knowledge with which it can reason about the other agent. In the wise men example the knowledge specifies how the other agent can reason; it gives an explicit representation of A's deduction system and A's knowledge. For example, part of the knowledge on A is the explicit meta-statement that if a fact X is derivable by A and A has knowledge that X implies Y, then Y is derivable by A (modus ponens). Agent B uses this knowledge of A to reason about A's reasoning, as shown in the knowledge base of B's component interpret agent info specified below. In this knowledge base the meta-statement rule(A, X, Y) denotes that A has the knowledge that X implies Y. The notation [X,Y] is interpreted as the conjunction of the statements X and Y, and derivable(A, X) denotes that A is able to derive statement X. The (meta-)fact observed(A, X) states that fact X is observed in the external world by A. Note that the I in this knowledge base refers to A, because it refers to A's own knowledge.

component interpret_agent_info

input atoms:
observed(A, hat_colour(B,C:Colour))   (** meta-level 2 **)

output atoms:
derivable(A, X)   (** meta-level 2 **)

knowledge base:
    rule(A, hat_colour(B,black), hat_colour(I,white)) ;

if	observed(A, X)
then	derivable(A, X) ;

if	derivable(A, X)
and	rule(A, X,Y)
then	derivable(A, Y) ;

if	derivable(A, X)
and	derivable(A, Y)
then	derivable(A, [X,Y]) ;

Refinement of the component maintain world information

The component maintain world information has two components: update current world information, which stores information on the world, and interpret world info, which interprets the available world information. Comparable to the composition described in the previous section, the first component only stores and updates information and does not reason. To interpret world information the component interpret world info has knowledge with which it can reason about the world. This knowledge is used by B to draw conclusions from information he has obtained from observation of A's hat colour: if B observes a black hat, then his own hat is white.

component interpret world info

input atoms:
hat_colour(A, C:Colour)   (** object level **)

output atoms:

hat_colour(I, C:Colour)   (**object level **)

knowledge base:
> **if**   hat_colour(A,black)
> **then**   hat_colour(I,white) ;

Note that both A and B can observe part of the external world, but that they observe *different* parts. This difference is expressed in the specifications by the different information links defined between the external world and the agents. The difference is also mirrored in the input information types of the two agents.

5. Analysis of the Example Reasoning Process in the Model

First the agent B generates a number of possible information acquisition strategies. As the agent is assumed to only perform one of these strategies at a time this entails a conflict between the strategies. This conflict is resolved by explicit knowledge that as long as observation has not been performed, it should be selected; otherwise if observation has been performed and communication has not, then (because the strategic knowledge specifies that observation is performed prior to communication), communication is selected, and so on.

Next, the agent deliberately aims at introducing another conflict, by making an assumption that may quite well turn out to be false: it assumes that its own hat is black (component **generate assumptions**). The subsequent process aims at falsification of the assumption. As a first step the deductive consequences of the assumption are derived, taking into account a model of the reasoning process of the other agent: the consequences of agent B's own hat being black, are that this would be observed by agent A and that agent A would draw the conclusion that its own hat is white, and communicate this. Conflict detection occurs when B compares the deductive consequences of B's assumption to observation results; the results contradict each other. After detection of the conflict (within the component **validate assumptions**), and determination of the assumption from which the conflict originates, the conflict is resolved within B's component (by blaming the assumption for the conflict, and making the opposite assumption).

6. Discussion

This chapter has addressed meta-reasoning and reflection in the context of conflict management, in particular with respect to agent abilities and architecture. An example of a reflective agent, based on a generic agent model, has been presented within which reasoning about (1) observation and agent interaction, (2) an agent's own information state and reasoning processes, (3) other agents' information states and reasoning processes, and combinations of these types of reflective reasoning, are explicitly modelled. To illustrate the transparency of the structure, partial specifications of the wise men's puzzle have been presented within which components at different meta-levels of knowledge and reasoning are distinguished. The agent is able to deliberately introduce a conflict, by making an assumption that is expected to turn out to be false. Conflict management is performed in a process aimed at falsification of the assumption. Conflict detection occurs when the deductive consequences of the assumption are compared to observation results. After detection of the conflict, the conflict is resolved by assigning a higher priority to observation results than to assumptions.

In the model presented in this chapter the dynamics of the combined pattern of reasoning, observation and communication is modelled: the specification explicitly expresses the strategy with which the problem is approached. Specification of the problem, abstracting from the dynamics, would also have been possible. However, in that case, either strategic knowledge to guide the problem solving has to be added at the implementation level, or a theorem prover or other program would need to search for the solution in the space of all possible alternatives. In the former case an implementation independent description of the dynamics of the system would be lacking. In the latter case the search process may be inefficient. Moreover, the system behaviour differs significantly from the way in which human agents most often approach problems such as this: human agents use strategic knowledge to guide the search.

The modelling approach adopted in this chapter distinguishes components reasoning at different levels in all cases where semantically distinct meta-levels can be found. An advantage of this approach is that the model has a rich structure with different constructs for entities that are semantically different. As a result a more complex problem may require additional meta-levels. This may be considered to be the price that has to be paid for the richer structure. An alternative approach is that all meta-levels are encoded in the highest meta-level. The price that is paid in this case is that the finer semantical distinctions between the different meta-levels found in practice are not explicitly represented.

CHAPTER 5

Difference: a key to enrich knowledge - Concepts and Models

Laurent Chaudron, Humbert Fiorino, Nicolas Maille, and Catherine Tessier

Onera-Cert Toulouse

The aim of the chapter is to show that differences among several agents can have positive effects in so far as they may generate original solutions and be a basis for a global enrichment of the agents' knowledge. Philosophical foundations of cooperation and of the positive aspects of conflicts are first explained. Our contribution next consists in i) a formal model devoted to the representation of the knowledge exchanged by the agents and to the characterization of their *common* knowledge; ii) a formal and implemented model allowing the *dynamic process* of common knowledge elaboration to be represented.

1. Introduction

Conflicts among several agents within a multiagent system may arise from different reasons (Reed and Long 1997): resource conflicts may occur when resources are limited or unavailable for all the agents; in dynamic contexts, knowledge conflicts may be created by the incompleteness and uncertainty of the agents' knowledge or beliefs; and differences in autonomous and heterogeneous agents' skills and points of view may generate conflicts if the agents' pieces of information are not comparable or if they come up with different answers to the same questions. Considering the last two cases, conflicts most often arise in contexts where a unique standpoint has to be worked out, e.g. situation assessment systems, multi-robot systems, intelligence systems, decision aid systems.

Considering research on multiagent systems, the focus has been much on how to avoid, solve or get rid of conflicts, via negotiation (Sycara 1989; Adler, Alvah, Weihmayer, and Worrest 1989; Rosenschein and Zlotkin 1994) or constraint satisfaction (Conry, Kuwabara, Lesser, and Meyer 1991; Khedro and Genesereth 1994). When choices have to be made, context-dependent likelihood or preference measures generally induce a total order on individual points of views, e.g. (Cholvy 1993), despite the fact that they may not be totally comparable with one another.

For instance, let us consider two agents α_1 and α_2 observing a given object in a dynamic environment. From his own sensors, α_1 can tell that there is a truck moving towards the building; α_2 tells that there are two vehicles moving with a 30km/h speed. α_1's and α_2's pieces of information cannot be compared, as it is shown on figure 1.1.

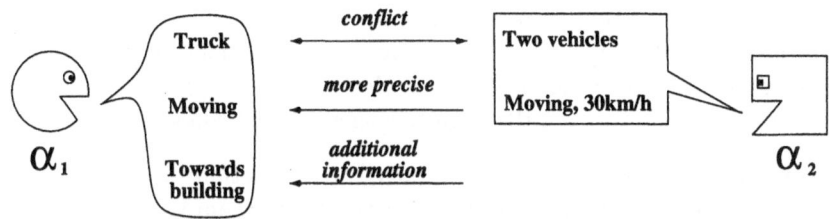

Fig. 1.1. α_1's and α_2's pieces of information

Such different points of view are obviously richer than a unique one, even if they are conflicting. Therefore, there is no *a priori* reason why one of them should be chosen instead of the other. Rather, positive effects can be searched for as those differences may generate original solutions and be a basis for a global enrichment of the agents' knowledge.

The context of this chapter is the elaboration of a common point of view by several agents (persons or machines) that may have a different knowledge on a given topic, or get different pieces of information coming from a dynamic environment. The motivations for this work are conceptual (fundamental notions are defined), theoretical (formal models are designed) and pragmatic (models are actually implemented for various real-world problems).

The chapter is organized as follows: philosophical foundations of cooperation and of the positive aspects of conflicts are first explained; then formal tools for knowledge representation and cooperation and conflicts management are defined; a situation assessment example is given and a final discussion on cooperation and conflicts is proposed.

2. Philosophical foundations

2.1 Cooperation maxims

Let us consider two *cognitive* agents interacting to progressively elaborate a common result; they may represent two human beings in a brainstorming meeting, or two machines solving a problem, or one human being and one machine in a situation assessment and decision making context. *Cognitive* (Sallantin, Szczeciniarz, Barboux, and Renaud 1991) means that each agent has deductive abilities: he can represent objects, qualify them with properties, set out statements and implement inferential processes. Moreover, only contexts where the explicit knowledge is preponderant in relation to the individual interpretative variations are considered. In real life situations (e.g. working groups, brainstorm meetings) the natural cooperative attitudes of the agents look as if they were governed by tacit rules. In order to describe these rules and following recent works (Evrard and Maudet 1998) dedicated to the exploitation of Grice's theory in dialogue analysis, we propose five *cooperation maxims* defining the cognitive agents' ideal cooperative work:

1. **purpose**: the agents are only involved in the action of elaborating a common result (for instance, they do not try to manipulate each other and they are aware of that);
2. **inter-operability**: the agents understand each other (the vocabulary is domain-limited and unambiguous – the same thing is understood under the same denotator);
3. **quality**: they follow Grice's theory assumptions (Grice 1975) and do not resort to control elements for the dialogue (e.g. "let me speak");
4. **protocol**: the mono-modal characteristic of oral communication is respected, different agents do not give their points of view at the same time (for example, statements are set out in turn by each agent);
5. **observability**: a current result or solution is available at each time t, either on a physical medium (blackboard, screen) or *via* a task-independent clerk.

We do not intend to assume that each cooperation process must verify all the above items. In fact, the whole set of cooperation maxims describes the class of perfect cooperative situations (as it is the case for Grice's maxims for dialogue situations).

As we want to focus on cooperative agents who are different, we will refer to a general rule of communication theory: "any communication exchange is symmetric or complementary, depending on whether it is based on equality or difference" (Watzlawick, Helmick Beavin, and Jackson 1967); hence, two main cooperation categories can be distinguished:

2.2 Symmetric cooperation

In this first case, there is no difference between the agents: they can be considered as clones within the cooperation context and they are purely redundant. Cooperation provides a result that is delivered more quickly or that is more reliable than when a single agent is involved (figure 2.1); in that sense, it is called *additive* cooperation (Tessier and Chaudron 1996).

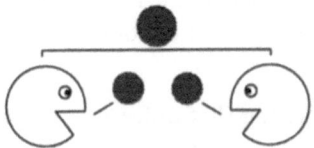

Fig. 2.1. Symmetric agents

2.3 Complementary cooperation, conflicts and suprA-cooperation

The second case involves different agents who are not interchangeable, i.e. they have different skills or points of view, or they may get different kinds of information from their environment. Those differences may allow a cooperative *construction* of knowledge to be achieved: in particular, conflicts may be a means to go further than a mere concatenation of the agents' initial knowledge bases. In that sense, cooperation is more than additive; we have called it *suprA-cooperation* (Tessier and Chaudron 1996).

At least three types of conflicts may arise between such agents:

- **difference**: two agents respectively give result a and result b to the same request. Here, only the agents' knowledge is involved in the conflict, not the agents themselves (remark: an optimal "conflicting" operator is provided by a negation operator, see hereafter).
  This case will be the main topic of this chapter.
- **refutation**: when both agents are able to apply inferential rules on their knowledge, they may respectively output formula ϕ and formula $\neg\phi$. This case is considered as the universal example of knowledge conflict in which one knowledge base is refuted by the other via the agents' interactions and a negation operator. Clearly both the knowledge and the agents are involved in the conflict. It must be noticed that the agents are supposed to share the refuting criterion the most common instance of which is the negation operator; nevertheless, many other algebraic means can be used to determine the refutation of a piece of knowledge by another one (Wansing 1996).
  The complex relations between the concepts of negation, knowledge and agents are currently under study. In the sequel, negation will be considered as an ordinary functional operator that contributes to the difference between two pieces of knowledge.
- **opposition**: the agents try to harm each other. In that case, knowledge is not a fundamental element, it is a question of relationships between individuals. Examples are hostility, aggression and fighting [see Castelfranchi's chapter].

As the study of agents' behaviours is more the concern of the psycho-sociological domain, this last case of conflict will not be considered here.

Remark: it is worth noticing that difference, refutation and opposition are not redundant: difference may exist without refutation, refutation does not suppose an opposition between the agents, and the agents may clash without being able to refute one another. The fact that refutation supposes difference is the only basic link.

The principle of suprA-cooperation is that conflicts can be used as a constructive basis to enrich the agents' common knowledge. The main conceptual grounding is Lakatos's approval-refutation cycle (Lakatos 1984) (see figure 2.2).

- when a conjecture[1] (or a theory T) and its proof are accepted, the conjecture is considered a theorem that can be refined by corollaries and examples (**C**);
- on the contrary, when the conjecture and its proof seem to be falsified by a counter-example δ, three solutions arise: rectification (1), exception (2), or search for a guilty-lemma (3).

(1) if δ is considered as an error, it has simply to be rectified in δ' and the new theory is still T.

(2) if δ is an exception, the conjecture and the counter-example have the same level of validity, and the exception is declared as such. The new theory is $T \cup \{except(\delta)\}$.

(3) Lakatos's third way is a sort of cognitive surgery in the body of the conjecture in order to find and rectify a so-called "guilty-lemma" λ responsible for the contradiction to the counter-example. The conjecture is modified, the ex-counter-example is integrated to form a new theory: $T - \{\lambda\} \cup \{\delta\}$ (**B and A**). New examples appear. Sometimes a new concept appears during the rectification of the proof, it is called a *proof-concept*.

---

[1] for epistemological considerations on the concept of "conjecture" see (Mazur 1997).

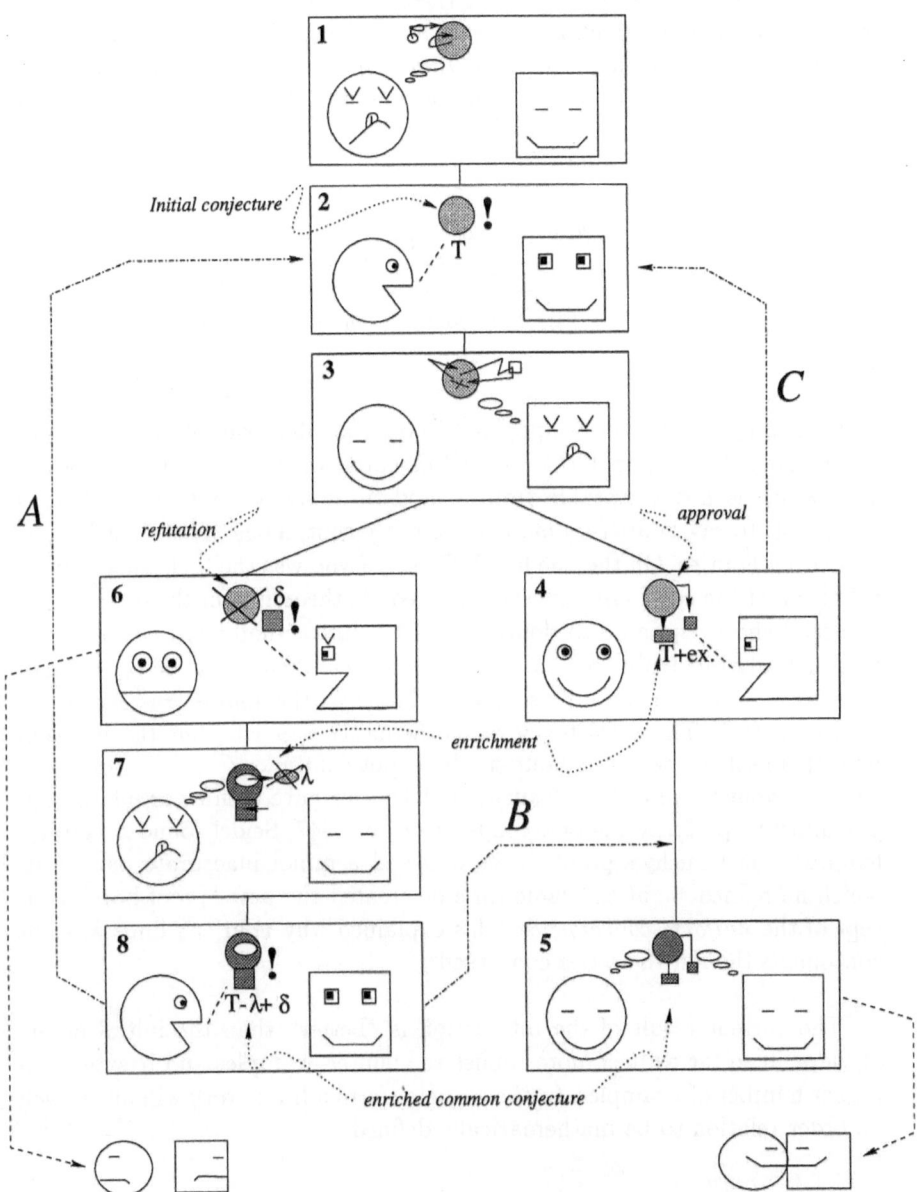

Fig. 2.2. Lakatos's cycle for suprA-cooperation

Example - the uniform convergence birth

This historical example of suprA-cooperation involves three famous mathematicians: Cauchy, Fourier, and Seidel.

In 1821, Cauchy enunciated a general theorem: $T = $ *The limit of a convergent series of continuous functions is continuous.* Nevertheless in 1822, Fourier discovered[2] a *convergent series of continuous functions* $\left(\sum_{n=0}^{\infty} \frac{1}{2^{2n+1}} cos(2n+1)x\right)$ *whose limit was <u>not</u> continuous*; the curve of this limit is the following figure 2.3:

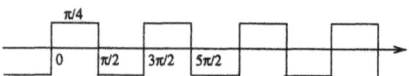

Fig. 2.3. Fourier's curve

Consequently, this series appeared to be a counter-example δ for the theory T: even if it is possible to draw this curve with one continuous pencil line (which is not acceptable from a modern analysis point of view), it is impossible to say Fourier's *function* is strictly continuous. Thus Cauchy was refuted by Fourier. On the one hand, Cauchy (who was the first one to give a definition of the continuity concept) proved his theorem. On the other hand, Fourier (who even came to doubt of his results) actually proved his series to be (slowly but truly) convergent. The classical "relegation of exceptions" method was the one and only solution: "Cauchy's theorem is true except for Fourier series". The consistency of mathematics was safe, but the problem was left unsolved: why was Fourier's limit not continuous?

The antagonistic models of Cauchy and Fourier gave a third agent the opportunity to perform a suprA-cooperation: in 1847, Seidel found a "guilty-lemma" λ in Cauchy's proof, as he detected a minor inaccurate part in it, which he refined[3] ; at the same time he created the new "proof-born" concept of the *uniform convergence*. This explained why Fourier's limit was not continuous though the series converged[4].

The current result of the interaction is "better" than the initial points of view, in so far as it is more robust to counter-examples and it satisfies a higher number of examples. In the sequel a formal framework will allow such an order relation to be mathematically defined.

---

[2] in fact Fourier won the Grand Prix de mathématiques with this result in 1812, but his memoir was published later in 1822.
[3] the refined assumption must be: "...the series is *uniformly* convergent..."
[4] the series is said to be simply convergent.

2.4 Requirements for a SuprA-cooperation model

In order to implement such a suprA-cooperation among agents, it is necessary both :

1. to be able to know how to accept or reject a new information, and to build new pieces of knowledge from the agents' current knowledge (e.g. a conjecture and an example; two conjectures; a general rule and an instance);

2. to have means to make the potentially conflicting agents evolve towards a common conjecture.

Section 3 proposes an algebraic structure to represent the agents' knowledge, which allows a true *enrichment* to be obtained, particularly when conflicts arise. Section 4 describes the dynamic aspect, i.e. the mechanism allowing the agents to reach a common conjecture. Both sections are exemplified with a multi-sensor surveillance problem that is derived from the PERCEPTION project (Chaudron, Cossart, Maille, and Tessier 1997; Barrouil, Castel, Fabiani, Mampey, Secchi, and Tessier 1998) and that involves *difference* conflicts, i.e. conflicts stemming from the fact that information comes from heterogeneous and scattered sources.

3. Agents' knowledge representation

3.1 A principle for building knowledge from difference

Let us consider again agents α_1 and α_2 with their respective assertions – unformally stated for the moment – *there is a truck moving towards the building* (A_1) and *there are two vehicles moving at a speed of 30km/h* (A_2). As it has been said before, (A_1) and (A_2) cannot be compared but in a subjective way. Moreover, as both agents are involved in a surveillance process, they are immersed into a dynamic environment within which criteria are heterogeneous and may vary with time. Instead of making an *a priori* choice on (A_1) or (A_2), the idea is to *characterize* what will be called the current *common conjecture* of agents α_1 and α_2.

The algebraic tool that is considered for this purpose is the lattice structure.

Given any couple of elements e_1 and e_2 of a set E, a lattice structure on E (see appendix for reminders on lattices) guarantees the existence of an *infimum* $inf(e_1, e_2)$ and a *supremum* $sup(e_1, e_2)$ embracing both initial elements. Assuming that no external knowledge is considered, any fusion process F is said to be *endogeneous* iff it verifies the following law:

$F(e_1, e_2) \in [inf(e_1, e_2), sup(e_1, e_2)]$. Such a principle guarantees that the result of the combination of a finite set of elements contains at least the common information but at most the mere union of all information.

If we consider a snapshot of interacting agents α_1 and α_2, the lattice structure gives the following framework (figure 3.1):

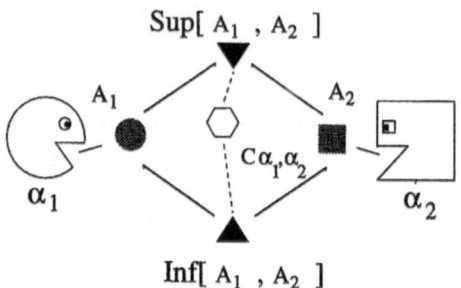

Sup[A_1 , A_2]

A_1 A_2

$C\alpha_1\alpha_2$

α_1 α_2

Inf[A_1 , A_2]

Fig. 3.1. Interacting agents within the lattice structure

As a matter of fact, initial assertions A_1 and A_2, together with their infimum $inf(A_1, A_2)$ (representing what the agents have at least in common) and their supremum $sup(A_1, A_2)$ (representing the whole spectrum of the possibilities) form a framework that characterizes the current knowledge c_{α_1, α_2} – the common conjecture – of α_1 and α_2.

3.2 Lattices and formal expressions of the language

As both human and artificial agents may be involved in the cooperation, agents' knowledge representation requires a formalism that is both understandable by humans and easily computable (Maille 1999). Therefore, agents' assertions are captured by the cube model (Chaudron, Cossart, Maille, and Tessier 1997) which is based on a classical first order language $(Const, Var, Funct, Pred)$ whose set of terms $Term$ is the functional closure of $Const \cup Var$ by $Funct$. The elementary properties are represented by literals.

Definition
A *cube* is a finite set of literals.

Thus, the set of cubes, $\mathcal{C}$, is the powerset of the set of literals. Cubes are interpreted as the conjunction of their literals and their variables are existentially quantified.

Example
Information "a red truck is moving" is captured by cube { *Type(truck)*,
Speed(x), *Color(red)*} which is associated to logical formula ($\exists x$ *Type(truck)*$\wedge$
Speed(x) $\wedge$ *Color(red)*).

As far as knowledge representation is concerned, we would like the order
relation induced on $\mathcal{C}$ to capture the intuitive notion of "knowledge enrichment". But such an "enrichment" can be obtained via different means: quantity of information, precision of terms, logical dependency.

Example
$\{Type(truck), Speed(30)\}$ is more informed than $\{Type(truck)\}$ for the number of literals is higher; but $\{Type(truck)\}$ is more informed than $\{Type(x)\}$
for the sake of precision. Unfortunately, the combination of both intuive criteria is a contradiction: $\{Type(x), Speed(30)\}$ cannot be consistently compared
to $\{Type(truck)\}$.

This example highlights the need for sound definitions for the intuitive
concepts of union and intersection of two finite information sets in accordance
to the following requirements: the infimum has to capture the common features; the supremum has to cope with the contradictory criteria: information
quantity *versus* information precision. If the definition of the supremum and
the infimum operators can be supported by the set union and intersection
within the propositional calculus frame, first order logic needs more sophisticated tools. Therefore we use the subsumption and reduction operators
defined by Plotkin (Plotkin 1970), but also adopt the approach of (Lassez,
Maher, and Marriot 1988) which allows a lattice on the set of terms to be
defined properly, thanks to the *anti-unification* operator.

Example
$p(x, g(y, b))$ is the anti-unified literal of $p(a, g(a, b))$ with $p(1, g(b, b))$.

In fact, anti-unification allows the infimum to generalize the terms so as to
properly enrich the set intersection on cubes. The result of the anti-unification
of two cubes c_1 and c_2 is defined as the union of the anti-unification of every
couple (l_1, l_2) based on the same predicate name and such that l_1 belong to
c_1 and l_2 to c_2.
Conversely, it is essential to reduce the mere set union of cubes in order to
define the supremum so as to discard redundancies and to guarantee the ver-
ification of the absorption law. The definition of such a reduction relies on
the class of the substitutions on terms.

Definition

A cube c is *reducible* iff$_{def}$ there exists a substitution θ such as $c\theta \subsetneq c$.

We have proved that an irreducible reduction of c always exists and is unique up to variable renaming. It is denoted $reduc(c)$. The reduction operator provides a means to capture in a unified way different conjunctions of properties representing exactly the same information.

Example

It is clear that $reduc(\{a(x), a(1)\}) = \{a(1)\}$, but $reduc(\{a(1, x), a(y, 2)\}) = \{a(1, x), a(y, 2)\}$.

If C^r denotes the subset of all the irreducible cubes of C, it is possible to define constructive operators on C^r:

Definition

Let c_1 and c_2 belong to C^r. The supremum and infimum operators $\cup_c$ and $\cap_c$ are defined as:

$$c_1 \cup_c c_2 =_{def} reduc(c_1 \cup c_2);$$
$$c_1 \cap_c c_2 =_{def} reduc[\text{anti-unif}(c_1, c_2)].$$

Theorem

$(C^r, \cup_c, \cap_c)$ is a non-modular lattice (see appendix).

Indeed, this lattice on cubes is an extension (defined in a constructive way) of the lattice on clauses defined in (Plotkin 1970).

From the theoretical point of view an extension to constrained cubes (such as: $\{Type(truck), Speed(v), 25 \leq v \leq 35\}$) has been formalized (Maille 1999).

Example

Let $\{Type(truck), Speed(30), Color(red)\}$ be agent α_1's assertion and $\{Type(x), Speed(25), Class(fire)\}$ be agent α_2's.

The elementary lattice built on these two pieces of knowledge is shown on figure 3.2.

In order to mix both initial pieces of knowledge so as to build a unique common conjecture, agent α_1 or α_2 may apply a dedicated fusion operator that chooses the "best" cube within this lattice structure (i.e. within interval $[inf, sup]$) according to his own integrity criteria. The fusion result is either the infimum, or $\{Type(truck), Speed(y)\}$, or $\{Type(x), Color(red), Speed(25)\}$, or..., or the supremum.

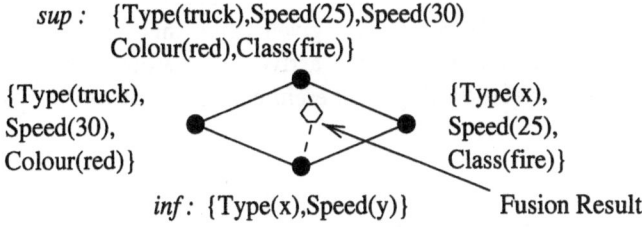

sup :   {Type(truck),Speed(25),Speed(30)
          Colour(red),Class(fire)}

{Type(truck),   {Type(x),
Speed(30),   Speed(25),
Colour(red)}   Class(fire)}

inf : {Type(x),Speed(y)}   Fusion Result

Fig. 3.2. Knowledge lattice of α_1 and α_2

It is intuitive that the common conjecture is something like an "average point" of the agents' beliefs: what has to be issued is an estimation of the current state of the observed world that is based on each agent's own beliefs on that world, even if they are conflicting.

An approach for conflict management through common belief is proposed in (Fiorino and Maille 1998).

4. The dynamic aspect: how to reach a common conjecture

4.1 Purpose

Agent cooperation for the elaboration of a common point of view is a dynamic process involving exchanges of points of views (Fiorino 1998). As the agents are designed to *cooperate*, *a priori* antagonistic agents, or agents with incompatible goals are not considered: building up a common conjecture is *the* common goal that is assigned to the multiagent system and conflicts result from "benevolent" agents making *different* assumptions. Contradictions are due to incomplete knowledge or erroneous data rather than to competing interests. Therefore, the common conjecture is not a *deal* resulting from a negotiation protocol (Rosenschein and Zlotkin 1994). Rather, agents locally update their points of view according to sensed data (Katsuno and Mendelzon 1991) and jointly elaborate a shared knowledge base. This is achieved by exchanging proposals and counter-proposals, i.e. by iteratively modifying the current conjecture. Clearly, those principles inherit some ground concepts from the blackboard approach (Lander 1994), but they especially aim at providing a formal model with demonstrable properties fitted to autonomous or man-machine systems.

A point that is worth noticing is that, contrary to problem solvers (Durfee, Lesser, and Corkill 1987), the convergence of the common conjecture cannot be searched for, as the agents are immersed in a dynamic environment from which new information regularly comes: consequently, if the agents succeed in converging on a steady result at a given time, this result may be in the balance again when new information arrives. Therefore, what is presented here is principles for elaborating a *coherent* common conjecture but not *convergence conditions*.

The cooperation principles that are proposed are based on the idea that two different types of functionalities are involved when designing cooperative agents, those defining the cooperation itself, and those linked to cooperation implementation. The position that is taken up is to design a cooperation model that encodes only what is a matter for cooperation, the implementation choices being included as parameters.

The model involves a set of agents and a function called the *federation clerk*, with the following features:

o the agents have the same generic goal which is to elaborate a common point of view: this data structure is called the *common conjecture*;
o the agents must state their decisions to carry on with this goal;
o the federation clerk monitors the agents' commitments to the goal and the status of the current conjecture.

4.2 Agent model

The inputs of a given agent are information coming from his own sensors, the current conjecture and the global state information delivered by the clerk; his outputs are the local state information delivered to the clerk and the updated conjecture if applicable.

The only two reasons for an agent α_i to access the conjecture are the following: he has updated his local knowledge base K_{α_i} with new information; or, the conjecture has been modified by another agent. When both conditions are true, the agent has to choose between updating his knowledge base or the conjecture.

Conjecture updating is based on Lakatos's approval-refutation cycle described in section 2.3.
The purpose for accessing the conjecture is restricted to assessing its *acceptability* from domain-dependent local criteria. For instance, let conjecture w be a propositional formula. A possible criterion is: w is *acceptable* if and only if $K_{\alpha_i} \vdash w$, and *unacceptable* otherwise (i.e. even if $K_{\alpha_i} \bigcup w$ is consistent); operator $accept_{\alpha_i}(w)$ is then applied. If the conjecture is acceptable, the agent may enhance it by adding knowledge from his knowledge base; operator $extend_{\alpha_i}(w)$ is then applied. If the conjecture is unacceptable, the

agent is allowed to modify it if and only if he is able to make it acceptable; operator $adjust_{\alpha_i}(w)$ is then applied, which implies to retract some pieces of knowledge from the conjecture. Figure 4.1 gives a Petri net representation of an agent's updating module:

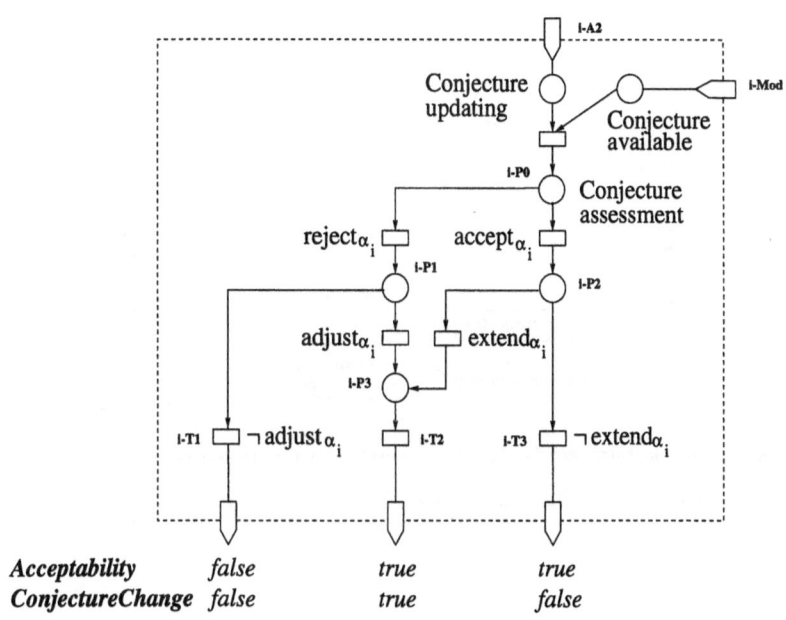

| Acceptability | false | true | true |
| ConjectureChange | false | true | false |

Fig. 4.1. Agent α_i's conjecture updating module

An agent must update his local states each time he accesses the conjecture. Those states are boolean(Fiorino and Tessier 1998): *Local Acceptability* asserts the agent's assessment of the conjecture; *Changed Conjecture* depends on whether the conjecture was modified or not. Furthermore *Local Commitment* to the joint task states whether the agent keeps on elaborating the common conjecture. When the agent decides to remain within the *federation*, operator $hold_{\alpha_i}$ is applied. Indeed, a coordinated behaviour cannot be guaranteed without the knowledge of the federated agents and their capabilities. The only reason for an agent to drop his commitment is that it is impossible for him to make the conjecture acceptable. Furthermore, uncommitment is irrevocable: this ensures that the convergence conditions to a common conjecture, when no new information enters the federation, are restricted to predictable issues (local criteria, knowledge bases and operators).

Therefore, the initial state for an agent is *committed*, *acceptable* and *unchanged*. The agent's generic functions are: update his knowledge base, update the conjecture, decide on whether to remain committed and assert his local states. It is worth mentioning that $extend_{\alpha_i}(w)$ and $adjust_{\alpha_i}(w)$ operators are strongly related to "classical" belief revision operators (Katsuno and Mendelzon 1991): they seem to be a valid counterpart of those operators for multiagent conjecture updating. Figure 4.2 gives a functional view of an agent's local activities.

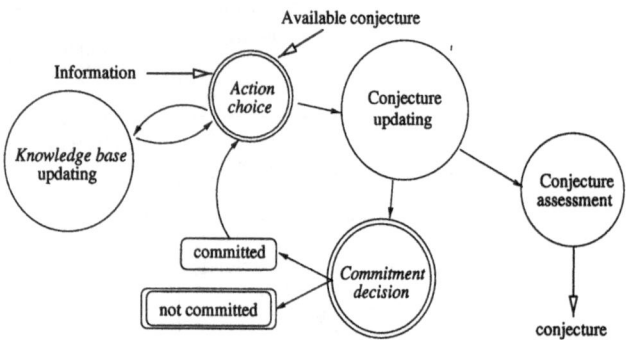

✗ *italics mean that the function depends on the application and on implementation choices*

Fig. 4.2. A functional view of an agent's local activities

4.3 Clerk model

The conjecture is a shared resource and there must be a single instance of the conjecture. Thus, it has to be dealt with like an exclusive resource, so as to ensure that two mutually inconsistent conjectures will never be generated. Communication within the federation is performed through the conjecture which is a statement from a shared language (e.g propositional logic).

The *clerk* is a global *function* that has got three roles:
(1) The cleck displays the current conjecture on a given medium, so that it should be available anytime for human or artificial decision makers.
(2) The clerk informs the agents each time the conjecture changes; therefore, the agents can decide to access the conjecture and assess it again.
(3) The clerk reflects the global state of the federation, which is a cooperation indicator enabling the designer or user to check whether the system is consistent *from the cooperation point of view*.

This cooperation indicator involves three variables (see figure 4.3):
- *Compliance* states whether the agents remaining within the federation are

able to achieve the joint task: compliance is the only stopping criterion provided by the model. Indeed, several agents are gathered together in order to achieve a global task: if the federation is assessed as not compliant anymore, because one or several agents failed or "died", this federation cannot carry out the joint task anymore. This task will have to be adapted to the remaining capabilities of the federation. Compliance therefore depends on the application.

- *Conjecture completeness* states whether all the agents have assessed the conjecture. This criterion is independent from each agent's point of view on the conjecture itself (i.e. whether he has assessed it as acceptable or not), and is *not* application-dependent.

- *Global acceptability* states the validity of the conjecture from the global viewpoint; this criterion depends on the application. For instance, the federation may rely on a voting procedure.

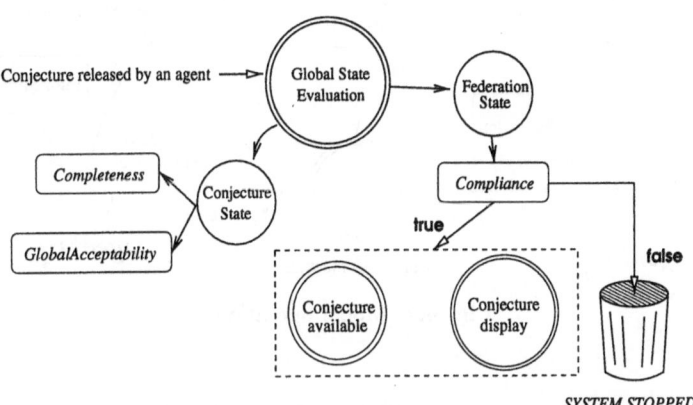

Fig. 4.3. A functional view of the federation clerk

The clerk is not necessarily intended to be an agent and it is not a centralized coordinator: on the one hand, it makes no decision concerning the interactions and plays no role at all in conjecture updating; on the other hand, it may be implemented as a distributed function among several agents of the federation. However, the global state has to be unique (as well as the conjecture itself); the implementation method must therefore guarantee that the agents will not be inconsistent with each other, *as far as this global state is concerned.*

4.4 Model operation

The interactions within the federation are based on a cycle of continuous exchanges between the clerk and the agents. One of the agents gets the conjecture, assesses it from his own point of view and possibly changes it. Then, the agent sends the conjecture back to the clerk, so as his local state.

The clerk aggregates the agents' assessments: if the group is not compliant to the joint task, the cycle ends. Otherwise, the conjecture becomes available again (figure 4.4).

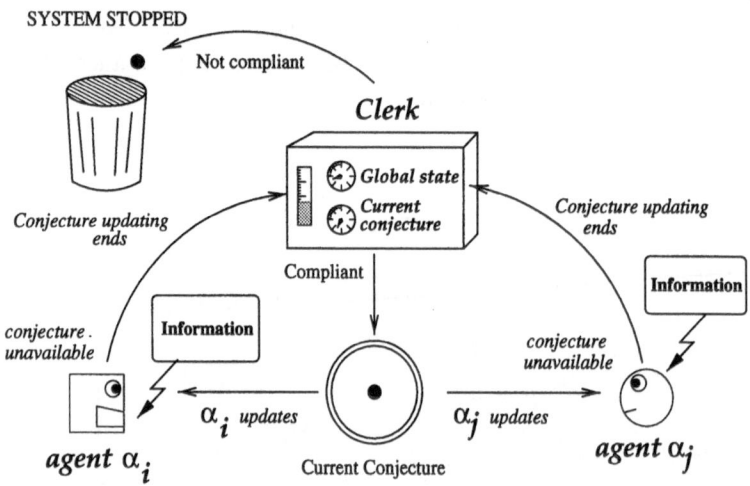

Fig. 4.4. Model operation

When does the process end? When no new information comes, and provided the compliance criterion is verified, the process stops when variables *Conjecture completeness* and *Global acceptability* are both *true*.

In a conflicting context, the following question may be raised: if the agents are involved in a conflict such as they continuously refute one another, either because the information they respectively get is contradictory or because their local knowledge does not enable them to change their point of view (stubborn agents), the common conjecture is likely to change each time one agent accesses it and consequently the whole process may enter an infinite loop (e.g. agent α_i says a and agent α_j says $\neg a$ and none of them can accept an empty conjecture nor the inconsistent conjecture $(a, \neg a)$. Is it possible to detect that?

The answer is yes. As a matter of fact, the clerk does not have the possibility to assess the conjecture from a semantical point of view. Therefore oscillations within the conjecture itself cannot be detected. Nevertheless, the *Conjecture completeness* variable allows these oscillations to be detected as, in this particular case, this variable will never switch to *true* (each time an agent assesses the conjecture, he changes it).

The properties of the cooperation model have been checked with Design/CPN (Meta Software Corporation 1993), a tool for modelling and simulation with coloured Petri nets (Jensen 1994). The computation of the occurrence graph leads to only two dead markings, respectively corresponding to the *compliance* stopping criterion and to the fact that the federation reaches a *complete* and *acceptable* conjecture. It is worth noticing that property checking can be processed with any communication protocol and therefore can help in choosing and adapting this protocol.

5. Example

Let us consider again agents α_1 and α_2 and their joint surveillance task (figure 5.1). Their common purpose is to elaborate a common conjecture relative to the moving objects they may observe *via* their own observation means. Under the assumptions that both agents remain committed to the global task, and can deliver their point of view in turn, the dynamic process is the following:

At time t, common conjecture c_t is empty and available; agent α_1 gets new information { *Type(truck)*, *Speed(30)*, *Color(red)*} and therefore modifies c_t. When it is released as c_{t+1}, it is *incomplete* (agent α_2 has to assess it).

At time $t + 1$, α_2 both gets new conjecture c_{t+1} and new information $I_2(t + 1) = \{$ *Type(x)*, *Speed(25)*, *Class(fire)*$\}$. He decides to reject c_{t+1} as such, as it is conflicting with his own local information, and to adjust it as c_{t+2}. The conjecture is chosen within the local lattice defined by c_{t+1} and $I_2(t + 1)$ as follows: $c_{t+2} \in [c_{t+1} \cap_c I_2(t + 1), c_{t+1} \cup_c I_2(t + 1)]$.

The same process of reject-and-adjust occurs with agent α_1 and conjecture c_{t+2}, which is released as c_{t+3} at time $t + 3$.

At time $t + 3$, agent α_2 gets both conjecture c_{t+3} and new information { *Action(surveillance)*}, that leads him to accept and extend c_{t+3}, the extensions being both a constraint specifying speed variable x, and { *Action(surveillance)*}. Common conjecture is released as c_{t+4}.

Agent α_1 then decides that c_{t+4} is consistent with new information { *Speed(28)*} and accepts it without extending it. c_{t+4} is therefore *complete* and *acceptable*. The process can stop provided no new information comes.

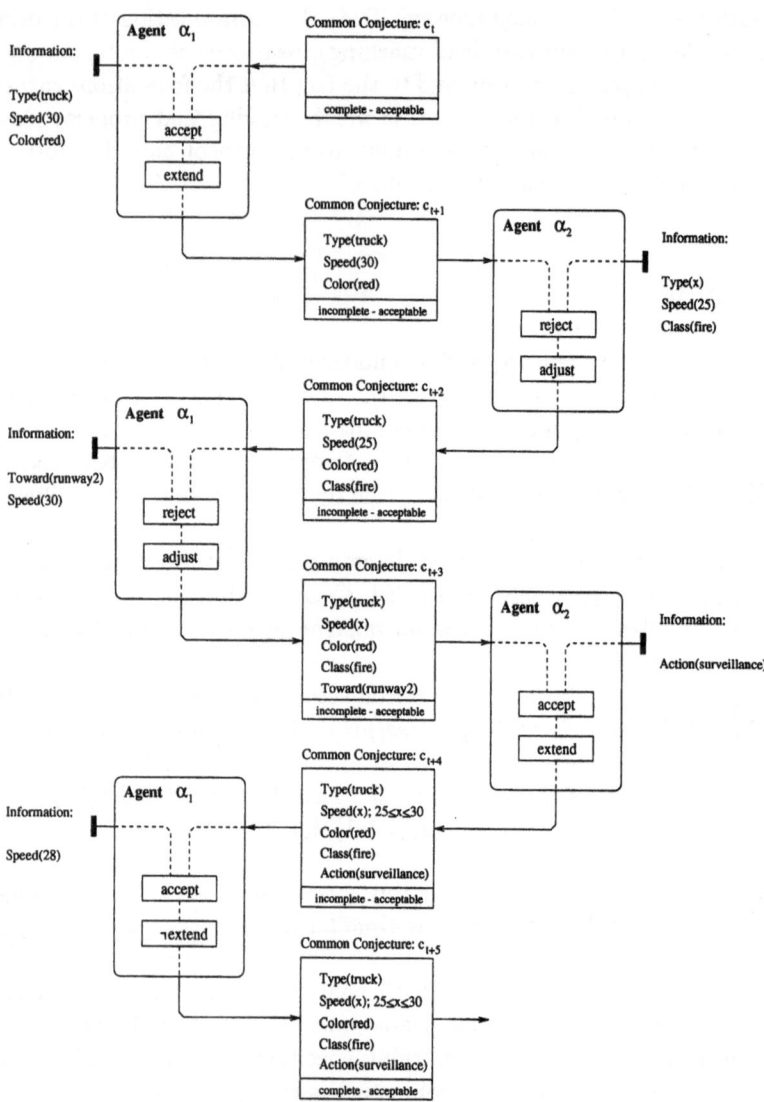

Fig. 5.1. Example

6. Conclusion

The keypoint of the framework that is proposed is that using conflicts is richer than getting rid of them if a certain amount of time is available: the enrichment of knowledge ΔK due to conflict exploitation by cooperative cognitive agents depends on the amount of time Δt that is freely available for the agents; ΔK is an increasing function of Δt.

In this context, when different (e.g. non interchangeable) agents are considered within a cooperative framework, it is obviously more interesting and powerful to consider the potential set of all the possible conjectures that can be built from their initial points of view or beliefs than to make a choice at once. Moreover, conflicting points of view may allow each agent to modify and enhance the common conjecture. As far as refutation conflicts are concerned and under the assumption that the agents are not stubborn, it may be interesting to keep the contradictory points of view (a and $\neg a$ for example) until the agents get new information. This allows the decision to be delayed and a least commitment process to be considered, which may be a good strategy for applications where the time constraint is flexible enough.

7. Appendix: lattice structures

As far as symbolic knowledge representation is concerned, the comparison of different pieces of information is a pivotal question.

Even on complex data, (logical formulas, graphs...) it is always possible to equip the knowledge set with at least a preorder relation, e.g. in a logical framework the implication defines a natural preorder relation upon the set of all well formed formulas. But if automatic processes are required (information fusion, decision making...) total orders are needed in order to guarantee the unicity of a "best result". This is the reason why numerical models (preference measures, belief functions...) are used to quantify symbolic data. Unfortunately, those models induce order relations between elements of knowledge that are not intrinsically comparable. Thus, there is a competition between correct knowledge representation means, generally based on preorders (but with limited and unefficient properties), and powerful numerical models (but with unrelevant links of comparison and no expression power). In order to enrich the models that are close to knowledge, the idea is to try to adapt the capabilities of preorders so as to get constructive properties, in particular when two pieces of knowledge are not comparable. The *lattice* structures are good candidates (Birkhoff 1940).

Definition
Given two internal operators $\sqcap$ *(infimum)* and $\sqcup$ *(supremum)* on a set E, $(E, \sqcap, \sqcup)$ is a *lattice*, iff$_{def}$: $\sqcap$ and $\sqcup$ are (i) idempotent, (ii) commutative, (iii) associative, and they verify the absorption law $x \sqcap (x \sqcup y) = x$ and $x \sqcup (x \sqcap y) = x$.

Examples
(1) (IN, hcf, lcm) is a lattice.
(2) If E is a set, the power set of E, $P(E)$, is a lattice with respect to the set union and intersection: $(P(E), \cup, \cap)$.
(3) Any totally ordered set is a lattice.

Contrary to what is usually found in the literature, it is not necessary to have the order relation prior to defining the supremum (the infimum) as the least upper bound (greatest lower bound): the axioms are sufficient to define a lattice properly and they allow a constructive definition to be programmed.
From a conceptual point of view, the lattice's conditions guarantees the information to be correctly processed.

Proposition
A lattice is an ordered set: relation $\leq$ defined on E as: $(x \leq y) \leftrightarrow_{def} (x \sqcap y) = x$ is an order relation for which $\sqcap$ and $\sqcup$ represent the greatest lower bound and the least upper bound.

For example, in a symbolic fusion context, the *endogeneous* fusion result of two elements of knowledge e_1 and e_2 is by definition an element f such that $f \in [e_1 \sqcap e_2, e_1 \sqcup e_2]$. The segment $[e_1 \sqcap e_2, e_1 \sqcup e_2]$ represents the potential set of all the solutions (figure 7.)

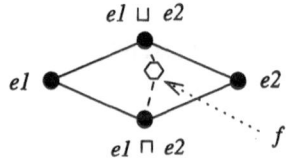

Fig. 7.1. Endogeneous fusion

Thanks to additional properties, various categories of lattices can be defined: *complemented* if there is a negation operator, *distributive* if the supremum and infimum are distributive, *complete* if any infinite set has a supremum and an infimum.

Definition
A lattice M is *modular* iff$_{def}$ it satisfies the modular law:
$\forall x, y, z \in M \; x \leq z \rightarrow x \sqcup (y \sqcap z) = (x \sqcup y) \sqcap z$.
Modularity is a weaker condition than distributivity as any distributive lattice is modular.

The cube lattice is non-modular; this restriction is of major importance for information processing results (Perception 1998).

CHAPTER 6

Detecting Temporal Conflicts in Integrated Agent Specifications

Guy Davies[1], Love Ekenberg[1,2], Paul Johannesson[2]

[1]Department of Information Technology, Mid Sweden University

[2]Department of Computer and Systems Sciences, Royal Institute of Technology and Stockholm University

We present a model for the analysis of temporal conflicts in sets of autonomous agents restricted in the sense that they can be described in a first-order language. The dynamic aspects of agents are modelled by means of the event concept. Various kinds of conflicts can occur in a system of agents. Agents may be in conflict with themselves or with each other, all depending on time. Conflicts between agents may be due to direct incompatibility inherent in their specifications, but it may also arise from the dynamic interactions protocols that govern multi-agent behaviour. The general theory for detecting conflict suggested here includes semantics for individual conflicts with respect to a first order action logic (FAL). Also introduced is the enrichment of agent systems with correspondence assertions. These express relationships between static or dynamic properties described in the formal specifications of agents. Correspondence assertions correspond to protocols for the system and can be analysed in relation to time. Representing agents as first order schemata, we construct a framework for determining when two schemata can be meaningfully integrated. We formalise this concept using the notion of non-conflict.

1. Introduction

Decentralised and co-operating information systems have become increasingly important as a result of organisational demands and as a consequence of technical advances in computer networking. When specifying and designing these kinds of systems, the concept of intelligent and co-operating agents has proved useful.

Agents are commonly described in mental and social terms such as beliefs, knowledge, capabilities, plans, goals, desires, intentions, obligations, commitments, etc. The agent metaphor has turned out to be most useful for describing complex software artefacts, see for example (Shoham 1993). There is a vast literature, ranging from philosophy and psychology to AI on different mental aspects, in particular on belief and knowledge (Russell 1995). In recent years, there has been a growing interest in those aspects that have to do with obligations and commitments, aspects that are essential for agent co-operation and co-ordination.

When co-ordinating their activities, agents create and fulfil obligations. They make and accept offers as well as request and commit themselves to actions, grant and revoke authorisations. Each agent holds its own little agenda of ever changing obligations and goals.

The first main issue of this chapter is the representation of agent interaction in an event driven first order setting using ideas from the theory of speech act.

'First order Action Logic' (FAL) is a language for specifying, creating, and monitoring obligations.

First order logic is used to model dynamics in (Benthem 1995), which argues in favour of this approach in contrast to that based on traditional temporal logic. Inspired by the work of van Benthem et al. we have attempted to fulfil two basic requirements: that FAL be executable; and that it have clear semantics.

FAL is similar to the language proposed in (Lee 1988), which provides constructs for deontic modelling in a first order framework; important differences between this language and FAL is that FAL handles the explicit creation of obligations through speech acts and can handle states of affairs as the subject matter of obligations. FAL is also similar to the extended situation calculus proposed in (Pinto 1993). We claim that this approach provides several advantages:

- Simple semantics - The meanings of the language constructs are easy to understand as they are given using a first order semantics. This makes FAL simpler to understand than modal approaches, which use various possible world semantics.
- Explicit creation of obligations - The language makes it possible to explicitly create obligations by means of speech acts. In this respect, it is similar to the approach proposed by Dignum et al. in (Dignum 1995).
- States of affairs as the subject matter of obligations - The language makes it possible to have actions as well as states of affairs as the subject matter of obligations. This feature makes the language more expressive than some recent approaches to deontic logic, such as (Meyer 1988), which only allow actions.
- Representation of time - The language provides explicit representation of time, which makes it possible to express, for example, that a certain action should be carried out during a specified time interval. We claim that an explicit representation of time is essential to providing adequate semantics to obligations.

Members of a multi-agent system may find that in creating and fulfilling obligations, they enter into conflicts in which their individual goals are incompatible (Katz 1993; Zlotkin 1991).

The second main issue of this chapter is to investigate how the concept of non-conflict can be generalised to the temporal and dynamic case and build a theoretical framework in which conflicts in multi-agent systems can be detected and analysed.

Many of the ideas in this work stem from research into database- and user view integration. A generic term, schema integration (Batini 1986), has been introduced to refer to both areas. In an earlier chapter (Ekenberg 1995), we argued the case for meaningful integration of two static schemata when the rules of one schema together with a set of integration assertions do not restrict the models of the other. Integration assertions express ontological overlap between the agent systems (Spanoudakis 1996), that is to say, terminological and structural differences between representations of the same reality. The theory was further extended in (Ekenberg 1996), where some general dynamic aspects of conceptual schemas were studied.

This chapter extends previous work on schema integration, which has considered only static and structural aspects (Biskup 1986), to handle general dynamic aspects too. Dynamics are formalised by means of the event concept which provides a natural progression into the dynamic realm.

The chapter is structured as follows: Section 2 describes the language used as a formalism for the rest of the chapter. Section 3 introduces a number of basics in conceptual modelling. Section 4 proposes several forms of temporal conflicts in multi-agent systems and shows how they are related. Section 5 discusses the dynamics of event rules and combinations thereof. Section 6 defines the several kinds of conflict. Finally, section 7 summarises the chapter and discusses topics for further research.

2. The Language FAL

This section introduces a language for specifying, creating, and monitoring obligations, called First order Action Logic (FAL). FAL is a first order language extended with the arithmetic required to handle discrete points in time. The extent to which FAL is used here warrants only a brief description of a subset of the language. In the simple examples the intuitive meaning should be apparent.[1]

---

[1] The interested reader is referred to [Assenova96) and [Johannesson98) for a complete description.

As is customary for first order predicate logic, the alphabet consists of a set C of constants, a set of variables, a set F of function symbols, a set P of predicate symbols, a set of connective symbols $\{\neg, \wedge, \vee, \rightarrow\}$ and a set of punctuation symbols. The UoD is considered to consist of different kinds of objects including agents, time points, actions, and states of affairs.

To make it possible to distinguish between terms denoting these different kinds of objects, they are typed: Ag for agents; T for time points isomorphic to the integers; A for actions; SoA for states of affairs; and AS for the contents of speech acts, which may be actions, states of affairs, or combinations of these. A and SoA are subtypes of AS. Further types are: SA for speech acts and IA for instrumental acts, both of which are subtypes of A.

Agents use speech acts, commissives and directives, in order to commit themselves and others to carrying out actions. To make it possible to construct different actions and states of affairs, some special sets of function symbols are defined:

- a set IP = {dir, com} of illocutionary points
- a set IAC $\subset$ F of instrumental acts constructors
- a set SoAC $\subset$ F of states of affairs constructors
- a set DO = {O, P} $\subset$ SoAC of deontic operators
- a set T $\subset$ C of time variables

All time variables are elements of **N** the set of natural numbers. The predicate symbols in FAL are <, =, 'done' and 'holds' with arity two and 'fulfilled' with arity three. The predicate symbols <, and = are used to give a partial order between the time points. The predicate symbols 'done', 'holds', and 'fulfilled' are typed as follows:

- holds: SoA $\times$ T
- done: A $\times$ T
- fulfilled: AS $\times$ T $\times$ T

Now follows an informal description of the meanings of a subset of these language constructs. A formal semantics based on a number of axioms can be found in (Assenova 1996).

Function symbols:

- dir(AgA, AgB, AS, T) - AgA asserts a request for AS that AgB is obliged to fulfil, by T at the latest
- com(AgA, AgB, AS, T) - AgA commits himself to AgB, to fulfil AS by T at the latest
- O(Ag, AS, T1, T2) - Agent Ag is obliged to fulfil AS between T1 and T2 inclusive

- P(Ag, AS, T) - Agent Ag is permitted to fulfil AS at T

Predicate symbols:

- holds(SoA, T) - The state of affairs SoA holds at T
- done(A, T) - The action A has been performed at T
- fulfilled(AS, T1, T2) - AS is fulfilled in the interval [T1 T2]. This means that AS is done in [T1 T2] if AS is an action, or else if AS is a state of affairs, that AS has been adequately dealt with in [T1 T2].

Example

The following formula in FAL expresses that agent A1, at time point 15, has committed himself to agent A2 to ringBackOffPeak at time point 18:

done(com(A1, A2, ringBackOffPeak, 18), 15)

This speech act will result in an obligation for agent A1 to fulfil his commitment. The following is derivable from the formula above:

holds(O(A1, ringBackOffPeak, 18), 15)

3. Conceptual Modelling

In the model described below, agent process specifications are represented and studied as formulae in the logic FAL. Such a structure will be referred to as a conceptual schema. Naturally, any suitable representation could have been used instead, but familiarity with conceptual schemata and their formal properties is widespread. Furthermore, the representation in FAL has some convenient features from a theorem proving perspective.

The definitions below assume an underlying language L of formulae in FAL. First a formal definition of a conceptual schema is provided[2]. Such a schema is a structure consisting of two parts. The first part, the static part, expresses rules and the model's static characteristics – the state space of the model. The second part expresses all possible state transitions using event rules.

Definition 3.1

Let S be a variable not in L and t ∈ **N**. A *schema* S is a pair <SR, ER> consisting of *static rules* SR and *dynamic rules* ER. SR is a finite set of first

---

[2]   The unfamiliar reader is referred to (Boman 1997).

order formulae in a language L. ER is a set of *event rules*. Event rules describe possible transitions between different states of a schema and will be described below.

L(SR) is the *restriction of L to SR*, i.e, L(SR) is the set {p | p ∈ L, but p does not contain any predicate symbol that is not in a formula in SR}. The elements in SR are called *static rules* in L(SR).

Example

The following example of a static rule in a schema. It expresses that the charge levied at all time points must be non-negative:

$$\forall x \forall t(holds(rate(x), t) \rightarrow x \geq 0)$$

In order to compare the semantics of schemas and not just their structural information capacity, some kind of semantic mapping is required. Static integration assertions serve this purpose.

Definition 3.2

Let t be a time variable in L. A *static integration assertion* that expresses an equivalence between schemata S_1 and S_2 at a given time t is a formula:

$$\forall \mathbf{x} \ (R(t) \rightarrow (F(\mathbf{x}, t) \leftrightarrow G(\mathbf{x}, t)))$$

where R is a formula containing no other predicate symbols than = and > (or some semantically equivalent symbols). $F(\mathbf{x}, t)$ is a formula in $L(S_2)$ and $G(\mathbf{x}, t)$ is a formula in $L(S_1)$ and $\mathbf{x}$ is a vector of variables.[3]
A set of such assertions will be denoted FALIA(t) below.

The intuition behind static integration assertions in FAL is that they express a static relationship between objects in the two schemata in relation to a point in time t. Thus, in a sense, they define a time dependent protocol for relationships between agents. This protocol may vary over time depending on global aspects of the system or changes in agents' internal goals. Note that both the static and the dynamic parts of a schema are functions of time. This allows protocols to be updated. This definition is a generalisation of that defined in (Ekenberg 1996) which permits only a single predicate on the left hand side of the equivalence.

---

[3] We can without loss of generality, in the definitions below, assume that the set of predicate symbols in $L(S_1)$ and $L(S_2)$ are disjoint.

Example

Assume that there are two agents A_1 and A_2 represented by the schemata S_2 and S_1. These agents monitor the rate of telephone charges but use different terminology and knowledge of possible states, which means that we have a case of ontological overlap. The first agent can only distinguish between 'dear' and 'cheap' while the second agent can distinguish between integral rates. Furthermore, the different representations vary over time. Formally, we have the following integration assertions given $t \in T$:

FALIA(t) =

$\{\forall x((t \geq 18 \vee t < 7) \rightarrow (holds(dear, t) \leftrightarrow holds(rate(x), t) \wedge x > 24)),$

$\forall x((t \geq 18 \vee t < 7) \rightarrow (holds(cheap, t) \leftrightarrow holds(rate(x), t) \wedge x \leq 24)),$

$\forall x((t \geq 7 \wedge t < 18) \rightarrow (holds(dear, t) \leftrightarrow holds(rate(x), t) \wedge x > 27)),$

$\forall x((t \geq 7 \wedge t < 18) \rightarrow (holds(cheap, t) \leftrightarrow holds(rate(x), t) \wedge x \leq 27))\}$

Next, the semantics of the static part of conceptual schemata is defined by introducing diagrams.

Definition 3.3

A *time-independent diagram* D(S) for a set SR of static rules of a schema S in a language L, is a Herbrand model for SR, extended by the negation of the ground atoms in L that are not in the Herbrand model. Thus, a diagram for L is a Herbrand model extended with classical negation.[4]

Diagrams can also be defined taking time into account. A time dependent diagram is D(S, t), $t \in \mathbf{N}$, is a subset of a time-independent diagram D.

Definition 3.4

Given a schema S = $\langle$SR, ER$\rangle$ and a non-negative integer t, a *diagram* D(S, t) for SR is a diagram for SR, but where all occurrences of time variables are substituted by the value t.[5]

---

[4] For our purposes, this is no loss of generality by the well-known result that a formula is satisfiable iff its Herbrand expansion is satisfiable. For a discussion of this expansion theorem and its history, see, e.g. (Dreben 1979).

[5] In the sequel, we will sometimes omit negations in the diagrams presented, i.e. we present them as Herbrand models.

Example

Consider the rule holds(cheap, t) $\leftrightarrow$ holds(rate(x), t). An example of a diagram, $D(S, 5)$, for this rule is {holds(cheap, 5), holds(rate(24), 5))}.

A diagram in this sense is very similar to the concept of a time independent diagram, but makes the time explicit.[6] This definition can be used to represent sets of current, past and future possible states.

Definition 3.5

Let S be a schema $\langle SR, EP \rangle$. By the *diagram set* $D(S, t_1, t_2)$ for S, where t_1 and t_2 are non-negative integers and $t_1 \leq t_2$, we mean the set {$D(S, t)$ | $D(S, t)$ is a diagram for SR and $t \in [t_1, t_2]$}.

Example

Continuing with the rule from the example above, setting $x = 26$, yields the following diagram set, $D(S, 6, 7)$:

{{holds(cheap, 6), holds(rate(26), 6)}, {¬holds(cheap, 6), ¬holds(rate(26), 6)}, {holds(cheap, 7), holds(rate(26), 7)}, {¬holds(cheap, 7), ¬holds(rate(26), 7)}}

Using diagram sets makes it simple to describe all possible states up until time t_1 using {$D(S,0,t_1)$} and the possible future states between t_1 and t_2 using {$D(S,t_1,t_2)$}, $t_1 \leq t_2$.

The dynamic semantics of a schema is based on transitions between diagrams using the event concept. The dynamic part ER of a schema consists of event rules that describe transitions. Intuitively, an instance of an event is a transition from one diagram to another in accordance with an event rule. An event rule may be enabled by the environment of the agent system or by another agent in the system.

Definition 3.6

An *event rule* in a language L is a structure $\langle P(z), C(z) \rangle$. $P(z)$ and $C(z)$ are formulae in L, and z is a vector of variables in the alphabet of L.[7] In terms of conceptual modelling, $P(z)$ denotes the precondition of the event rule, and $C(z)$ the post condition.

---

[6]   Needless to say $D(S, t_1)$ is equal to $D(S, t_1, t_1)$.

[7]   The notation $A(x)$ means that x is free in $A(x)$.

Note that an event rule is non-deterministic, i.e. if a diagram σ satisfies the precondition of an event rule then any diagram ρ satisfying the event rule's post condition will give rise to a basic event (σ, ρ). In this way, our approach to the dynamics of a schema differs from the traditional transactional approach in the database area, where an event deterministically specifies a modification of the information base (Abiteboul88).

Definition 3.7

The set of *basic events E for a schema S* $=\langle SR, ER \rangle$ *spanning* $[t_1, t_3]$ *and* $[t_4, t_6]$ is a relation $E \subseteq D(S, t_1, t_3) \times D(S, t_4, t_6)$ where $t_1 \leq t_3$ and $t_4 \leq t_6$ and where $D(S, t_1, t_3)$ and $D(S, t_4, t_6)$ are diagram sets for SR. An element (σ, ρ) belongs to E iff either of the following cases hold:

(i) $\rho = \sigma$ and $\sigma \in D(S, t_1, t_1)$ and $\rho \in D(S, t_1, t_1)$, for any t_1. This will be called an *identity transition*.

(ii)   there is a rule $\langle P(z), C(z) \rangle$ in ER, and a vector e of constants in L, such that $P(e)$ satisfies σ and $C(e)$ satisfies ρ, and also that there are two time points t_2 and t_5 where $t_1 \leq t_2 \leq t_3$ and $t_4 \leq t_5 \leq t_6$, such that $\sigma \in D(S, t_2, t_2)$ and $\rho \in D(S, t_5, t_5)$ and $t_2 \leq t_5$. In this case the *basic event* (σ, ρ) will be said to *result* from the event rule.

$P(z, w)$ can be thought of as a precondition that the initial diagram σ must satisfy, and $C(z, w)$ as a post condition that ρ must satisfy. The choice of weak order between t_1 and t_2 allows events to take place instantaneously as well as from one point in time to the next. The diagram sets may overlap in any way as long as time points $t_2 \leq t_5$ exist for σ and ρ within the interval of their respective diagram sets, so as to ensure that ρ does not precede σ. This prevents events from going back in time.

The definition is general and allows events to occur between specific time points if the relation is $D(S, t_1, t_1) \times D(S, t_2, t_2)$ as well as instantaneously for $D(S, t_1, t_1) \times D(S, t_1, t_1)$.[8]

Events between discrete and precise time points are a special case of events between intervals. In this chapter events between precise consecutive time points form the theoretical basis for dynamics.

In this chapter, the focus is on connecting events given the restriction that they may only connect diagrams for identical or consecutive time points.

---

[8] However, the definition is not the most general since it is realistic to require that in order for an event to be enabled its preconditions be fulfilled over a period of time.

Definition 3.8

A set of basic events E for a schema $\langle SR, ER \rangle$ spanning intervals $[t_1, t_1]$ and $[t_2, t_2]$ is a set of *connecting events EC for a schema S = $\langle SR, ER \rangle$ between t_1 and t_2*.

Definition 3.9

A set of basic events E for a schema $\langle SR, ER \rangle$ spanning intervals $[t_1, t_1]$ and $[t_1, t_1]$ is a set of *instant events EI for a schema S = $\langle SR, ER \rangle$ at t_1*.

Definition 3.10

A set of basic events E for a schema S spanning $[t_1, t_3]$ and $[t_4, t_6]$, such that t_1, t_3, t_4, and t_6 are all greater than or equal to 0 is a set of *basic events E for a schema S*.

Example

A possible event rule for a schema is: $\langle holds(a, t), holds(b, t) \rangle$. Let the diagram set D(S, 1, 1) of the schema be:

$\sigma_1 = \{holds(a, 1), holds(b, 1)\}$

$\sigma_2 = \{\neg holds(a, 1), holds(b, 1)\}$

$\sigma_3 = \{holds(a, 1), \neg holds(b, 1)\}$

The set of basic events at time 1 for this schema is the union of the identity transitions and the events resulting from the event rule in accordance with cases (i) and (ii) respectively in definition 3.7:

$\{(\sigma_1, \sigma_1), (\sigma_2, \sigma_2), (\sigma_3, \sigma_3)\} \cup \{(\sigma_1, \sigma_1), (\sigma_1, \sigma_2), (\sigma_3, \sigma_1) (\sigma_3, \sigma_2)\}$

An extension of a schema is a structure consisting of all diagrams for a schema, together with all the transitions that are possible with respect to the basic events for the schema.

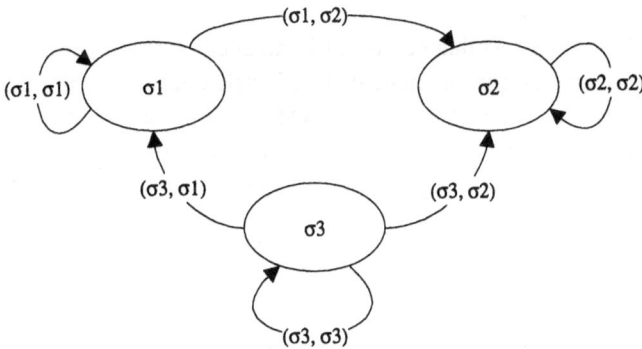

Fig. 3.1 The extension of the schema at time 1

Definition 3.11

The *extension of a schema S at time t_1* is a digraph $\langle D(S, t_1, t_1), E \rangle$, $E \subseteq D(S, t_1, t_1) \times D(S, t_1, t_1)$ is the set of instant events at time t_1 for S. This is a special case of the following.

The *extension of a schema S between t_1 and t_2* is a digraph $\langle D(S, t_1, t_1) \cup D(S, t_2, t_2), E \rangle$, such that for all $(\sigma, \rho) \in E$, (σ, ρ) is an instant event for S at t_1 or (σ, ρ) is an instant event for S at t_2 or (σ, ρ) is a connecting event for S between t_1 and t_2

The constraints on t_3 and t_4 ensure that events do not go back in time and that they occur within the designated period $[t_1, t_2]$.

Example

Fig. 3.1 illustrates the digraph $\langle D(S, t_1, t_1), E \rangle$ for the event rule in the previous example. The arrows in the figure represent basic events and the ellipses represent the diagrams for the schema.

4. Temporal Conflict Detection

This section introduces the basics of static conflict detection.

4.1 Inconsistency

Of the various kinds of conflicts that can occur in an agent system, perhaps the most basic is when a schema for an agent system is self-conflicting at a given time, otherwise known as inconsistent. We prefer to reserve the term 'con-flicting' for later when dealing with incompatibility between two schemata. Let us begin with inconsistency and gradually tighten the requirements on compatibility.

Definition 4.1

Let S be a schema. S is *consistent at* t_1 iff $D(S,t_1,t_1)$ is nonempty. Otherwise S is *inconsistent at* t_1

Definition 4.2

Let S be a schema and $[t_1, t_2]$ be an interval starting at time point t_1 and ending at time point t_2.

Given a time point t_1, S is *consistent from* t_1 iff S is consistent at all t where $t \geq t_1$.

Given a time point t_2, S is *consistent up until* t_2 iff S is consistent at all t where $0 \leq t \leq t_2$

Given an interval $[t_1, t_2]$, S is *consistent during* $[t_1, t_2]$ iff S is consistent at t for every $t \in [t_1, t_2]$.

S is *always consistent* iff S is consistent at all t.

Through the definition it is implied that a schema that is consistent for an extended period must have a least one diagram for all t in that period. If this were not the case fleeting conflicts could exist but pass by unnoticed which could invalidate the correctness of all subsequent transitions.

Example 4.3

Assume that the static part of the schema representing an agent A_1 contains the following rule meaning that the agent A_1 has made a commitment at time point 3, that from t_1 onwards, obliges him only to fetch data if the charge rate is 24 units:

$R_1 = \{ \forall t_1 \ \forall t_2 \ (t_1 = t_2 \wedge t_2 \geq 5 \rightarrow \text{holds}(O(A1, \text{fetchIf}(\text{rate}(24)), t_1, t_2), 3)) \}$

Furthermore, assume that the agent has also made a commitment at time point 4, that at t_3 obliges him until t_4, only to fetch data if the charge rate is 26 units

$R_2 = \{\forall t_3 \forall t_4 ((t_3 = t_4 \wedge 7 \leq t_4 \wedge t_4 \leq 9) \rightarrow \text{holds}(O(A1, \text{fetchIf}(\text{rate}(26)), t_3, t_4), 4))\}$

Given that the agent always fulfils its obligations the agent A_1 is not consistent in the interval [7, 9]. A_1 is consistent up until time point 4 upon which A_1 harbours impending inconsistency until time point 7 when the inconsistency is immediate. Note also that although the schema is consistent at 1 it is not consistent *from* 1. However, it is consistent again after 9.[9]

4.2 Integration Assertions and Conflicts

Systems of agents can also be in conflict with respect to the protocol of the agent system. The basic idea in the definitions below is that if for a specified period two agent representations are non-conflicting, then neither agent obstructs the other during that time.

Assume each agent to be represented by a schema specification. Intuitively, two schemata are in conflict at time t_1 with respect to a set of static integration assertions if the static rules of one of them, in union with the integration assertions, restrict the set of diagrams to the empty set for the other schema at time t_1, or vice versa.

Definition 4.4

Let $FALIA(t_1)$ be a set of static integration assertions in FAL expressing a partial equivalence between S_1 and S_2 at time t_1. S_1 *compromises* S_2 *at* t_1 *with respect to* $FALIA(t_1)$ iff for any $\sigma \in D_2(S_2, t_1, t_1)$ no diagram $\tau \in D_1(S_1, t_1, t_1)$ exists such that $\sigma \cup \tau \models FALIA(t_1)$;

Definition 4.5

S_1 and S_2 are *in conflict at* t_1 iff either S_1 compromises S_2 at t_1 with respect to $FALIA(t_1)$ or S_2 compromises S_1 at t_1 with respect to $FALIA(t_1)$. Otherwise S_1 and S_2 are *non-conflicting at* t_1 *with respect to* $FALIA(t_1)$

If two schemata S_1 and S_2, representing the agents A_1 and A_2, are in conflict at time t_1, they are not necessarily in conflict at time t_2, and similarly for non-conflict. The definition defines a general state based concept. However, this definition of conflict differs from that in (Ekenberg 1996) in that it is symmetric and that the check for conflict is dependent on the time. It is also stronger. The definition can also be generalised for time intervals in several ways similar to definition 4.2 for consistency in the single agent case.

---

[9] A machinery that forces the agents to always fulfil their obligations is assumed here.

The generalisations below are not the most general. They are based on the assumption of a bijection between the extensions of S_1 at a given time and S_2. That is to say, every time point for which there is an extension to schema S_1, there is exactly one extension to schema S_2 and vice versa. In keeping with this, every set of integration assertions is assumed to express equivalences between schemata only for one point in time, not between time points. The consequences of loosening these restrictions for a more general theory is the subject of our continuing research.

Definition 4.6

Given a time point t_1, S_1 and S_2 are *non-conflicting from t_1* iff S_1 and S_2 are non-conflicting at t with respect to FALIA(t) for every $t \in [t_1, t_2]$

Given a time point t_2, S_1 and S_2 are *non-conflicting up until t_2* iff S_1 and S_2 are non-conflicting at t with respect to FALIA(t) for all t where $0 \le t \le t_2$

Given an interval $[t_1, t_2]$, S_1 and S_2 are *non-conflicting during $[t_1, t_2]$* iff S_1 and S_2 are non-conflicting at t with respect to FALIA(t) for every t where $t_1 \le t \le t_2$.

S_2 and S_1 are *always non-conflicting* iff S_1 and S_2 are non-conflicting at all t with respect to FALIA(t)

Example

Assume that there are two agents A_1 and A_2, and a set of integration assertions:

FALIA(t_1,t_2) =

$\{\forall x \ ((t < t_1 \vee t_2 \le t) \rightarrow (holds(dear, t) \leftrightarrow holds(rate(x), t) \wedge x > 24))$,

$\forall x \ ((t < t_1 \vee t_2 \le t) \rightarrow (holds(cheap, t) \leftrightarrow holds(rate(x), t) \wedge x \le 24))$,

$\forall x \ ((t_1 \le t \wedge t < t_2) \rightarrow (holds(dear, t) \leftrightarrow holds(rate(x), t) \wedge x > 27))$,

$\forall x \ ((t_1 \le t \wedge t < t_2) \rightarrow (holds(cheap, t) \leftrightarrow holds(rate(x), t) \wedge x \le 27))\}$

where $t_1 = 7$ and $t_2 = 18$

Suppose now that an agent, A_1, has made a commitment at time point 3, that from time point 5 onwards, obliges him to set the charge rate at 25 units and keep it there:

$R_1 = \{\forall t_1 \ \forall t_2 \ (t_1 = t_2 \wedge t_2 \ge 5 \rightarrow holds(O(A1, setRate(25), t_1, t_2), 3))\}$

Suppose also that a different agent, A_2, has made a commitment at time point 4, that at 6 obliges him until 8, to set the charge rate to cheap:

$R_2 = \{\forall t_3 \forall t_4 ((t_3 = t_4 \wedge 6 \le t_4 \wedge t_4 \le 8) \rightarrow holds(O(A2, makeCheap, t_3, t_4), 4))\}$

Assume that the agents always fulfil their obligations. As we step through each point in time t, the integration assertions together with the two rules above interact as follows.

At t = 3, only A_1 has made a commitment and there is no conflict. At t = 4, A_2 makes his commitment and a potential conflict has arisen between A_1 and A_2. Unless one of the agents is released from his obligation, conflict will occur at t = 6. At t = 5, A_1 begins fulfilling his commitment by setting the charge rate to 25. Still no conflict has occurred. At t = 6 however A_1 and A_2 are in conflict: A_2 is bound to set the charge rate to 'cheap' which for A_1 corresponds to 24 or lower, whilst A_1 is bound to maintain the charge rate at 25. However, without either agent's obligations expiring, the conflict is resolved at t = 7 because then the integration assertions state that A_2's value 'cheap' corresponds to 27 or lower, which accommodates A_1's rate of 25. At t = 8 A_2's obligation ends.

Although the conflict in the above example resolves itself, the reliability of ensuing states is dubious to say the least. Conflict is equivalent to the empty diagram, so without further semantics it is not clear what it actually means to arrive at any state coming from an empty diagram set. A frame rule for handling this may be a good way in which to give meaning to this turn of events. The question lies open for future work.

The above example illustrates some of the subtleties that arise when both integration assertions and schema formulae are assigned time constraints.

As the definitions are formulated, the general problem of determining non-conflict is undecidable. In most cases it is reasonable to assume that there is a finite number of relevant objects in the agent system as well as in its environment. In this case a language with a finite number of constants may be used. Complexity results for such a logic are provided in (Ekenberg 1995).

5. Events Paths and Pairs

This section investigates how compound events can be constructed by combining the basic event rules of a schema.

5.1 Event Paths

Events may be sequentially composed to form a path linking diagrams together in a chain. This concept is useful when defining non-conflict from the dynamic perspective of two schemata. A path includes all diagrams that the compound event traverses.

Definition 5.1

Let $S = <SR, ER>$ be a schema, $V = V_1 \nabla \ldots \nabla V_k$ be a sequence of event rules in ER.

An *instant path in S for V at t*, $\Pi(S, V, t)$, is a set of sequences of diagrams for S, $(\sigma_1, \sigma_2, \ldots, \sigma_{k+1})$, such that (σ_i, σ_{i+1}) is an instant event resulting from V_i at t. The *event path extension for S*, $\Pi(S, t)$, is the union of $\Pi(S, V, t)$ for all sequential combinations V of event rules in ER.

A *connecting path in S for V between* t_1 *and* t_2, $\Pi(S, V, t_1, t_2)$, is a set of sequences of diagrams for S, $(\sigma_1, \sigma_2, \ldots, \sigma_{k+1})$, such that for $1 \le i \le k+1$ there is a sequence of diagrams $(\sigma_1, \sigma_2, \ldots, \sigma_i) \in \Pi(S, V, t_1)$ and a sequence of diagrams $(\sigma_{i+1}, \sigma_{i+2}, \ldots, \sigma_{k+1}) \in \Pi(S, V, t_2)$ and a connecting event (σ_i, σ_{i+1}) between t_1 and t_2.

The *connecting path extension of S between* t_1 *and* t_2, $\Pi(S, t_1, t_2)$, is the union of $\Pi(S, V, t_1, t_2)$ for all sequential combinations V of event rules in ER.

Fig. 5.1 exemplifies an event path. The dots represent diagrams and the arrows represent basic events. The basic events labelled in the graph to the left corresponds to the sequence labelled in the graph to the right.

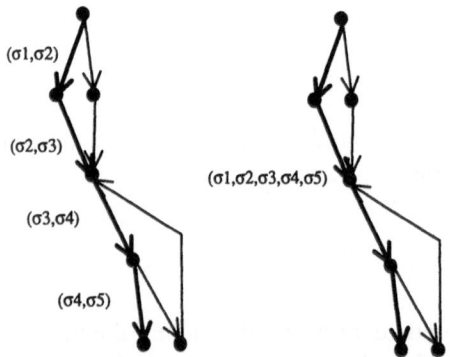

$(\sigma1,\sigma2)$

$(\sigma2,\sigma3)$

$(\sigma1,\sigma2,\sigma3,\sigma4,\sigma5)$

$(\sigma3,\sigma4)$

$(\sigma4,\sigma5)$

Fig. 5.1 A sequence of events and the corresponding event path

When events are mapped between schemata their paths may differ in length. In this case the first and last diagrams of the respective paths are of particular interest since these should be compatible. The following definitions couple the first and last diagrams of an event path into a pair, and define as events all such pairs including basic events.

Definition 5.2

Let $S = \langle SR, ER \rangle$ be a schema, $V = V_1 \nabla \ldots \nabla V_k$ be a sequence of event rules in ER.

The set of *connecting events in S for V between* t_1 *and* t_2, $\Lambda(S, V, t_1, t_2)$ is $\{(\sigma_1, \sigma_{k+1}) \mid$ there is a sequence of diagrams $(\sigma_1, \sigma_2, \ldots, \sigma_{k+1}) \in \Pi(S, V, t_1, t_2)\}$.

The set of *events in S for V at t*, $\Lambda(S, V, t)$ is $\{(\sigma_1, \sigma_{k+1}) \mid$ there is a sequence of diagrams $(\sigma_1, \sigma_2, \ldots, \sigma_{k+1}) \in \Pi(S, V, t)\}$.

The *connecting event extension of S between* t_1 *and* t_2, $\Lambda(S, t_1, t_2)$ is the union of $\Lambda(S, V, t_1, t_2)$ for all sequential combinations V of event rules in ER.

The set of *event extension of S at t*, $\Lambda(S, t)$ is the union of $\Lambda(S, V, t)$ for all sequential combinations V of event rules in ER.

The *event extension of S*, $\Lambda(S)$ is the union of $\Lambda(S, t)$ for all t.

An *event for S*, is a pair $(\sigma, \rho) \in \Lambda(S)$.

The elements of $\Lambda(S)$ will be called *lambda pairs*.

The above concepts can now be employed in dynamic integration. Section 4 defines the set FALIA of static integration assertions as equivalences that given two schemata, expresses formulae in one schema in terms of formulae in the other. The dynamic counterpart to these provides the semantics for dynamic integration by asserting correspondences between event rules in one schema in terms of event rules in the other.

6. Dynamic Integration

This section suggests an extension of the conflict concept and shows some effects this entails.

6.1 Dynamic Conflict

There are many ways of defining conflict both for the static and the dynamic aspects of schemata. An exploratory exposition of several definitions of conflict and their properties is to be found in (Ekenberg 1996) the static definition of which is identical to that used in this chapter. The various definitions of dynamic non-conflict were all found to be equivalent to static non-conflict. However, this leads to some unsatisfactory situations as the following example illustrates. The propositional case and instant events suffice to show this.

Example

Let there be two agents A_1 and A_2, one irresponsible and one protective, represented by schemata $S_1 = <SR_1, ER_1>$ and $S_2 = <SR_2, ER_2>$ respectively.

$D(S_1, 1, 1) = \{\sigma_1, \sigma_2\}$

$D(S_2, 1, 1) = \{\sigma_3, \sigma_4, \sigma_5\}$

where

$\sigma_1 = \{holds(normal, 1)\}$

$\sigma_2 = \{\neg holds(normal, 1)\}$

$\sigma_3 = \{holds(stable, 1), \neg holds(crash, 1)\}$

$\sigma_4 = \{\neg holds(stable, 1), \neg holds(crash, 1)\}$

$\sigma_5 = \{\neg holds(stable, 1), holds(crash, 1)\}$

$ER_1 = \{[(holds(normal, 1)), (\neg holds(normal, 1))]\}$

$ER_2 = \{[(holds(stable, 1), \neg holds(crash, 1)), (\neg holds(stable, 1), \neg holds(crash, 1))]\}$

$FALIA = \{\forall t((t > 0) \rightarrow (holds(normal, t) \leftrightarrow holds(stable, t)))\}$

Events for ER_1 and ER_2 are:

$\Lambda(S_1, t) = \{(\sigma_1, \sigma_1), (\sigma_2, \sigma_2), (\sigma_1, \sigma_2)\}$

$\Lambda(S_2, t) = \{(\sigma_3, \sigma_3), (\sigma_4, \sigma_4), (\sigma_5, \sigma_5), (\sigma_3, \sigma_4)$

This is illustrated in Fig. 6.1. In S_1 it is possible to get from a normal state to abnormal state, whereas in S_2 it is possible to get from a stable state to an unstable state. However it is not possible in S_2 to get to a crashed state. In this light, agent A_1 can be seen as irresponsible and agent A_2 as protective. Taken together, S_1, S_2 and the static integration assertion, satisfy the conditions of static non-conflict. Since dynamic non-conflict in (Ekenberg 1996) is equivalent, the example also satisfies dynamic non-conflict. However, the static integration assertion leads to a combined schema S_3 with the following diagram sets:

$S_3\sigma_1 = \sigma_1 \cup \sigma_3 = \{holds(normal, 1), holds(stable, 1), \neg holds(crash, 1)\}$

$S_3\sigma_2 = \sigma_2 \cup \sigma_4 = \{\neg holds(normal, 1), \neg holds(stable, 1), \neg holds(crash, 1)\}$

$S_3\sigma_3 = \sigma_2 \cup \sigma_5 = \{\neg holds(normal, 1), \neg holds(stable, 1), holds(crash, 1)\}$

These correspond to the dashed lines in Fig. 6.1. Now it becomes clear that agent A_1 can get to both $S_3\sigma_2$ and $S_3\sigma_3$ from $S_3\sigma_1$. Which of these occurs is immaterial to A_1, indeed it is non-deterministic, and so although agent A_2 does not permit a transition to a crashed state in schema S_2, in S_3 he is powerless to prevent it.

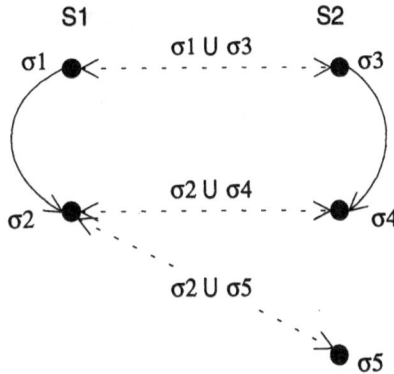

Fig. 6.1 Static non-conflict and dynamic conflict

According to (Ekenberg96) this situation is not classified as conflicting. A suggestion follows, for new definitions of dynamic non-conflict that prevent this problem. The definitions are intended to be general and intuitive. Intuitively, two schemata are dynamically non-conflicting with respect to a set of static integration assertions if for every event e1 in one schema it holds that for every pair of diagrams compatible with the static integration assertions together with event e_1, there is *some* rule that will result in that pair. More formally:

Definition 6.1

S_1 and S_2 are *dynamically non-conflicting at t with respect to* FALIA(t) iff it holds for every $(\sigma, \rho) \in \Lambda(S_1, t)$ that for all σ' where $\sigma \cup \sigma'$ satisfies FALIA(t) and for all ρ' where $\rho \cup \rho'$ satisfies FALIA(t); $(\sigma', \rho') \in \Lambda(S_2, t)$. Otherwise S_1 and S_2 are *dynamically conflicting at t with respect to* FALIA(t)

Note that this definition does not require that a single event rule or sequence of rules in S_2 must be able to result in all the events compatible with all the events resulting from a single rule or sequence of rules in S_1. This is a stronger requirement, and is what is demanded by dynamic integration assertions.

With this definition the example above no longer qualifies as dynamically non-conflicting because $\sigma_1 \cup \sigma_3$ and $\sigma_2 \cup \sigma_5$ both satisfy FALIA(t), and although there is an event $((\sigma_1, \sigma_2) \in \Lambda(S_1))$ there is no event $(((\sigma_3, \sigma_5) \in \Lambda(S_2))$.

The definition of dynamic non-conflict presented here is essentially different from that in (Ekenberg 1996). Static non-conflict does not imply dynamic non-conflict and dynamic non-conflict does not imply static non-conflict. The example last given shows the first conjuct since it is statically non-conflicting but dynamically it is conflicting.

The following example shows the second conjuct. Again the propositional case and instant events suffice.

Let there be schemata $S_1 = <SR_1, ER_1>$ and $S_2 = <SR_2, ER_2>$ respectively.

$D(S_1, 1, 1) = \{\sigma_1, \sigma_2, \sigma_3\}$

$D(S_2, 1, 1) = \{\sigma_4, \sigma_5\}$

where

$\sigma_1 = \{holds(a, 1), \neg holds(b, 1), holds(c,1)\}$

$\sigma_2 = \{\neg holds(a, 1), holds(b, 1), holds(c,1)\}\}$

$\sigma_3 = \{\neg holds(a, 1), \neg holds(b, 1), \neg holds(c,1)\}\}$

$\sigma_4 = \{holds(d, 1), holds(e, 1), \neg holds(f,1)\}$

$\sigma_5 = \{holds(d, 1), \neg holds(e, 1), holds(f,1)\}$

$FALIA(t) = \{\forall t ((t > 0) \rightarrow (holds(c, t) \leftrightarrow holds(d, t)))\}$

$ER_1 = \{[(holds(a, t)), (holds(b, t))],[(holds(b,t)),(holds(a,t))]\}$

$ER_2 = \{[(holds(e, t)), (holds(f, t))],[(holds(f,t)),(holds(e,t))]\}$

Events for ER_1 and ER_2 are:

$\Lambda(S_1, t) = \{(\sigma_1, \sigma_2),(\sigma_2,\sigma_1)\}$

$\Lambda(S_2, t) = \{(\sigma_4, \sigma_5),(\sigma_5,\sigma_4)\}$

The example satisfies the conditions for dynamic non-conflict because for each event in $\Lambda(S_1, t)$ there is an event in S_2 such that the requirements are fulfilled. However for the diagram σ_3 in S_1 there are no diagrams in S_2 that satisfy $FALIA(t)$, and therefore S_2 compromises S_1, and they are conflicting. The schemata in the example are thus dynamically non-conflicting and statically conflicting.

The independence of static and dynamic non-conflict is important because it allows greater freedom in the expression of constraints between two schemata. This means that compatibility between two schemata when based on the definitions of non-conflict given here, will be less dependent on the static integration assertions alone, and rest instead upon a number of properties of the schemata in question.

6.2 The Demands of Dynamic Non-conflict

When dynamic non-conflict is required between schemata that are statically non-conflicting, certain patterns of correspondences between schemata, can force a large number of events to be required. The simplest case is that shown in the example illustrated in Fig. 6.1. An event (σ_3, σ_5) is required for dynamic non-conflict to be fulfilled. Extending the problem further leads to an integration structure like that shown in Fig. 6.2, which is dynamically conflicting. The event (σ_1, σ_3) requires event (σ_2, σ_4) which in turn requires (σ_3, σ_5) which in turn requires (σ_4, σ_6) and so on. The demands that one schema makes on the other ricochet back and forth propagating down the statically integrated structure in a chain reaction.

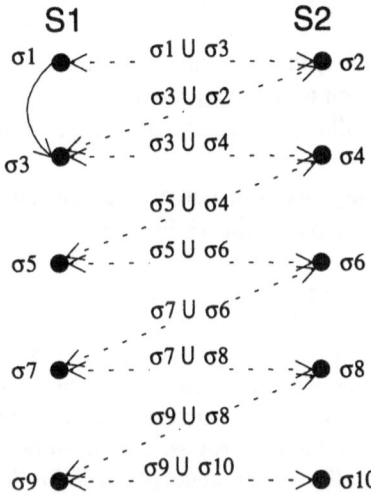

Fig. 6.2. Striving for dynamic non-conflict sets off a chain of demands

This growth of the requirements on events has consequences not only for the size and complexity of the integration process but also for coping with the plethora of events required. The considerable increase in choices of events that results during schema execution can have grave consequences for computational efficiency.

Recognising the kinds of structure that result in chain reactions of this type may be a useful way of checking for static integration assertions that can result in a taxing integration procedure or worse, an operationally unwieldy integration. Integration assertions or the schemata could be adjusted to avoid creating unfavourable correspondence patterns.

7. Concluding Remarks

The work described in this chapter includes temporal aspects in determining whether a multi-agent system is in conflict when features such as intentions, obligations and commitments are important. Such features are represented in the first order action language FAL, which is a first order language with extended semantics for handling certain speech acts, and with arithmetic for dealing explicitly with discrete time.

The definitions treated herein take both static and dynamic aspects of multi-agent specifications into consideration. Non-temporal dynamic aspects are examined in (Ekenberg 1996), from which ideas have been brought into the theory described here. These provide a model for event driven systems, which can be extended to include schemas with more complex data structures.

In (Abiteboul 1995), three fundamental ways of restricting updates to a database are described:

- Specify constraints (static as well as dynamic) that the database must satisfy and reject any update that leads to a violation of the constraints.
- Restrict the updates themselves by only allowing the use of a set of pre-specified update rules.
- Permit users to request essentially arbitrary updates, but provide an automatic mechanism for detecting and repairing constraint violations.

This chapter, relates to the first two of these points by introducing static and dynamic rules as well as the event concept. The third point above is studied in the emerging field of active databases (Simon 1992). An active database supports the automatic triggering of updates as a response to events. One possible extension to our work on schema integration is to investigate how this form of automatic updates can be incorporated into the proposed framework.

Another research direction is to change the event concept used in this chapter. Our event concept is deliberately weak and it could be argued that it does not capture common intuitions about events, in particular our approach implies that from a given state infinitely many states can be reached from just one event rule with one instantiation.

To remedy this situation, it is straightforward to introduce an alternative event concept, by means of an information processor that obeys some form of a frame rule. This would render our event concept more similar to traditional transactional update approaches in the database area, where updates are provided by means of transactions composed of sequences of insertions, deletions, and modifications (Abiteboul 1988).

Acknowledgements

This work was supported by the Graduate School of Teleinformatics.

CHAPTER 7

Conflict Management in Concurrent Engineering: Modelling Guides

N. Matta, O. Corby

INRIA (ACACIA) Sophia Antipolis

In Concurrent Engineering, several designers (participants) aim at designing a system (artifact), given requirements. Conflict Management in Concurrent Engineering is a complex task in which it is difficult to identify conflicts and to solve them. Reuse of generic components is generally considered as a good help to guide complex task modelling. An overview of our study to define a library of generic components to guide conflict management modelling is presented below. Conflict management methods, proposed in the literature, are classified and associated to each concurrent engineering subtask. This classification provides help to index these methods, considered as generic components in a library.

1. Introduction

Concurrent Engineering (CE) aims at facilitating a product development process requiring different specialities, and at achieving better product quality (Schreiber, Wielenga and Van de Velde 1994). So, it is important to facilitate teamwork and collaboration between participants in the development process. The main problems in CE ensue in communication between participants and collaborative decision making.

Conflict management remains a complex task in Concurrent Engineering (CE) (Klein 1995). On the one hand, it is difficult to detect conflicts and their nature precisely, and on another hand, it is complex to determine appropriate methods to solve them.

Our main objective is to define generic models for the conflict management task in CE. These models will provide generic components to be used as building blocks in conflict management task modelling for a specific application. This work is a part of the Genie[1] project, in which the CE task is analysed in order to provide guides for modelling this task and for defining corporate memory.

---

1 Genie project is a common project between INRIA and DASSAULT AVIATION.

Our generic models are represented in CML formalism (Schreiber, Wielinga and Van de Velde 1994) and organized in the same way as the generic components in the Common-KADS library (Breuker and Van de Velde 1994), which offer models to guide several task types modelling. So we have represented all studied methods and models from the literature in a single formalism. This allows to analyse their characteristics and to reveal their respective contributions. The generic models, provided by CommonKADS library for tasks such as diagnosis, design, etc., are described in CML. Therefore, it seemed natural to exploit CML to represent our generic models.

Before describing guides to model conflict management (2, 3, 4, 5 and 6), let us define some conflict types handled in CE (Cf. 1).

2. Conflict in Concurrent Engineering

At least, two Classes of conflicts can be handled in CE:

1. First, *conflicts between design and requirements*. In other words, the design made by a participant does not satisfy corresponding requirements. This type of conflicts is handled in the same way as in mono-expertise design, when a designer tries to generate a design in order to satisfy requirements. CommonKADS library (Breuker and Van de Velde 1994) and Brazier in (Brazier, Van Langen and Treur 1995) offer a number of generic models to assess the design respecting the requirements. We do not study this class of conflicts.

2. Second, *disagreements between some participants* in the designers group, according to their design propositions. Such conflicts arise from problems caused by strategies used and propositions made by designers: 1) *Strategic conflicts* ensue from the inconsistency in methods and tools used by designers and in the allocation of tasks to each designer. Divergence between the participants responsibilities and failure in their cooperation (Brazier, Van Langen and Treur 1995) causes also strategic conflicts. 2) *Conflicts about propositions* made can appear from: a) misunderstanding of the participants' terminology and their points of view, b) unacceptance of the conditions under which a proposition is made and of consequences by which a proposition constrain the design cycle. Preconditions problems can be revealed from preferences like needs (Sycara, 1991), from the use of the same resources and from difference in the requirements evaluation by the designers. Constraints imposed by the proposition and its interaction with other propositions can generate consequences problems. Note also that the quality of a proposition can cause its unacceptance (Figure 2.1.) shows a typology of such conflicts. In this typology objects about which problems can appear and the nature of conflicts revealed are emphasised.

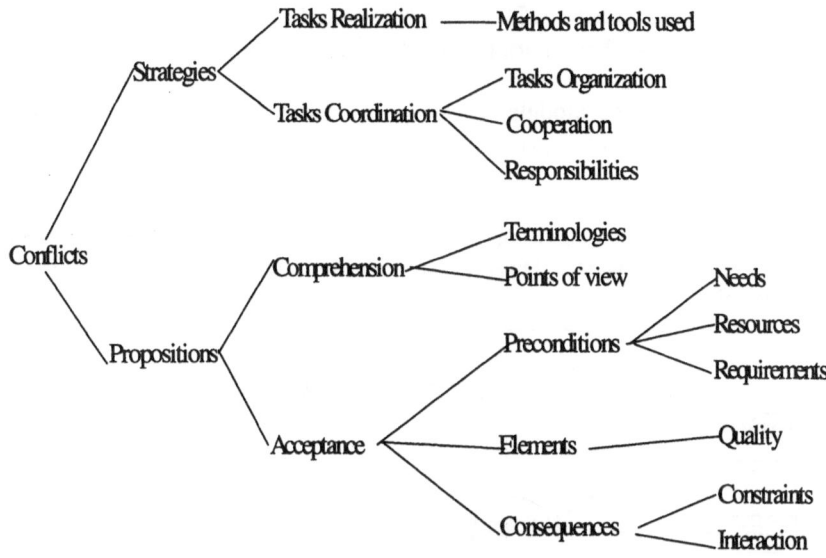

Fig 2.1. A Typology of Conflicts.

It is necessary to define the nature of such conflicts and explicit their contributors, to determine appropriate methods to solve them. We offer in a library a number of methods presented like generic components to manage these types of conflicts between participants.

3. Management conflict in Concurrent Engineering

To determine in which step in CE task conflicts can appear and how to manage them, we first studied a model for the CE task itself. A number of models for this task are presented in the literature like Bond's model (Bond, 1990) and Brazier et al's model (Brazier, Van Langen and Treur 1995). We can distinguish some CE particularities from these models like:

1. The existence of a shared model and private models (Bond, 1990) in CE. Each one of the private models belongs to a participant of the CE task and describes his knowledge. In fact, a private model is the expertise model (an explicitation of the model of his knowledge) of a participant. These expertise models are private and they are not shared. However, shared model describes shared knowledge of the system to be designed.

2. Modifications can be made in requirements as well as in artefact (Brazier, Van Langen and Treur 1995). So conflicts can be revealed and managed in requirements as well as in artefact model modifications.

After studying these models, we propose a generic model for concurrent engineering task, in which private propositions are combined with coordination (Figure 3.1).

After studying such models of CE task, we propose a generic model for the concurrent engineering task (Figure 3.1). We distinguish three main subtasks in this model:

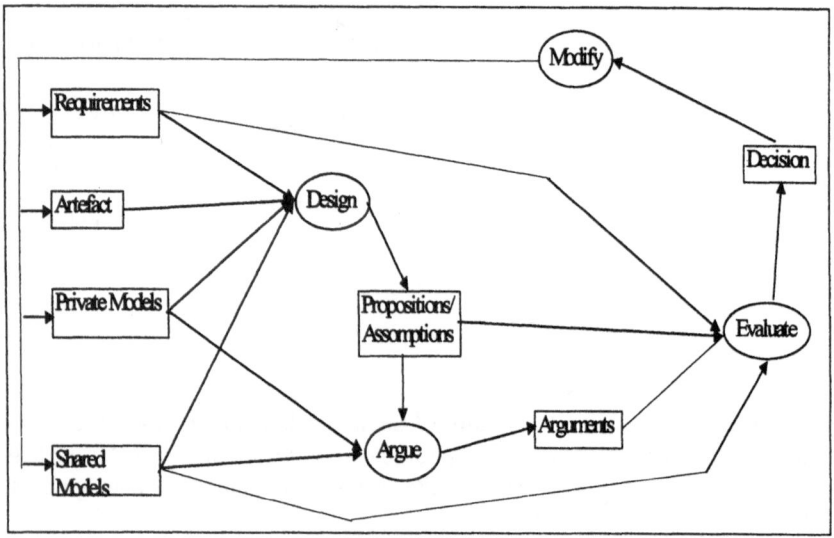

Fig 3.1. Concurrent Engineering data flow.

- *Design task*: Relying on his private knowledge (Private model), each designer generates some propositions to satisfy given requirements. His task is similar to a design task. Generic design model represented in the CommonKADS library (Breuker and Van de Velde 1994) can guide the modelling of this task.

- *Argue task*: To promote the acceptance of his propositions by the group, a participant justifies them with a number of arguments. Assumptions made in the design task are used to determine arguments and to define them. Argumentation tries to change other participant's opinion by justifying the utility and the necessity of a proposition (Castelfranchi 1996). It forms an important part of negotiation which aims at solving a conflict.

- *Evaluate task*: The group evaluates the integration of propositions in the artefact. Propositions may not satisfy participants' needs and conflicts can appear. So, the principal subtask in this evaluation consists of detecting and solving conflicts.

Propositions can concern the requirements or the artefact model. Decisions about which object (requirements or artefact model) can be modified in the next process cycle and in which part modifications can be made, are taken in the design control (a subtask of "Evaluate")

Shared model can be reorganized and modified, because other shared knowledge can be learned at each cycle.

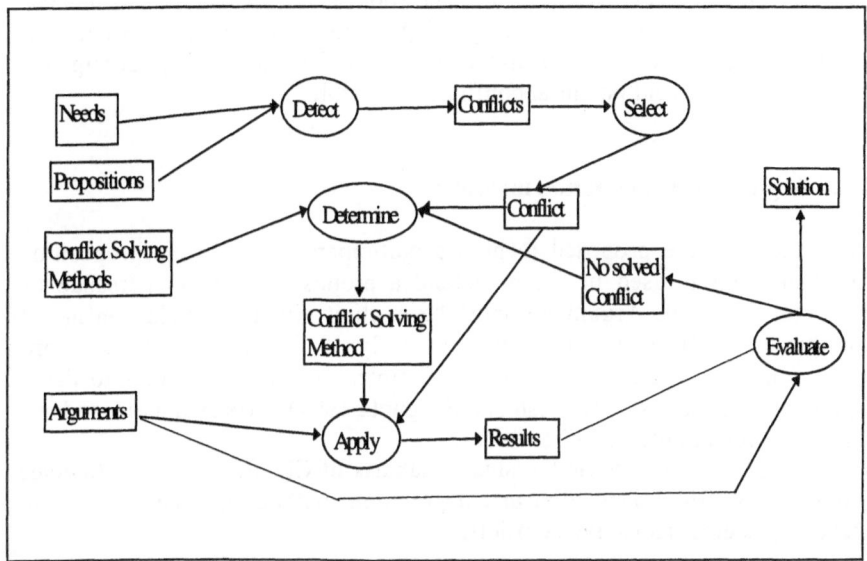

Fig 3.2. Conflict Management data flow.

Conflict management task consists of first detecting a conflict (its nature) and then solving it. Detection task can be assimilated to a diagnosis task in which a default (i.e.: the conflict) is located (well defined). Once detected, to solve a conflict, a solving method is selected and applied. The result is then evaluated to determine if the conflict is solved or not. In the last case, another method can be selected and applied and so on. (Figure 3.2).

Emphasising the characteristics of the tasks performed in the CE, specially the players in each task allowed us to express the nature of conflicts which can be detected in CE and the types of methods which can be used to solve them.

4. Methods to manage conflicts for each CE subtask

We associated several conflict management methods proposed in the literature, to CE subtasks as generic components in the library.

4. 1. "Design": Prevention methods

In CE, several designers in different specialities collaborate together. Each designer has a specific viewpoint due to his speciality. B. Ramesh proposes to share part of private knowledge to avoid terminology and interpretation conflicts (Ramesh and Sengupta 1994). S. Easterbrook relates potential conflicts to group member characteristics (Easterbrook et al. 1993). He recommends some strategies to form a group respecting members' characteristics and relationships. Such methods can be associated to the Concurrent Engineering "Design" subtask to avoid potential conflicts if possible.

4. 2. "Argue": Argumentation methods

Other methods are proposed to help a participant to argue his proposition. Argumentation is used in CE to defend a proposition and to persuade the group to choose it. Arguments must be explicit either to avoid conflicts if possible or to determine their nature precisely. K. Sycara (Sycara 1991) proposes some strategies using general principles and heuristic rules to define arguments. B. Ramesh (Ramesh and Sengupta 1994) favours interdependency sharing to detect potential differences.

The important step in the "Evaluate" subtask of CE (Figure 3.1) is to detect and solve conflicts. Detection and negotiation methods can be used to (respectively) detect and solve conflicts.

4. 3. "Evaluate Propositions": Conflict detection methods

Methods to detect conflicts and to determine their nature are not well defined in the literature. Klein considers a conflict as an exception in the CE cycle and provides a typology of the nature of exceptions (Klein 1995). He recommends also some strategies to handle exceptions depending on their nature. Conflict detection can be assimilated to a diagnosis task in which conflicts (faults) are to be determined (located). So, diagnosis methods like those presented in (Benjamins 1993) can be used to detect conflicts. Conflict symptoms can be first detected and contributors (opposed propositions and arguments) are analysed as hypothesis in order to define explicitly conflict causes. Our conflict typology (Figure 2.1) helps to determine the nature of a conflict and to detect elements which cause it.

4. 4. "Evaluate Propositions": Negotiation methods

A large number of negotiation methods can be used to solve detected conflicts. Some of them like "Locate a consensus", where a consensus is located and a solution is then chosen, can be applied to solve mixed-motive conflicts (Ramesh and Sengupta 1994). Another method like "Introduction of a Third party", where a third party imposes a solution (Easterbrook et al. 1993) is defined to solve resource conflicts and also strategic conflicts.

Other methods are proposed in some conditions. For example, to apply Case-Based Reasoning (CBR) (Sycara 1991), first a number of past cases must be stored and second, at least one case similar to the current one must be selected. CBR recommends to retrieve conflict solution from an appropriate previous case and to adjust it as a solution to the current conflict. Another method proposes a Goal Graph Search to add goals or to substitute rejected goals in order to modify tasks decomposition and attribution (Sycara 1991). To be applied, this method needs goal graphs organized as influence trees. Defining a "Counter-proposition" or modifying a rejected proposition (Sycara 1991) are also recommended.

5. Representing conflict management methods in the library

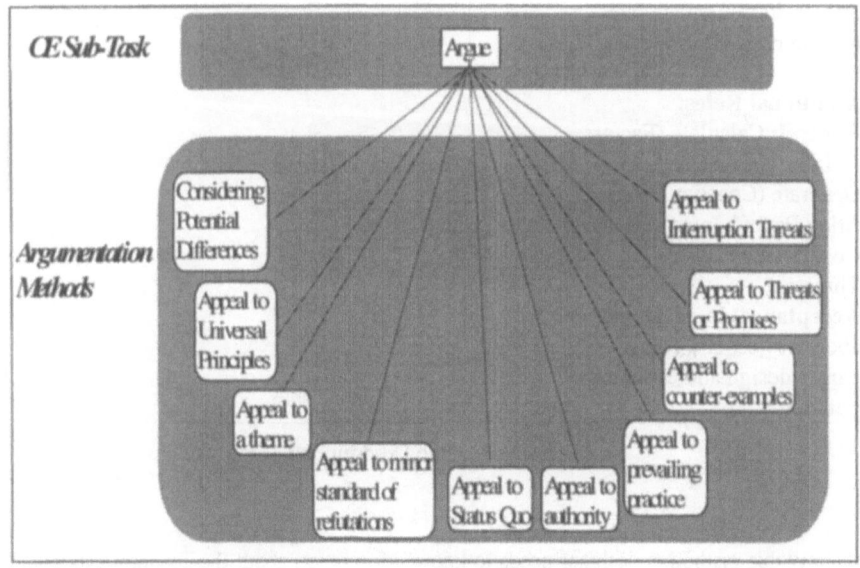

Fig 5.1. Argumentation methods.

A global view of the associations between CE subtasks and conflict management methods can guide a knowledge engineer to determine appropriate methods to manage conflicts in a particular application. So, trees of associations CE-subtasks/corresponding methods are presented in the library. For example, representing, a number of argumentation methods (Figure 5.1), shows a global view of possible strategies which can be used to justify a proposition. These trees are used also to mark out the description of a method.

The competence and the acceptance described in a method inform the knowledge engineer what the method is able to perform and in which conditions can be applied. For example, the "Interruption Threats" method guide to formulate arguments by using interruption threats in order to incite designers to accept a proposition.

Method "Interruption Threats":	Method "Interruption Threats": Data Flow
Competence: Guide to generate threats. If a conflicted proposition is not considered in the solution, the overall design process can be interrupted. **Input:** Factors (Project Information), Conflicts **Output:** Interruption Threats **Sub-tasks:** Calculate interruption cost, Generate threats **Additional Roles**: **Control:** Calculate (Factors -> Interruption Cost) Generate (Conflict, Proposition Payoff, Interruption Cost -> Interruption Threats) **Acceptance:** Information about project and company's design and economic policies.	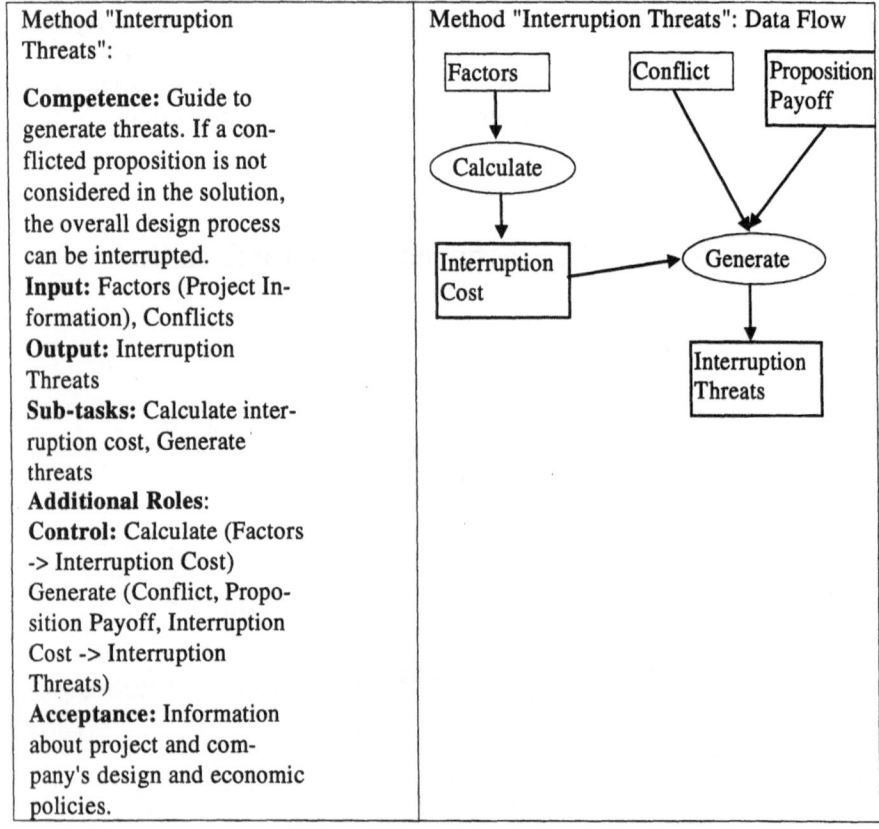

Fig 5.2 A Method Description.

To apply this method, a designer needs to know information about the economic state and the politics of the company. He will use these information to calculate the interruption cost of the design process. This cost helps to formulate threats as arguments in which acceptance of the corresponding proposition as a necessary condition of the design process progress, is emphasised. Data flow shows the interaction between tasks and roles which can be played by the application static knowledge (Figure 5.2).

Each task is then described, with its goal, I/O roles,... (Figure 5.3). For example, the task "Calculate" allows to determine the design process "Interruption Cost" using the company's economic information as factors. A definition of agents which will realise the task and to which task results must be communicated, is also made (Figure 5.3). This definition emphasises players in each level in CE task (personal, inter-personal or group level). For example, the task "Calculate" will be realised by one designer. The result of this task is used by the same designer to generate arguments which will be communicated to the group. So, the "Interruption Threats" methods is performed at the inter-personal level, in which a designer executes all the method subtasks, and the results are then communicated to others (the designers group).

Sub-Task "Calculate":	Allocation and Communication
Definition: **Goal:** Determine the Interruption Cost. **Specification:** To calculate the interruption cost, a number of factors like information about economic situation of the company and of the industry overall, about the project itself and about the specific design sector are considered. **Input:** Factors **Output:** Interruption Cost **End definition.**	
Sub-Task "Generate":	Allocation and Communication
Definition: Goal: Generate Interruption Threats. **Specification:** To determine a number of Threats as arguments. These arguments emphasize that the corresponding proposition is a necessary condition to the progress of the design process and it is costly to interrupt the design process. **Input:** Interruption Cost **Output:** Interruption Threats **End definition.**	

Fig 5.3. Tasks Description.

Let-us show another example of the description of methods in the library. A number of negotiation methods are presented as guides to help conflicts solving (Figure 5.4).

The "Locate Consensus" method, presented in (Ramesh and Sengupta 1994) can be described as (Figure 5.5 and 5.6) in the library. The "Locate" task recommended by this method are described as in Figure 5.6.

These associations are not exhaustive. We plan to study other methods and enrich these associations.

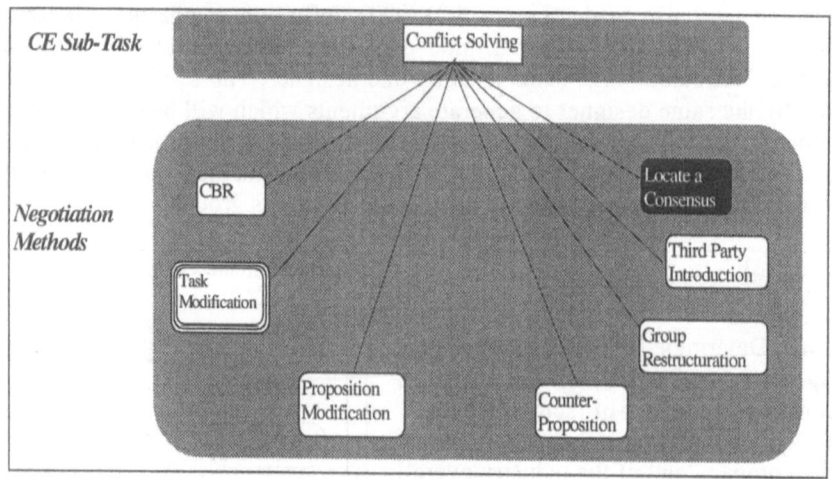

Fig 5.4. Negotiation methods.

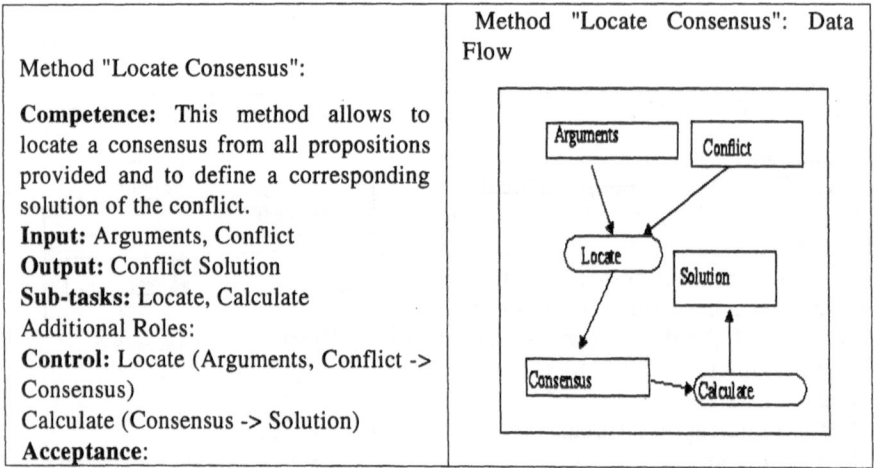

Method "Locate Consensus":

Competence: This method allows to locate a consensus from all propositions provided and to define a corresponding solution of the conflict.
Input: Arguments, Conflict
Output: Conflict Solution
Sub-tasks: Locate, Calculate
Additional Roles:
Control: Locate (Arguments, Conflict -> Consensus)
Calculate (Consensus -> Solution)
Acceptance:

Method "Locate Consensus": Data Flow

Fig 5.5. The "Locate Consensus" method description.

Sub-Task "Locate":	Allocation and Communication
Definition: Goal: Locate a consensus. Specification: Find an area of agreement, with evaluating valid propositions and determining norms which define the guidelines of a solution as a potential consensus. Input: Conflict, Arguments Output: Consensus End definition.	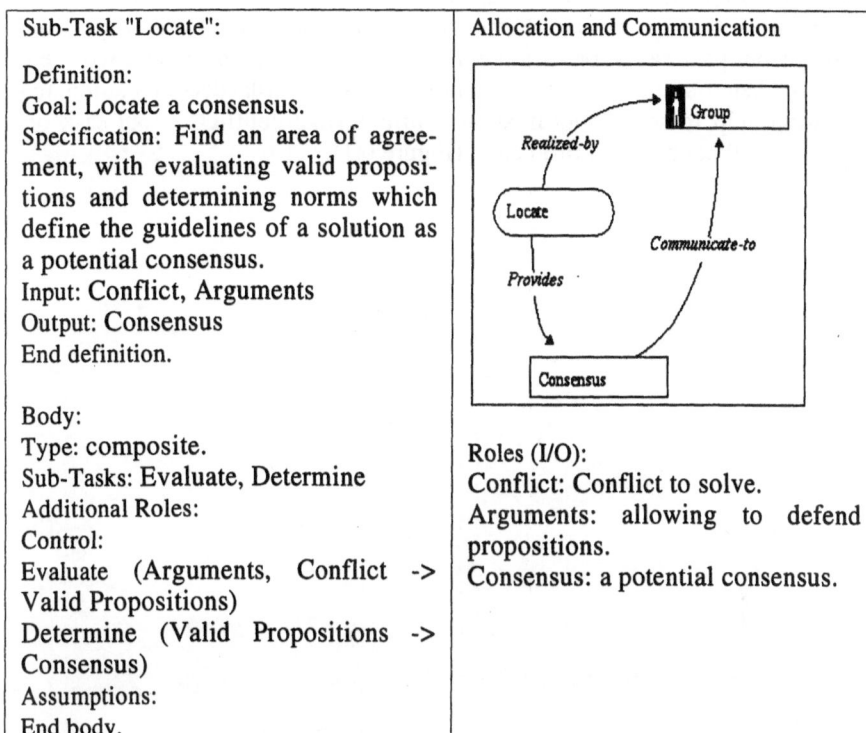
Body: Type: composite. Sub-Tasks: Evaluate, Determine Additional Roles: Control: Evaluate (Arguments, Conflict -> Valid Propositions) Determine (Valid Propositions -> Consensus) Assumptions: End body.	Roles (I/O): Conflict: Conflict to solve. Arguments: allowing to defend propositions. Consensus: a potential consensus.

Fig 5.6. The "Locate" task description.

6. Conflict types as another library index

To facilitate the selection of methods from the library, we use the conflict typology (illustrated in Figure 2.1) as another index. The associations of prevention, argumentation and negotiation methods to conflict types which can be managed by these methods, guided us to determine a number of selection criteria as index.

6. 1. Strategic Conflicts

To manage strategic conflicts, the appeal to the authority, to Threats or Promises and to Interruption Threats, can be used in the argumentation. Group Restructuring, or The Introduction of a Third Party will help conflict solving. Conflicts came out from tasks realisation like conflicts about methods and tools used or from missing in the responsibilities to execute tasks, can be managed with an appeal of a minor standard of refutations rules or an appeal of rules relative to a particular theme, as argumentation methods. Extracting solution from past cases, or locating a consensus between designers will help also in the negotiation. However, The modification of tasks decomposition and attribution help to solve coordination conflicts (like conflicts about task organization and cooperation problems) (Figure 6.1).

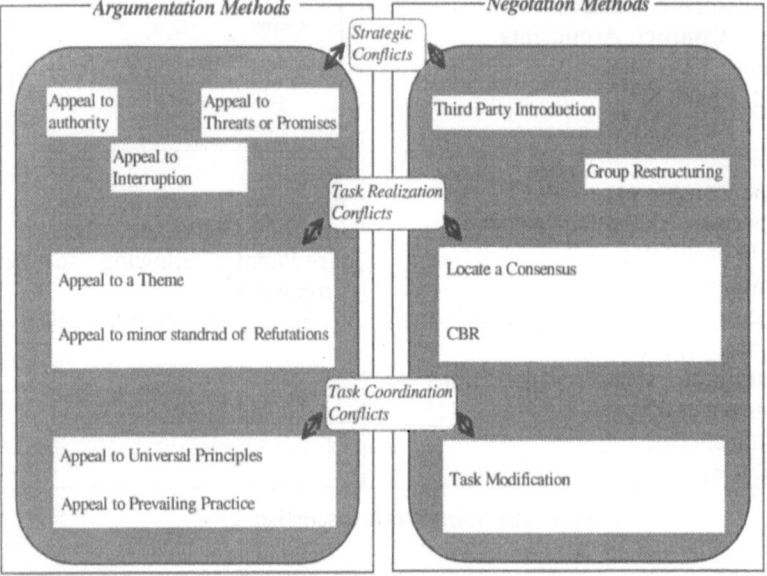

Fig 6.1. An example of Conflict types/Generic methods association: Methods to manage strategic conflict.

6. 2. Conflicts about propositions

Knowledge sharing is necessary to prevent problems caused from a misunderstanding of propositions provided (Ramesh and Sengupta 1994). Considering Potential differences and Appealing to a particular theme's rules can be used in this case as argumentation methods. Propositions Modification is an interesting method to be used in the negotiation.

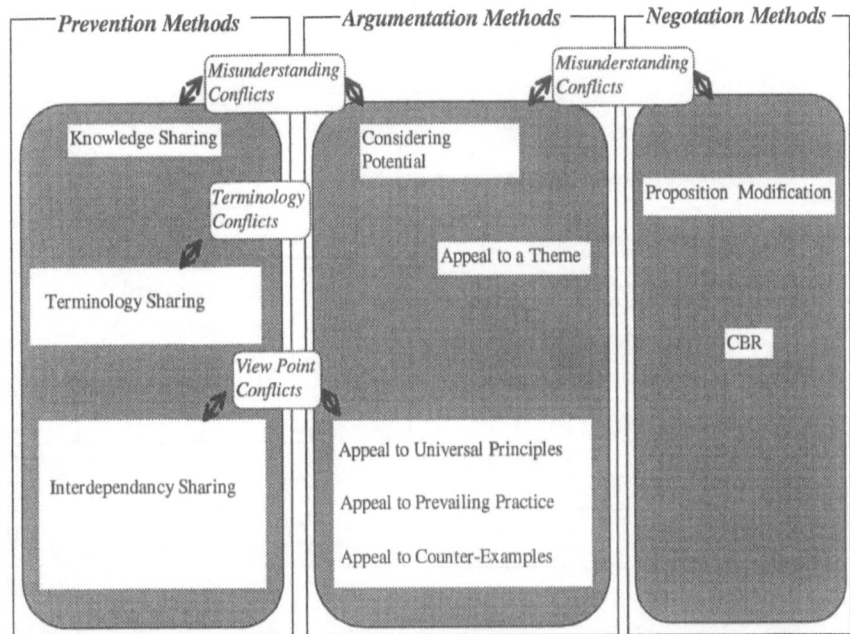

Fig 6.2. An example of Conflict types/Generic methods association: Methods to manage conflicts that appeared from misunderstanding of propositions.

To manage acceptance conflicts, the negotiation can be oriented in order to locate a consensus. To solve those caused from different evaluation of preferences or of requirements, negotiation methods like Propositions Modifications and Counter-Proposition will be used. To solve resources problems, the Introduction of a Third Party Decision is noticeable. The Appeal to authority, to Threats or Promises or to Interruption Threats can be also used as argumentation methods in this case. Problems about the acceptance of the quality of propositions can be solved using the Appeal to Prevailing Practice, to Minor Standard Refutations rules, to Threats or Promises or to Interruption Threats as argumentation methods. Negotiation methods like the modification of tasks decomposition and attribution, Proposition modification, Counter-Proposition and Introduction of a Third Party decision will help also to deal with this type of conflicts.

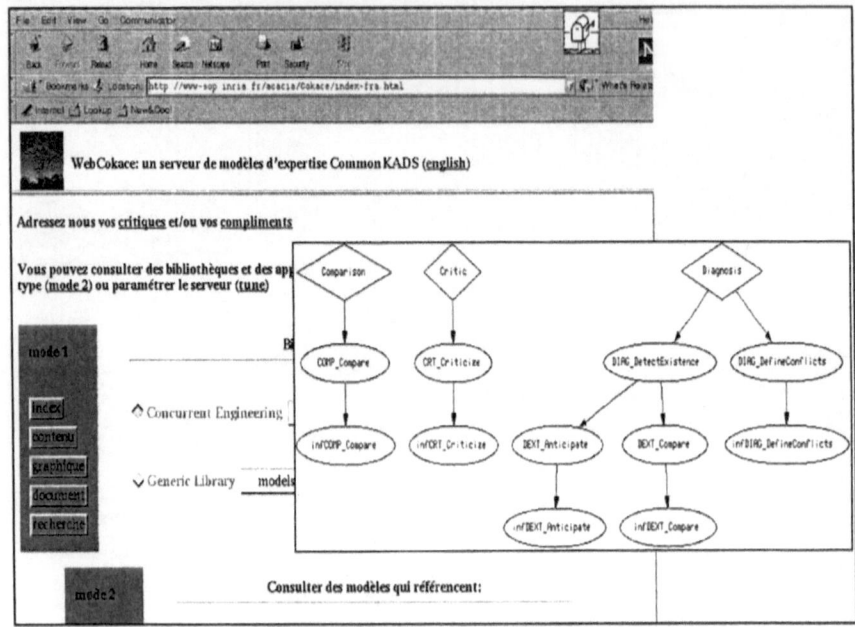

Fig 6.3. Access to components via Task/Methods Index. For example, Methods (Comparison, Critic and Diagnosis) which can be used to detect conflicts.

7. An easy access to the library

We expressed a formal representation of this library in the CML language, using Cokace, a CML dedicated environment (Corby and Dieng 1996), in order to facilitate its exploitation. An HTML format is also generated automatically using this tool. The library is accessible via a knowledge server called "WebCokace", defined in our team (Corby and Dieng 1997), at the URL: http://www.inria.fr/acacia/Cokace.

7.1. The knowledge server WebCokace

The knowledge server WebCokace (Corby and Dieng 1997) provides an easy access and an intelligent knowledge search from knowledge bases. This server is based on requests on knowledge represented with CML language (Schreiber, Wielinga and Van de Velde 1994). An editor (Cokace), we defined, allows to represent knowledge with CML and to generate an HTML format accessible through the WebCokace server.

The ergonomic analysis (Ros 1997) of the server user's task and needs provided us a number of recommendation to make WebCokace more useful and more usable. In fact, the server can be used by knowledge engineers to define conceptual models of applications in particular domains. It can be used also by another type of users who search information about problem solving. For example, participants in CE applications can look for knowledge about nature of conflicts and methods to solve a particular conflict, etc., using this server.

So, functions in WebCokace server is defined considering different types of users. and knowledge is presented close to natural language and in different ways (graphical, Index, formal,...).

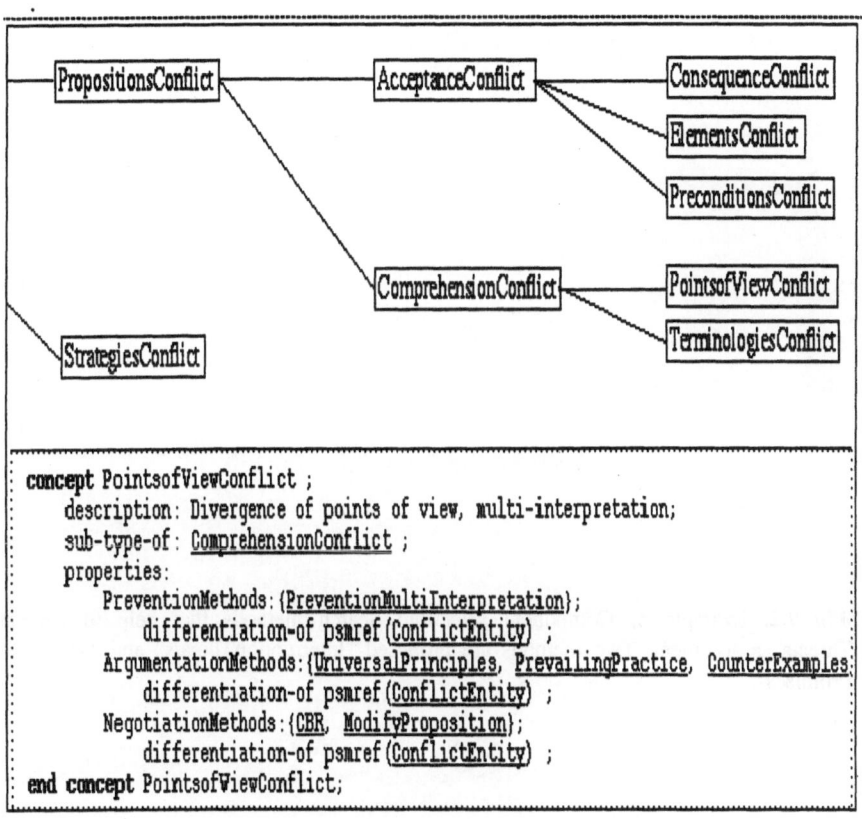

Fig 7.1. Example of the Conflict/Methods Index.

WebCokace offers different types of access on components on the library. It helps designers to search knowledge (methods, tasks, conflicts,...) and learn strategies to manage similar situations

We present in the following examples of such types of access to knowledge from the CE library using WebCokace.

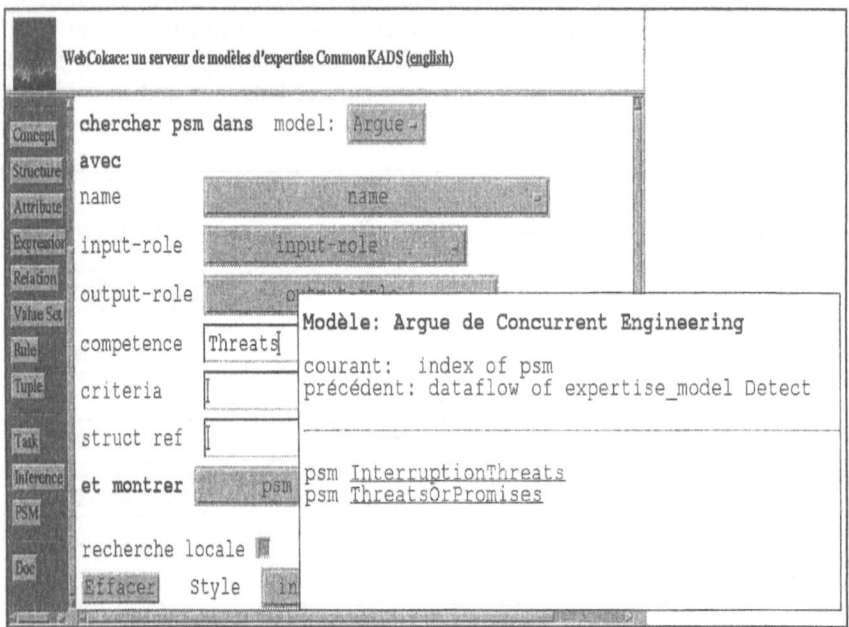

Fig 7.2. Example of Component selection: Search methods that help to generate Threats as argument. Two methods are proposed "InterruptionThreats" and "ThreatsOr-Promises".

7.2. Examples of access to the library using the knowledge server

Different ways of access to our library (described in CML) are offered via WebCokace. In fact, in addition to the index (Associations Task/Methods (Figure 6.3) and Associations conflict/Methods (Figure 7.1)), the server provides dedicated user interface for searching main CML entities such as: concept, method, task, etc.

For example, if a user needs methods that generate threats to argue its propositions, he selects "Argumentation" as the type of task (or "Argue" model in "Concurrent Engineering Library") and then, he chooses the "PSM" interface, through which he requires methods that "Competences" can generate "Threats". An index of all methods that allow to generate threats is shown (Figure 7.2). A simple click on each method allows to show its description (how generate threats, Inputs needed,...) For example, one method found suggests to use an influence tree of goals and to analyse the influence of the conflict on others' goals in order to generate threats. The user can also ask the data flow of methods, by choosing the "data flow" look (Figure 7.3). So, a graph that shows the relation between inputs, tasks and outputs is presented. It emphasize how knowledge are used by tasks to achieve a goal (for example, "generate Threats").

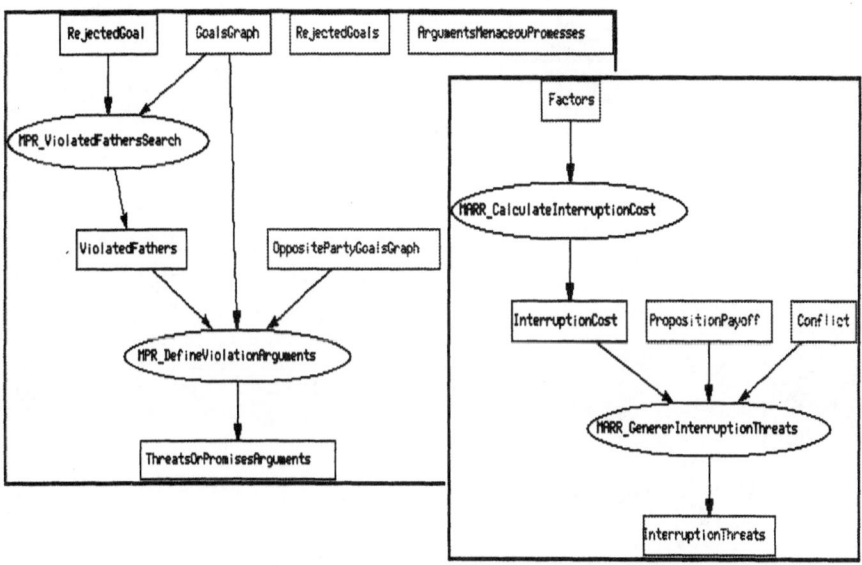

Fig 7.3. Example of Component selection: Search methods that help to generate Threats as argument. The data flow of found methods can be also shown.

Another example: search tasks that give an artefact as output. So, in the Task interface, "Artefact" can be asked as "Output Role" of the task (with for example, the look "text"). The description of two tasks are shown: "CE" and "update" (Figure 7.4). The first one describes how to design an artefact and the second one shows that an artefact must be updated by integrating the right design propositions.

The use of a knowledge server like WebCokace, carries away different problems due to Hyper-text navigation, like localization and processing (Foss 1989) of knowledge and also orientation problem of the user with respect to his initial search goal (Conklin 1987). To minimize these problems, we recommend a global presentation of the content of knowledge that WebCokace server allows to access (Ros 1997). User needs a clear representation of the server: its structure, its search logic and the semantic of links used. Dedicated interfaces help also users to search appropriate knowledge.

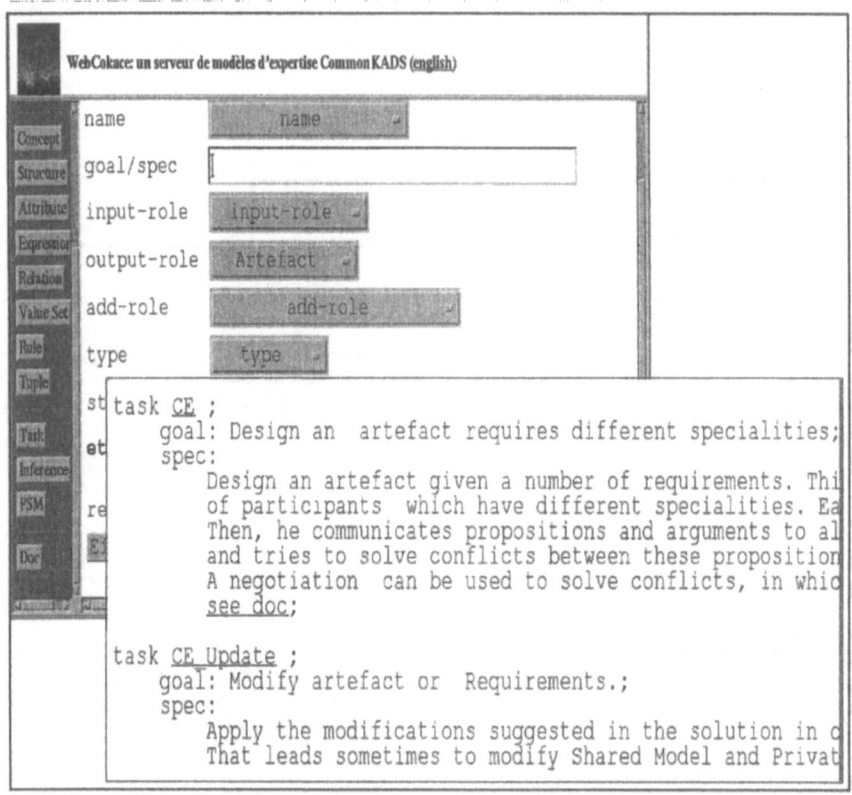

Fig 7.4. Example of Component selection: Search tasks that help to define an artefact. Two tasks are proposed "CE" and "CE-Update".

8. Conclusion

Conflicts ensue essentially from divergence of different fields implicated in a CE project. So, the management of this type of conflicts requires to detect first the discordance between proposals of different designers and to negotiate modifications to be done in order to find a coherence between design propositions and to integrate them in a single product.

In negotiation, a designer tries to change with arguments, the opinion of others in order to minimise modifications on his propositions. The main objective of this chapter is to provide guides which help to detect this type of conflicts and to negotiate a solution.

Determining generic components as guides to model CE task and specially Conflict Management task is an innovative aspect of the research in CE. Representing conflict management as generic components allowed us to characterise the nature of different types of conflicts. Prevention, argumentation and negotiation methods are organized to manage these types of conflicts.

We analyse conflict types as conditions of conflict management methods selection and application. This helps to index these methods considered as generic components in the library. Other work in indexation is also studied for this purpose.

Generic components libraries offer guides for a large number of users. The use of the Web makes easier their sharing. As far as we know, there is no study to offer such libraries via the Web and especially to facilitate the search of components from them by making them accessible via a knowledge server.

The development of a server like WebCokace needs an ergonomic analysis of users' activities and their motivation to search knowledge from the library. So, we plan to study the use of the server in real applications. We plan also to a use real application in aeronautics to validate components selection from the library and their adaptation to specific applications.

We plan to study the representation of shared knowledge in CE applications using multi-perspective structures (Ribière, Matta and Cointe 1997). A multi-agent architecture is in development in our team (Cointe 1997). This architecture aims at helping a group of participants to design an artefact. It guides participants to share their propositions by structuring them in a single formalism and to detect and solve conflicts by facilitating propositions comparison and by recommending conflict management methods extracted from our library. This architecture is based on the generic CE task model.

Acknowledgements

We deeply thank the French "Ministère de l'Enseignement Supérieur et de la Recherche" and DASSAULT-AVIATION (Genie Project) that funded this research for their partial funding. We thank also Dr. R. Dieng for her remark.

CHAPTER 8

Modeling Conflicts Between Agents in a Design Context

David C. Brown and Ilan Berker

Computer Science Department, WPI, Worcester USA

This chapter discusses the use of fine-grained agents to investigate conflicts during multi-agent design. Our goal is to study in detail the interactions, conflicts and conflict resolution that is possible with such a multi-agent system. The approach is to use Single Function Agents (SiFAs), each of which can perform a very specialized task, from a single point of view. These different points of view usually cause conflicts among agents, and these conflicts need to be resolved in order for the design process to be successful. This chapter presents a model of conflicts and negotiations in the SiFA framework, including a hierarchy of possible conflicts.

1. Agents in a Design Context

The goal of our work[1] has been to make conflicts explicit during design activity. By having design knowledge represented by many fine-grained agents we are able to realize this goal.

The goal was originally conceived by the realization that many conflicts in the multi-agent design systems and design support systems that we were building were internal to an agent. In addition, many of the conflicts were being "compiled out" at system-building time (Dunskus et al. 1995).

By "breaking open" these systems into fine-grained agents the conflicts became visible, and thus available for study (Berker and Brown 1996). Hence, internal conflicts, with their hidden resolution, become visible conflicts with visible resolution – intra-agent conflicts become inter-agent.

In addition, by deliberately avoiding encoding only "normal" solutions we paved the way for more unusual designs. Also, as success and failure are the standard stimuli for learning, conflicts and lack of conflict – now revealed more clearly – can be used to investigate learning in multi-agent systems that do design (Grecu and Brown 1998) (Grecu and Brown 1999).

Another important realization was that when building design systems we had been providing each agent with a specialized task, and a particular target (e.g., some portion of the design to complete, or check). While making the agents finer grained, it was clear that we were also giving agents a "point-of-view".

---

[1] This chapter is based on text that appeared in (Brown 1996) and (Berker and Brown 1996).

Consequently, our agents are Single Function Agents (SiFAs). A SiFA is an agent that performs a single function on a single target from a single point of view (Dunskus et al. 1995).

The function performed by a SiFA determines its type. At present only a limited number of functions have been used for design problems. We conjecture that a set of agents with these functions is sufficient for most design problem solving activities. The key agent types with which we have worked are Selector, Estimator, Evaluator, Critic, and Praiser.

The target of a SiFA is a single aspect the design, such as a parameter. The point of view of an agent is some aspect of the design that the agent considers while doing its work. Usually, the point of view of the agent is a goal that the agent is trying to satisfy or optimize. Examples of points of view for design agents are cost, strength, and style.

Taking the multi-agent paradigm to such an extreme results in Single Function Agents (SiFAs), where each agent performs a single function in the design process and therefore contains knowledge that is very specialized. As with a human team, each SiFA will have different goals and different knowledge. As each SiFA does far less than a normal team member, many more agents are required. Current SiFA research focuses on parametric design.

1.1 Agent Size

Our goal is to study *in detail* the interactions, conflicts and conflict resolutions that are *possible* with such a multi-agent system. This work is not meant to literally simulate a real team, but rather to try to discover what is at the *core* of a team's decision-making. We are concerned with the "primitives" of knowledge and reasoning for design, redesign, and conflict resolution.

Other work on multi-agent systems that do design has tended to use large agents with powerful capabilities and large quantities of knowledge (e.g., see (Lander and Lesser 1991)). With so much power and knowledge it is hard to discover what is *essential* in the system. Although research with large agents is very valuable, it has other goals.

In our approach we have stripped down each agent to an extremely simple form, in order to more closely study the behavior of the team, the functionality required, the interactions that are possible and necessary, the amount and types of knowledge needed, and the conflicts that occur. In this way we can build a better understanding of design agent conflict management.

SIFAs are not the same as the large-grained agents in systems that try to incorporate legacy systems, such as constraint solvers, or data-base retrieval engines (Kuokka and Harada 1995), as although those also have restricted functionality they are usually very general, and may not be knowledge-based.

1.2 Conflicts and Negotiation

The use of agents brings with it the possibility of conflicts. Although it may be possible to build a system where all conflicts are resolved during development time, in most design problems this is either impossible or extremely difficult.

There are many advantages of run time conflict resolution. Such interaction supports concurrent engineering. Conflicts and their resolution cause the behavior of the system to emerge from the requirements of the particular problem at hand. The system is more flexible and does not suffer from the brittleness problem of traditional expert systems.

One way of resolving run time conflicts is for the agents to negotiate. This is the most general and flexible way of resolving conflicts. With SiFAs, many more conflicts become visible, due to the small size of each agent – conflicts can't appear and be resolved within an agent. This is very important if we wish to understand the essence of conflict management.

Conflicts in SiFA systems are indicated:

- by pairs of Selectors, Estimators or Evaluators producing apparently different responses (i.e., values, estimates, or evaluations) for the same parameter;
- by a Critic objecting to a Selector's value;
- by opposing opinions (i.e., Praise and Criticism); or
- by an agent discovering that a previously decided value that it wants to use to perform its function is incompatible with its knowledge.

Conflicts occur in SiFA systems for a variety of reasons:

- Conflicts from agents having different points-of-view;
- Conflicts from agents having different knowledge;
- Conflicts from agents not providing the right information (e.g., less accurate than required).

At present, SiFAs do not contain plans, and consequently conflicts between plans cannot occur. However, acting with a point-of-view (e.g., the goal of keeping cost low) could be seen as an intention, and thus point-of view conflicts could be seen as weak clashes between intentions.

A Conflict can be thought of as a process. It has actors, location and a duration. The location is, loosely, the object of the conflict (i.e., values, evaluations, etc.). This is important for characterizing conflicts. A conflict can be thought of as existing until the conflict resolution process is complete.

1.3 What is the Function/Role of Conflicts?

The main role of conflicts in a SiFA system is to detect and drive the exploration of the search space – in particular, examination of the possible boundaries of the acceptable design space. We refer to "possible boundaries" as, due to conflict resolution via negotiation, the boundaries may well be flexible. These conflicts usually correspond to (hard or soft) constraint violations. Conflicts can also indicate the incompleteness or incorrectness of an agent's knowledge.

In addition, although this has not been explicitly implemented in SIFAs – although it was in DSPL (Brown and Chandrasekaran 1989) – a conflict may indicate a mismatch between the current situation and the conditions under which an agent's knowledge should be used. In such a case the conflict is between the request for an agent to act and the inability of that agent to act.

Another important role of conflicts, as indicated above, is as a trigger for learning (Grecu and Brown 1998). As conflicts and their resolution involve resources (e.g., time), agents may wish to avoid them. This might be accomplished by inductive learning about the general and specific situations in which conflicts occur (Grecu and Brown 1996), and by learning why they occur, using exchanged design rationale (Lee 1997).

1.4 How Are Conflicts Possible?

Conflicts are possible in SiFAs because there is no assumption that the design knowledge comes from a single, consistent source. There might be a different source of knowledge for each agent. Hence, even for a single parameter, there might be agents that have completely different methods for producing a value, and different underlying (deep) knowledge or assumed models (e.g., for the role that parameter plays in the function, structure or behavior of the artifact). In addition, the experience that formed (compiled) the knowledge of each source may be quite different.

The point-of-view of an agent might be concerned with any phase of the life-cycle: for example, design, manufacturing, assembly, packaging, distribution, use, servicing, or recycling.

Point-of-view derived goal-goal conflicts can easily occur during the design process. For example, concern with strength may imply using more material, which increases cost. Thus, agent's goals are linked by dependencies. Lack of knowledge of these dependencies, due to the lack of a global model, is an underlying cause of conflict.

Conflicts can be implicit or explicit. There can be many possible, implicit conflicts. As agents attempt to complete a design to everyone's satisfaction, each agent can be thought of as searching through their space of allowable responses. The path is shaped by preferences or constraints. Preferences distort the surface of the space, making some areas more appealing. The path produced is also shaped by conflicts. Conflicts with other agents cause unexpected changes in direction. These changes, due to the interaction that results from attempting to resolve conflict, may then lead to other conflicts with other agents. Thus explicit conflicts emerge.

1.5 How Can Conflicts Be Modeled?

We are studying and categorizing conflict types in terms of SiFA types. We have investigated types of conflicts and their possible resolution by considering all possible pairs of SiFA types. By building a matrix with SiFA types as both the row and column we can systematically attempt to fill in the elements of the matrix to explain how such a conflict might occur (Dunskus et al. 1995).

These conflicts can also be arranged in a domain-independent taxonomy. This is discussed below. The fine-grained nature of a SiFA means that cause of the conflict is closely related to the types of agent involved.

2. Selected Previous Work

2.1 Agents and Multi-Agent Systems

In recent years there has been increased interest in agent based systems. The concept of an agent has become important both in Artificial Intelligence (AI) and in other fields of Computer Science (Wooldridge and Jennings 1994). Agents also have a direct influence on Distributed Artificial Intelligence (DAI) research because of their potentially concurrent nature (Bond and Gasser 1988). Many difficult tasks, including design, have parallel decompositions that result in easier subtasks than serial decompositions. Parallel decompositions allow opportunistic collaboration among the subtasks.

2.2 Conflict Resolution

Klein (1991) suggests a model of conflict resolution having a hierarchy of conflicts with the most abstract conflicts at the top and most concrete conflicts at the leaves. There is a corresponding hierarchy of resolution strategies, resulting in domain dependent and domain independent conflicts and their associated resolution strategies. The nodes higher in the hierarchy represent the domain independent conflicts while the lower nodes become more domain dependent.

Klein's agents all have their own design knowledge and conflict resolution knowledge (Klein and Lu 1990) (Klein and Lu 1991). The agents have differing design expertise, but their conflict resolution knowledge is identical.

Other related, recent work on Conflict Management can be found in an AI EDAM special issue (Smith 1995).

2.3 Negotiation

Negotiation is a common approach to conflict resolution in the design domain. Sycara defines negotiation to be the process by which resolution of inconsistencies is achieved in order to arrive at a coherent set of design decisions

(Sycara 1988) (Sycara 1990). The negotiation process proceeds with generation of a proposal, generation of a counter proposal based on feedback from dissenting agents, and then communication of justifications and supporting evidence (Sycara 1990).

Lander and Lesser (Lander and Lesser 1991) use the negotiated search paradigm for conflict resolution among heterogeneous and reusable expert agents in their TEAM framework. This paradigm allows agents to be both logically and implementationally heterogeneous.

Werkman's Designer Fabricator Interpreter (DFI) is a system where agents with different points of view cooperatively evaluate different suggestions for a design parameter (Werkman and Barone 1992). Unlike SiFA systems, DFI uses an arbitrator as a means of central control through which agents communicate.

Polat, Shekar and Guvenir (1993) describe a problem-solving environment that supports multi-agent conflict detection and resolution. They include a flowchart that describes the general conflict resolution process between agents. This has many similarities with our approach.

2.4 Single Function Agents

Although there has been a lot of work done on multi-agent systems, Single Function Agents (SiFAs) are a relatively new way of building multi-agent systems. The first SiFA system, I3D (Victor et al. 1993), integrated part design and manufacturing plan production for Powder Processing applications. The agents were carefully sequenced, and all possible conflicts that might occur were anticipated in advance and removed during development of the system.

I3D+ (Victor and Brown 1994) had agenda-based scheduling of the agents and allowed conflicts about the values of parameters to occur among agents. The conflicts were classified into six types depending on the relation between agents' local goals and the global goal.

SNEAKERS (Douglas, Brown and Zenger 1993) was built to train users in Concurrent Engineering. The user interacted with agents that had different functions and points of view.

Based on these systems, SINE was developed as a platform to build multi-agent design systems using SiFAs (Brown, Dunskus and Grecu 1994). It was possible to simulate the negotiation behavior of I3D+ using SINE.

3. The Single Function Agent Paradigm

3.1 What is a SiFA?

A SiFA is an agent that performs a single *function* on a single *target* from a single *point of view* (Dunskus et al. 1995).

The function performed by a SiFA determines its type. At present only a limited number of functions have been used for design problems. We conjecture that a set of agents with these functions is sufficient for most design problem solving activities, although we admit that this is far from clear for more conceptual design activities.

These agents types are:

Selector: Selects a value for a parameter by picking a value from a list of possible values. These are usually suitable for discrete valued parameters.

Advisor: Produces a value for a parameter by some means other than picking a value from a list. Advisors are more suitable for real valued parameters. Advisors and selectors are the agents where most of the design knowledge is stored.

Estimator: Produces estimates of values for a parameter. Unlike selectors, estimators can work with insufficient information, so the values they produce are just estimates of what the final value should be.

Evaluator: Evaluates the value of a parameter, producing a value of goodness for that value, usually represented as a percentage.

Critic: Criticizes values of parameters by pointing out constraints or quality requirements that are not met by the current values.

Praiser: Praises values of parameters by pointing out why the values are desirable.

Suggestor: Suggests what to do to remove an existing conflict or to avoid a conflict altogether.

The target of a SiFA is a single parameter of the design. For example, for wine glass design, the targets include cup radius, and stem length.

The point of view of an agent is some aspect of the design that the agent considers while doing its work. Usually, the point of view of the agent is a goal that the agent is trying to satisfy or optimize. Examples of points of view for agents in wine glass design are cost (as in all design, the cost should be minimized), style (the glass should look nice), stability (the cup should not fall over because of a very large cup and a small base), and volume (the cup should hold a reasonable amount of liquid).

In the SiFA paradigm, an agent is characterized by a single function, a single target, and a single point of view. In contrast to agents that perform general tasks, such as an equation solver, SiFAs are very specialized knowledge-based agents. A naming convention for individual SiFAs is to specify the target first, then the point of view and lastly, the function. So a selector whose target is the cup radius and is trying to maximize stability of the cup is a *cup radius stability selector*.

SiFAs implement the basis of Concurrent Engineering, i.e., early consideration of aspects of the product's life-cycle, by allowing agents, such as selectors and critics, to represent the points of view of these aspects at any decision making point in the design. Hence a decision about a length might be made from the points of view of packaging and of maintainance, and criticized from the point of view of cost.

3.2 SiFA Communication & Control

SiFAs communicate by sending each other messages. Each agent can communicate directly with any other agent. The communication language used is based on KQML (Knowledge Query and Manipulation Language) (Finin et al. 1993). Even though agents exchange messages directly, the current state of the design is stored centrally and is accessible to all agents in the system.

The SIFA research makes very little commitment to the system architecture to be used, as this is not currently the primary focus of the work. However, for current implementations an agenda mechanism is used to schedule agents. Agents are polled by the agenda and each agent indicates what it wants to do. Based on the replies, the agenda orders the agents according to the importance of the tasks they will carry out; e.g., conflict detection and resolution is more important than doing design. Then the agenda gives control to that agent. When the agent's work is finished, the cycle is repeated.

4. Extensions to the SiFA Paradigm

4.1 The Parameter Block

In previous work with SiFAs, the critiques, praises, or evaluations they produced were not stored separately. This prevented some potential, realistic actions of agents. This work extends the SiFA model to represent all value, estimate, criticism, praise, and evaluation *entities* separately, as *first class objects*. Being a first class object means that critiques, praises, and evaluations have the same status as the value of a design parameter. They are all directly accessible and they can all be the target of an agent. This is done by having value, estimate, criticism, praise, and evaluation entities organized in a structure called the *parameter block*, shown in figure 4.1. There is a block for each parameter. These blocks are stored centrally.

The root of the parameter block is the name of a parameter. The first *level of reference* has two entities. These are the parameter's value and estimated value. In the current model there can be only one value and one estimate at any time.

The second level of reference has evaluations, criticisms, and praises of the value and the estimate. These entities are said to reference the value or the estimate. There can be multiple criticisms, praises, and evaluations of the same value or estimate.

The third level of reference has evaluations, criticisms, and praises of second level evaluations, criticisms, and praises. These entities refer to the

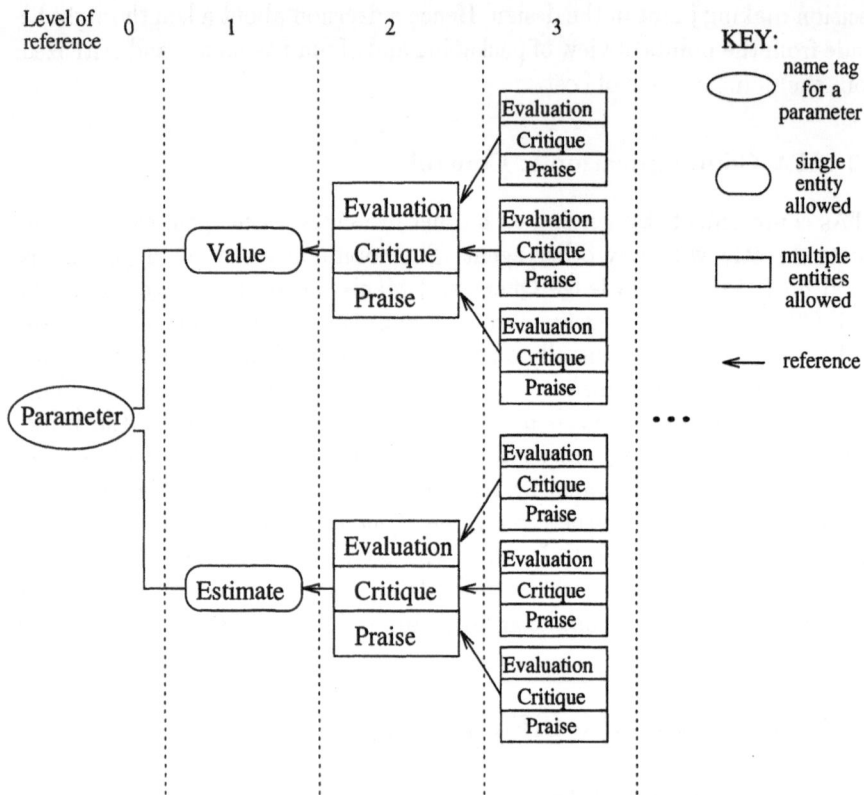

Fig. 4.1. The parameter block

second level entities which refer to the first level entities. These *chains of reference* uniquely determine what each entity refers to. So at the third level, there exist entities such as the evaluation of the criticism of the value of the parameter. The third level entities typically contain meta-level information about the design. Once again, there can be multiple evaluations, criticisms, and praises of the same second level entity.

It is also possible to imagine this structure growing into fourth, or even fifth level references. Although what the contents of such entities might be is not immediately obvious, the model allows such information to be represented if it is meaningful in any design problem.

It is clear that any complete model of the formation, detection and resolution of conflicts between agents with different points of view needs to be able to represent and reason about the information in at least the first three levels of the parameter block.

4.2 Targets of Agents

When all entities are represented as first class objects, they can all be the target of an agent. This means that the target of a critic is no longer just the name of a parameter, but more specifically, it is a criticism entity, such as the criticism of the evaluation of the estimate. Each agent can act on, or modify, the contents of its target. So a critic can store a criticism in the critique entity that is its target (Figure 4.2), and an evaluator can store an evaluation in the evaluation entity that is its target (not shown).

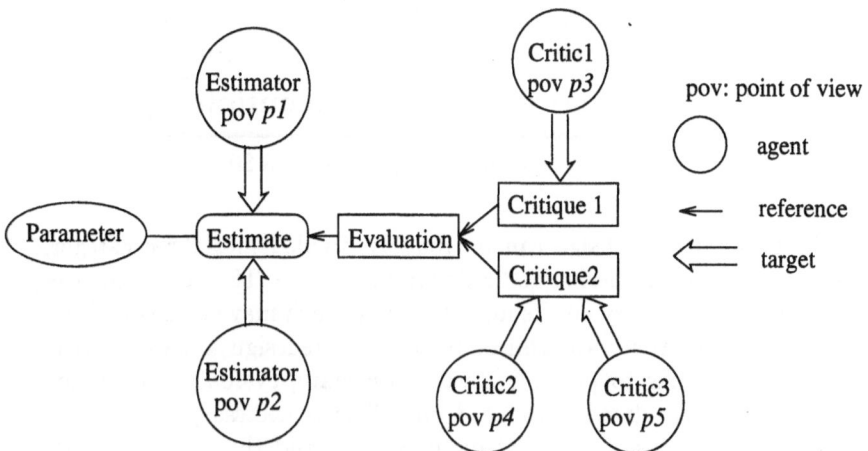

Fig. 4.2. Estimate evaluation critics

There can be more than one criticism of the evaluation entity, from different points of view. In that case there would be one agent for each of these criticisms, shown as Critic1 and Critic2 in figure 4.2. These critic agents would have different points of view and different targets, as they are acting on two different entities. It is also possible for two critics to have different points of view but the same target as is the case with Critic2 and Critic3, if it is not necessary to store both criticisms produced.

Only one value and one estimate are possible at any time in a parameter block, unlike evaluations, criticisms, and praises. There may be more than one selector or estimator agent, with different points of view, that have the same estimate or value as their target. This is also shown in figure 4.2. Note that this may lead to a conflict.

4.3 Knowledge in a SiFA

The knowledge that has to be present in a SiFA is determined by the tasks the agent has to carry out (shown in figure 4.3). Each agent has to have knowledge about how to perform these tasks.

Single Function Agent
Design
Redesign
Conflict Indication
Conflict Detection
Conflict Classification
Negotiation Strategy Selection
Negotiation Strategy Refinement
Negotiation Strategy Execution

Fig. 4.3. The knowledge contained in a SiFA

The types of knowledge can be roughly divided into three categories. The first one contains design and redesign knowledge. The design knowledge allows the agent to carry out its main function which may be one of selection, estimation, evaluation, criticism or praise. The redesign knowledge is used when the agent has to produce a value, estimate, evaluation, criticism or praise after it has already produced one. This is necessary when the first entity produced causes a conflict in the system and the agent is asked for another during negotiation.

The second category contains conflict indication, detection, and classification knowledge that is used to carry out the respective tasks of conflict handling. These typically involve checking if some constraints which are internal to the agent are violated or not. The knowledge in this category also includes the knowledge of the types of conflicts in which the particular agent can be involved.

The third category consists of negotiation strategy selection, refinement, and execution knowledge. This category of knowledge enables the agent to negotiate with other agents in conflict situations.

5. Hierarchy of Conflicts

The conflict hierarchy for SiFAs is shown in figure 5.1. The nodes represent conflict types. Each node is a specialization of its parent node and therefore inherits all of its properties. The root node, labeled *conflict*, encompasses all conflict types. Since advisors and selectors are involved in similar conflicts, we use the term *selector* to refer to both types in this hierarchy.

It would be possible to change the order of the criteria used at each level to specialize the conflicts. However, the hierarchy presented here does the best

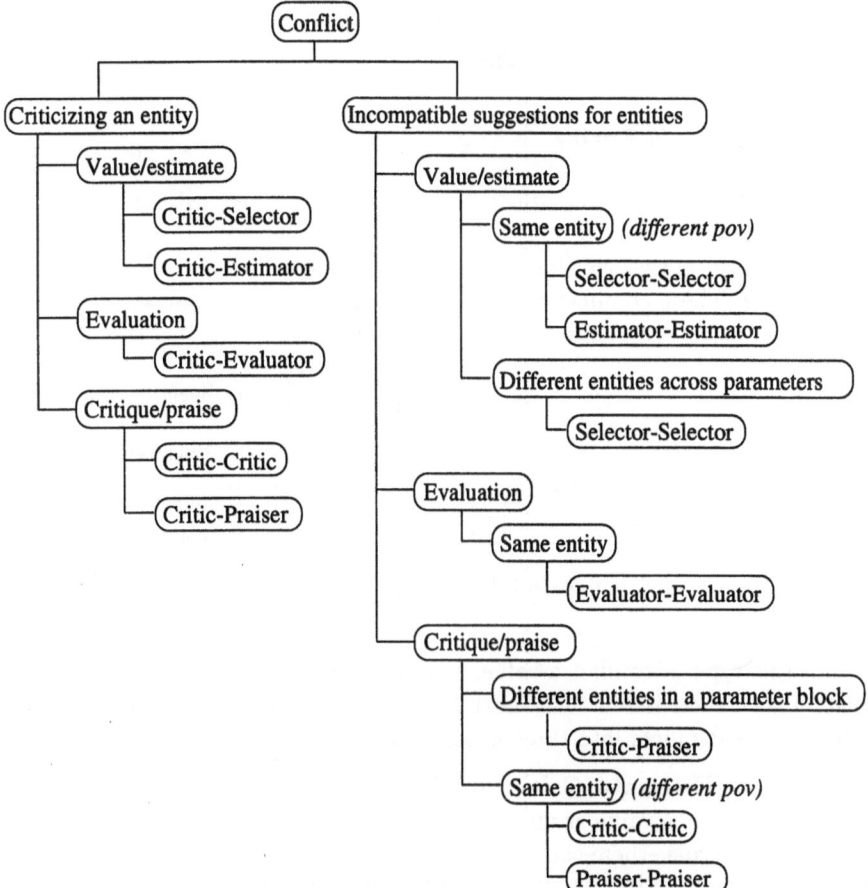

Fig. 5.1. The SiFA conflict hierarchy

job of grouping common aspects of conflicts into a single, more general node. The hierarchy is structured mainly by the way the conflicts manifest themselves, since in the SiFA paradigm this also provides information about the underlying cause of the conflict. The following sections describe the hierarchy of conflicts in detail.

Although this hierarchy is very fine grained, it is highly domain independent. It applies equally to all design problems that can be solved by SiFAs. This property allows us to investigate what type of knowledge is needed for each type of conflict, to form a more precise picture than already exists for multi-agent systems in a Concurrent Engineering setting.

The conflict taxonomy is structured by how the conflict occurs. An alternative is to structure conflict hierarchies by the fundamental underlying causes of the conflicts. We believe that SiFAs are fine-grained and specialized enough to be very close to the cause of each conflict. Interaction with the conflicting agent should refine the agents' knowledge of the cause. Precise classification of each conflict should provide indexing for retrieval of an appropriate remedy for that conflict.

5.1 Criticizing an Entity

This type of conflict occurs when a critic is not satisfied with the entity it is watching over. It produces a criticism and initiates a conflict. The entity being criticized is the one that is the critic's target. This situation is shown in figure 5.2. These conflicts are referred to as *criticism conflicts*.

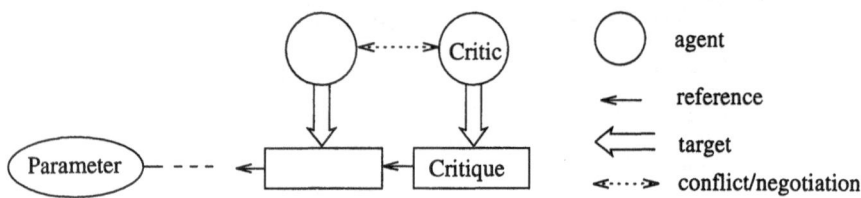

Fig. 5.2. Criticizing an entity

For this type of conflict a value, estimate, evaluation, criticism, or praise entity may be criticized. The next level of specialization of the hierarchy differentiates conflicts into three based on the type of entity being criticized.

5.1.1 Value/Estimate Criticism. In this group of conflicts, the entity being criticized is a value or an estimate. There are similarities between these two entities because there can be at most one value or estimate of a parameter at any time. Currently, the criticism of a value or estimate may be one of *too high*, *too low*, *wrong units* or *too imprecise*.

This group can further be broken down into two subgroups where the criticized entity is a value, and where it is an estimate, resulting in conflicts between a critic and a selector, and between a critic and an estimator, respectively. Both types of conflict are initiated by the critic.

5.1.2 Evaluation Criticism. An evaluation may be criticized because it is *too imprecise*, *too high*, or *too low*. All conflicts of this type are between an evaluator and a critic. The conflict is initiated by the critic.

5.1.3 Critique/Praise Criticism. Just as for any other entity, it is possible to have criticisms of either criticism or praise. Such a criticism may be one of *too negative*, *too positive*, *too imprecise*, or *not substantiated*. SiFAs are probably unique in their ability to express and act on this sort of meta-level knowledge. Such conflict-based interactions provide information that may enable learning to take place in the Concurrent Engineering team.

This conflict type may be divided into two groups, criticizing a critique, and criticizing a praise, resulting in conflicts between two critics, and between a critic and a praiser respectively.

5.2 Incompatible Suggestions

If there are two or more agents with the same target, or if there is a relationship between the targets of two agents, then there is a possibility for conflict among these agents. If the results of these agents are not compatible in some way, there is conflict. These conflicts are also referred to as *incompatibility conflicts*.

Similar to the left hand side of the hierarchy, the next level of specialization is based on the entity that is the subject of the conflict. Here, the subject of the conflict is not what the criticism refers to, but it is the target of the agents suggesting incompatible values, estimates, evaluations, etc. Analogous to the right side of the hierarchy, the conflicts are divided into three groups.

5.2.1 Value/Estimate Incompatibility. Incompatible suggestions for values and estimates can occur in two ways. The first is when there are two agents with the same target and the suggested values, or estimates, are incompatible. This will cause a conflict because only one value (or estimate) may be stored in the target entity. This situation is shown in figure 5.3. Both agents have to be the same type, selector or estimator. So the conflict is between two selectors or two evaluators. The points of view of the conflicting agents have to be different.

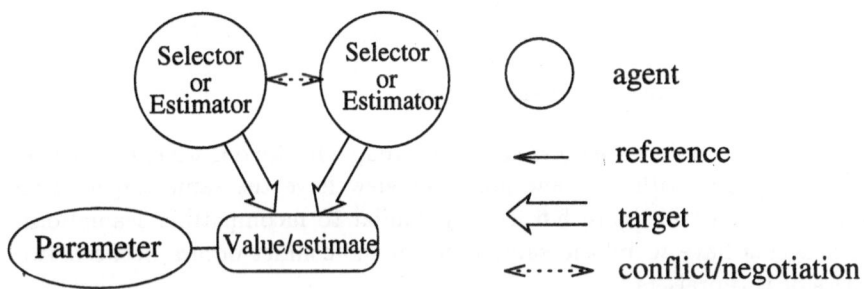

Fig. 5.3. Incompatible suggestions for the same value/estimate entity

The second kind of conflict can occur between two entities across parameters. This happens when the value of one parameter is not compatible with the value of the other parameter as shown in figure 5.4. The two value entities have to be in different parameter blocks since each parameter can have only one value entity. This type of conflict is possible only between two selectors. As a simple example, consider the case in the wine glass design where the a base radius selector generates a value for the base radius and then checks the internal constraint that the base radius has to be greater than the stem radius. If this constraint is violated, then the base radius selector will be in conflict with the stem radius selector.

5.2.2 Evaluation Incompatibility. Incompatible suggestions for an evaluation entity occurs when two evaluators with different points of view have

158   D. C. Brown and I. Berker

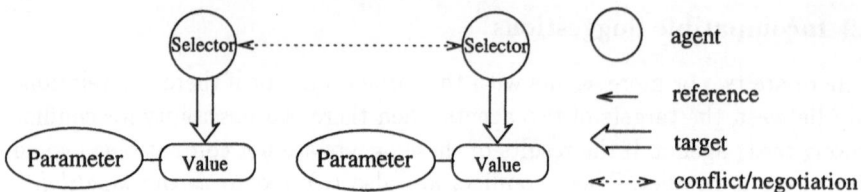

Fig. 5.4. Incompatible suggestions for different value entities

the same evaluation entity as their target, as shown in figure 5.5. This kind of conflict will occur only between two evaluators.

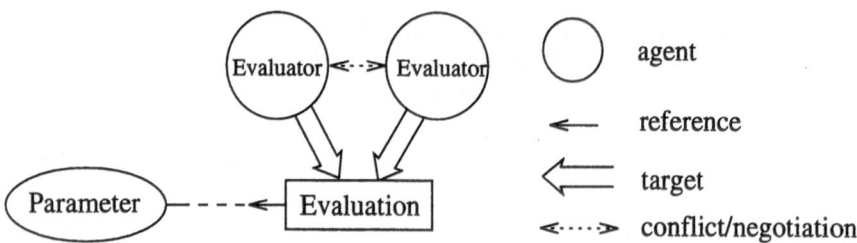

Fig. 5.5. Incompatible suggestions for an evaluation

5.3 Critique/Praise Incompatibility

Two kinds of conflicts are possible in this group. One kind is when two critics, or two praisers, with different points of view have the same target. This situation, shown in figure 5.6, is very similar to incompatible evaluations. Both agents have to be the same type, so the conflict occurs between two critics or two praisers.

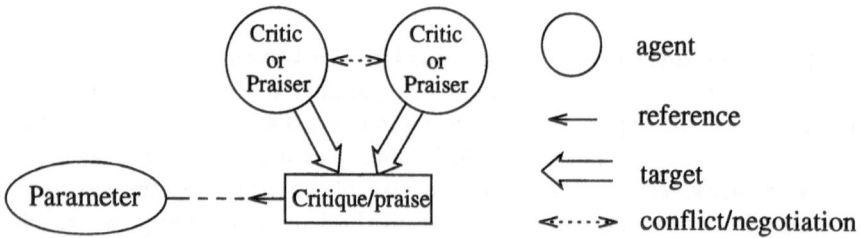

Fig. 5.6. Incompatible suggestions for the same critique/praise entity

The other kind happens when there is an incompatibility between a criticism and a praise of the same entity. In this situation, shown in figure 5.7, the targets of the agents in conflict are different but the targets refer to the same entity. In other words, the criticism and the praise of an entity are not compatible. This conflict occurs between a critic and a praiser and can be initiated by either of them. The agents in conflict have to have targets in the same parameter block at the same level of reference, since the incompatible critic and praise refer to the same entity. This conflict is not meaningful across parameters.

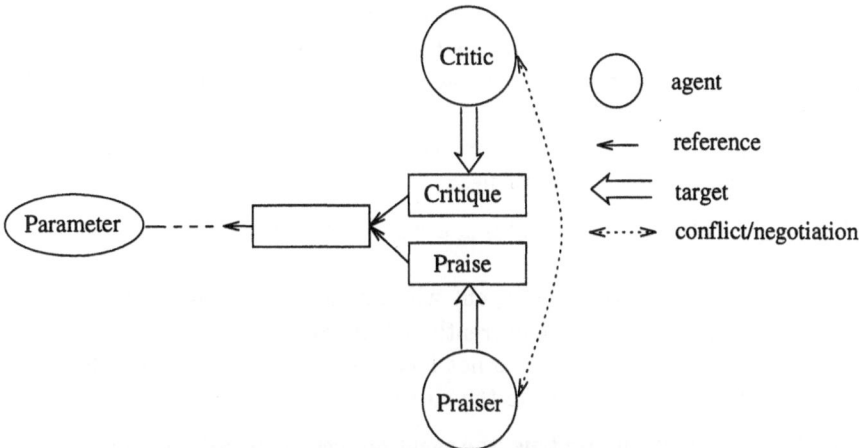

Fig. 5.7. Incompatible suggestions for different critique/praise entities

6. SiFA Negotiations

The system has to go through several steps during a conflict. These are *Indication of a possible conflict, Detection of the conflict, Selection of a negotiation strategy to use, and Refinement of that strategy.* The actual negotiation is simply the execution of the selected strategy. All of these steps put together is called the *negotiation process.* The result of the process is either a solution to the conflict or the signaling of a failure.

After conflict indication, detection, strategy selection and refinement, the agents are finally ready to negotiate. The negotiation consists of the initiator's and the partner's execution of their respective strategies. Examples of some simple strategies, and their potential for supporting learning, are described in (Grecu and Brown 1996).

6.1 The Conflict Indication Step

Agents need to be able to notice situations where there is the possibility of a conflict. This act of realizing a potential conflict is called *conflict indication.* Conflict indication is a very simple task for the agents in the SiFA paradigm.

Each time an agent acts on its target by modifying it, the state of the overall system changes, therefore there is potential for a conflict. How a possible conflict is indicated depends on the general conflict categories to which it belongs.

6.1.1 Indication of a Criticism Conflict. Conflicts which are caused by the criticism of an entity, the ones on the left hand side of the conflict hierarchy, are noticed by the critic producing the criticism. Each time a critic produces a criticism, there is a conflict indication.

6.1.2 Indication of an Incompatibility Conflict. Whenever an agent acts on its target by producing a value, estimate, evaluation, praise, or criticism, it checks to see if there is the possibility of a conflict.

For an agent to indicate a incompatibility conflict, all of the three conditions given below have to be satisfied:

- The target entity already contains a value, estimate, evaluation, critique, or praise;
- The owner of the entity (the agent who put in the current contents) is a different agent from the one currently acting; and
- The old content of the entity is not identical to the new content that the agent is attempting to store in the entity.

If all these conditions are true, the agent notices the possibility of a conflict and "indicates" it. The indication of a conflict does not mean that there is necessarily going to be a conflict. This is the work of the conflict detection knowledge.

6.2 The Conflict Detection Step

The agent that indicates a conflict is responsible for determining whether there actually is a conflict. Suppose there is a 0.01% difference in the values proposed by two different selectors for the value entity of a parameter. Unless that value is extremely sensitive, this small difference does not constitute a conflict. Thus indication of a conflict does not necessarily mean that there is actually a conflict.

Conflict detection, for human or SiFA, is a *knowledge-based* task and it is not always trivial. How detection works in the SiFA paradigm depends on whether the conflict is a criticism conflict or an incompatibility conflict.

6.2.1 Detection of a Criticism Conflict. As soon as a critic produces a criticism it has to decide if that actually signals a conflict or not. This is usually an easy task since the critic knows the reason why it produced that particular criticism. If the criticism was due to the violation of a hard constraint that tests some physical properties or user requirements, then there is probably a conflict. On the other hand, if the criticism just reflects a preference, then there is no conflict. The criticism stays on the blackboard and the agents whose targets were criticized may take it into consideration if they wish.

6.2.2 Detection of an Incompatibility Conflict. Detecting an incompatibility conflict requires more knowledge and is usually a more complicated task than detecting criticism conflicts. There are three possible cases.

Same Entity Conflicts: Once the agent notices that what is already stored in its target entity is not identical to what it wants to store, and indicates a conflict, it has to decide if the two are compatible. If they are, then there is no conflict, even though the two may not be identical.

For example, suppose a design parameter can take on continuous numeric values, and its current value has been set to 5.00 by selector A. If later, selector B calculates a value for the same parameter from a different point of view and comes up with 5.01, it indicates a possible conflict, but has to do more work in order to decide if there is indeed a conflict. If selector B allows up to 1% difference in the value of the parameter, then there is no conflict. Selector B can leave the value as 5.00. Similar situations can occur with other agent types and entities.

Different Entities Within a Parameter Block: Detecting this kind of conflict is the same as detecting conflicts involving one entity as far as the knowledge-based reasoning is concerned. The difference is that the agent is not comparing something that is already in its target with what it wants to store, but is comparing it to some other entity in the parameter block. Critics and praisers are the only kind of agents that can get into such conflicts because of incompatible criticisms and praises of the same entity.

Different Entities Across Parameter Blocks: This case is very similar to detection of conflict involving entities within a parameter block. The only difference is that only selectors can have such conflicts. This means that selectors need to know what values are related to the value they are producing and check for the constraints between these values.

6.3 The Conflict Classification Step

After an agent detects a conflict, it has to decide what kind of conflict it is. This is a very simple task in the SiFA paradigm, as each agent can be involved in a very limited set of conflicts. Also, the detection process already gives the agent enough information to immediately classify the conflict as one of the leaf nodes of the conflict hierarchy.

If a critic detects a conflict after producing a criticism because some hard constraint is violated, then it knows that it is involved in a criticism conflict. It also knows if the conflict is about a value, estimate, evaluation, criticism or praise. The type of the agent with which it is in conflict follows immediately from the entity type – e.g., a value entity means that the other agent is a selector. Finally, it can easily figure out which particular agent it is in conflict with by inspecting the *owner* field of the entity that is the subject of the conflict. Similar reasoning allows the agents to deal with incompatibility conflicts as well.

6.4 The Negotiation Strategy Selection Step

A *negotiation strategy* is a body of knowledge, usually representable by a set of rules, that allows the agent to carry out a negotiation. After a conflict has been detected and classified, the SiFA that detected the conflict has to start negotiating, as the *initiator*, with the conflicting agent, referred to as the *partner*. In order to do that, it has to select a negotiation strategy. The partner also has to select a strategy.

Since the conflicts a SiFA can be involved in are very specific, the number of strategies an agent can have for any conflict are also limited. As the number of possible agent-agent conflict types is also small, the total number of strategies it needs is small as well.

If an agent has a single negotiation strategy for the conflict it is in, then the strategy selection task is trivial. If the agent has more than one strategy for a particular conflict, then it needs a criteria to select its negotiation strategy. This criteria may be the point of view of its partner or the particular value, estimate, evaluation, criticism, or praise that is the the subject of the conflict. For example, it might choose its negotiation strategy by using a rule such as "if the difference is less than 10% use strategy 1 else use strategy 2".

6.5 The Negotiation Strategy Refinement Step

The negotiation strategy selected may still be a generalized strategy that has to be instantiated by giving values to some variables of the strategy. The main reason why an agent would have generalized strategies is to save space. The agent may need a few different strategies for a type of conflict, and if these strategies are very similar except for a few minor points, then it is better to have only one generalized strategy rather than storing all these similar strategies separately.

Another reason why a generalized strategy may be useful is if the agent does not have enough information to select a strategy before the negotiation starts. In this case, the agent can start negotiation using the generalized strategy and then instantiate it during the negotiation as more information becomes available.

7. Future Research

One direction for future research is to formalize the meaning and use of the parameter block's higher level entities, where meta-level knowledge about the design resides. It is not very clear what, or in what form, the information should be stored in the third level criticisms, praises, and evaluations in order to help the design process.

In addition, the current negotiation behavior of the agents is very primitive. The simplicity of the negotiation process among the agents is one of the promises of the SiFA paradigm. However, more work is needed to construct and test a library of negotiation strategies for each SiFA type.

Another direction is to provide SiFAs with history keeping capabilities. Even very simple history keeping would improve the system drastically. For example, if an agent keeps a record of its proposals that led to a conflict, it can avoid those in the future (Grecu and Brown 1996). Learning could improve the quality of the final design, reduce the time required to do the design, and provide better conflict anticipation, avoidance, and resolution.

As SiFAs are very fine-grained, an agent must be available for every possible decision that needs to be made. This suggests the possibility of cloning SiFAs on demand. This is possible due to the relatively small amount of knowledge that each contains, and because of the families of agents that the Function + Point-of-View + Target dimensions produce. We have done some small experiments with this idea, and it seems quite plausible to produce SiFAs by inheritance along the dimensions followed by specialization.

8. Conclusions

8.1 Main Contributions

The first contribution of this work has been to extend the SiFA paradigm with the concept of a parameter block. The parameter block enables knowledge about the design to be presented explicitly, and related. It also allows multiple levels of meta-knowledge to be represented, through levels of reference. This allows comments about the decisions and comments of other agents.

Another contribution is the analysis of conflicts in the SiFA framework. Since SiFAs provide the building blocks of a multi-agent design system, the conflicts between them represent the primitives of conflict situations in any design. The conflict hierarchy enables general methods for handling the various tasks involved in the negotiation process, i.e., a method for detecting incompatibility conflicts will work for a whole group of conflicts under the incompatibility conflicts branch of the hierarchy.

The SiFA-based model provides a very powerful tool with which to build and study design systems. The model allows a designer to build a system that will consider many different points of view while designing an artifact, without having to predict all possible conflicts between these points of view when building the system. The separation of conflict knowledge from the design knowledge in the agents also has very important consequences in terms of the maintainability and the understandability of a system.

SiFAs reflect a Concurrent Engineering approach by allowing agents to represent the point of view of any life-cycle aspect at any decision making point in the design. The SiFA framework provides a new perspective to study conflict management in Concurrent Engineering.

8.2 Discussion

To date we have yet to build a large, real-world SiFA-based design system. This is because we are using this paradigm as the basis of small systems with which to experiment. However, it should be clear that SiFAs are more suited to parametric design that is routine or near-routine. Design that requires configuration has yet to be investigated.

The fine-grained, restricted nature of SiFAs allows Knowledge Acquisition to be done quite easily. However, although each agent is easy to acquire, this is somewhat offset by the fact that there tend to be a lot of them.

One distinct advantage of SiFAs is that once a SiFA establishes the type of agent with which it is in conflict, it can assume quite a lot about that agent, as there are only a few possible SiFAs in a particular design situation. This is helpful for our experiments with learning in multi-agent design systems, as, for example, it allows easy construction of a model of the other agent with only a small exchange of information.

The main disadvantage of the SiFA model from a practical perspective is that the fine-grained agent size is less efficient than using larger agents: every conflict produces inter-agent communication, producing high overhead in anything but the most routine situations. However, we anticipate that the understanding gained from SiFA research will show how functionality should be grouped, and learning added, to produce more efficient systems.

In conclusion, SiFAs continue to provide a useful and interesting vehicle for experimentation. The major gain in building SiFA-based design systems will be to discover more about the essence of conflict management and negotiation. It is doubtful whether this approach will be practical for large real-world design systems. However, they are very revealing to use, and force examination of assumptions. SiFAs have proved to be very helpful in gaining insight into many design related research issues and they have revealed new research paths that should be explored further.

CHAPTER 9

Conflict Management as Part of an Integrated Exception Handling Approach

Mark Klein

Center for Coordination Science ,MIT Sloan School of Management , Cambridge USA

Collaborative design conflicts are an important type of process "exception", i.e. a real-life contingency such as a process change, execution error or missed opportunity that leads to sub-optimal performance of a collaborative process. This chapter presents an integrated computational approach to collaborative process exception handling that avoids important weaknesses in current conflict management methods through the synergistic integration of conflict, workflow and rationale technology. The approach is based on an inclusive dependency language plus coordination services for dependency capture, process enactment and exception handling. An initial implementation of this model called "iDCSS" is presented and challenges for future evolution of this technology are identified.

1. Limitations of Current Conflict Management Technology

Collaborative design processes are typically distributed across multiple functional perspectives that address inter-related aspects of a single product design. The design of an airplane, for example, involves groups dedicated to many different structures (e.g. wings, doors, struts), systems (e.g. fuel, electrical, hydraulic), analysis disciplines (e.g. noise propagation, stress analysis) and manufacturing functions (e.g. major assembly planning, detailed part planning, tool design). The functions/groups working on these different perspectives are highly interdependent. When many perspectives are involved, maintaining consistency (i.e. avoiding and/or resolving conflicts) among these design activities becomes a significant challenge with major potential impacts on product cost, quality and timeliness. The manual conflict management currently approaches taken in large manufacturing concerns (i.e. interface conventions, multi-disciplinary design teams, coordination memos, mockups and design change boards) are being overwhelmed by the sheer scale of current collaborative design activities.

Conflict management technology is emerging to address these issues by providing computer-supported detection and resolution of design conflicts (Klein 1991a), (Lu 1991), (Smith 1991), (Bowen 1993), (Mark 1994), (Tiwari 1994), (Gross 1994) (Sussman 1980), (Fox 1984), (Descotte 1985), (Brown 1985), (Marcus 1987), (Goldstein-75), (Hewitt 1986), (Wilensky 1983),   (Lander 1988), (Robinson 1994), (Ramesh 1994), (Easterbrook 1994), (Bahler 1994), (Kannapan 1994). While much progress has been made, deployment of these technologies in commercial settings has been limited.

This limited deployment is largely due to several key weaknesses in current technology. Detecting, understanding and resolving conflicts typically requires a formal representation of the inter-dependencies between the design decisions involved in the conflicts. The dependency languages used in current conflict management systems lack expressiveness (e.g. do not capture the goals or history underlying design decisions) and are not integrated with design decision capture (i.e. CAD) tools. Another key challenge is the difficulty of scaling up the conflict detection process; untrammeled dependency propagation can quickly become computationally intractable and overwhelm designers with floods of information on the impact of multitudes of design changes made elsewhere. Finally, most conflict management systems provide a single algorithm, typically mathematical in nature, that typically is suitable for representing only a subset of the full range of collaborative design conflict resolution strategies.

2. The iDCSS Design Coordination System

The central claim of this chapter is that key limitations in current conflict management technology can be addressed if we view it as the *exception handling* component of an integrated set of collaborative design coordination services. We shall consider below what this set of integrated services is and how conflict management fits in.

Three kinds of coordination technology have evolved to address the different ways inter-dependent actions (that therefore require coordination) can be distributed. Cooperative work can be distributed across the three orthogonal axes of time, agents and perspectives:

- distribution across agents (both human and computational) requires support for orderly flow of tasks and information among them; this is addressed by process management (i.e. workflow, structured conversation, planning / scheduling / project management) technology.
- distribution across perspectives arises because the participants involved work on different interacting aspects of the design and/or have different goals; consistency among their design actions can be maintained with the support of conflict management technology.
- distribution across time arises because the content and rationale for design decisions made earlier often are needed later on, for example to support redesign; this is addressed by rationale capture technology.

This division was undoubtedly helpful to allow the component technologies to reach some level of maturity while dealing with a more limited set of requirements. It is, however, an artificial distinction and no longer necessary or even useful. Current coordination technologies are now encountering fundamental limitations that derive in large part from this schism (Klein 1995).

Limitations in current coordination technologies can best be addressed I believe by viewing them as synergistic components of a single integrated approach to coordination among inter-dependent actions however distributed. Collaborative work (of which collaborative design in an instance) consists of the interleaved *definition* of work processes and results (including their logical inter-dependencies), the *enactment* of work processes (during which time the human and computational agents perform the actual work) and the *redefinition* of these processes in response to *exceptions* (including design conflicts as well as changes in requirements or available resources, mistakes in performing or routing tasks,, unforeseen opportunities etc.). Services for dependency capture, process enactment and exception handling when taken together thus represent a comprehensive approach to coordination in collaborative design.

A preliminary implementation of this philosophy called iDCSS (the Integrated Design Collaboration Support System; pronounced „IDEX") has been developed. iDCSS is the latest result of five years of work including empirical studies of collaborative design (Klein 1990) as well as several previous systems including the DCSS conflict management system (Klein 1991a), the DRCS design rationale capture system (Klein, 1993) and the TCAPS workflow system (Faragher-Horwell 1992). We will consider iDCSS's architecture and functionality in the sections below, highlighting how this integrated approach provides a powerful framework for handling collaborative design conflicts.

2.1 The iDCSS Architecture

iDCSS is based on three core services, for dependency capture, process enactment and exception management, that generalize and integrate current coordination technologies. The dependency capture service records the dependencies among the process and product decisions made when defining and enacting work processes. The process enactment service routes work goals and output artifacts (e.g. documents) among participating agents according to these processes. The exception management system attempts to anticipate/detect and avoid/resolve coordination problems that occur during process definition and enactment as effectively as possible.

These services are deployed using the following *functional* architecture (Figure 2.1):

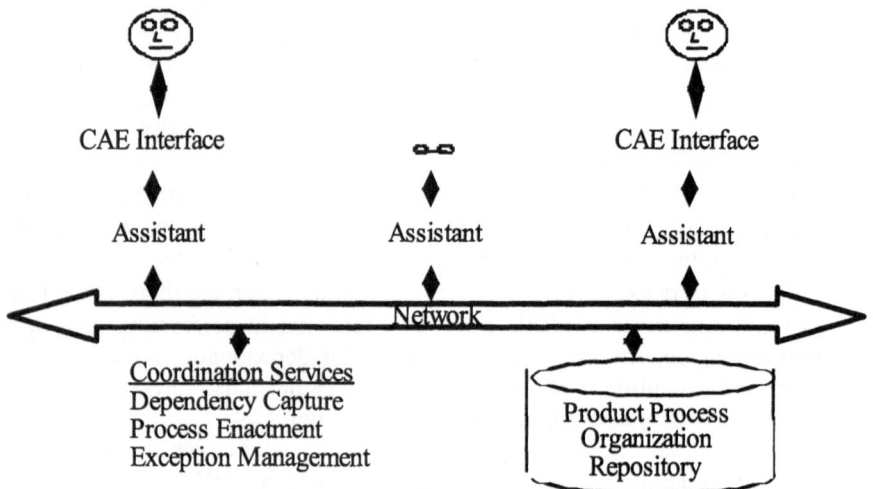

Fig 2.1. The iDCSS Functional Architecture.

The coordination services, as well as a repository for all product, process and organizational decisions plus their interdependencies, are accessible over a network. All agents (be they human participants or computational systems) access the shared services and repository using an "assistant" system. Message traffic is omni-directional; the coordination services can for example access the repository contents as well as address queries and notifications to the agent/assistant pairs.

Note that the *implementational* architecture can be highly distributed; the coordination services may for example be realized as collections of specialist agents and the repository may be distributed over multiple servers.

Note that iDCSS does not attempt to help make the process or product decisions taken by individual agents. This is the job of existing technologies such as requirements capture tools, CAD tools for product decisions as well as planning, scheduling and other tools for capturing process decisions. iDCSS focuses, rather, on helping to ensure that these different decision sets fit together into a well-coordinated whole in dynamic environments.

2.2 The Dependency Capture Service

The core of iDCSS is a service for capturing all process, product and organizational decisions and their inter-dependencies (Figure 2.2):

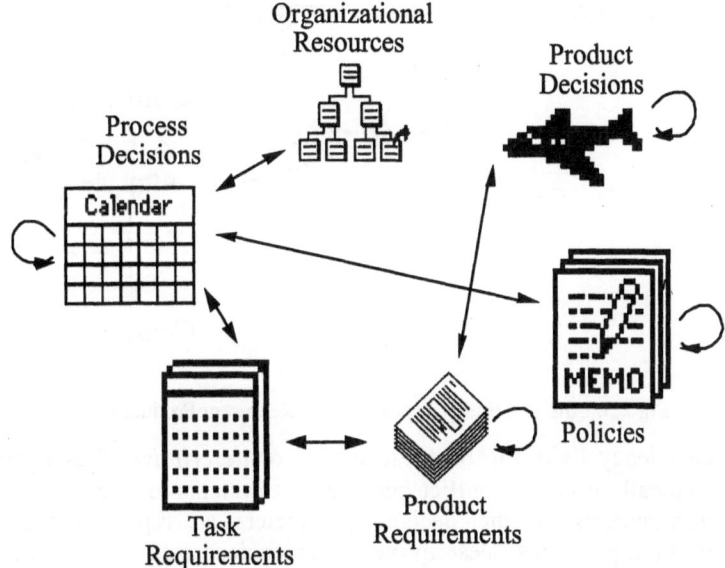

Fig 2.2. iDCSS Captures Design Decisions and Their Inter-Dependencies

The iDCSS language uses a vocabulary of assertions consisting of *entities* like modules, tasks, specifications and versions as well as *links* between these entities representing their inter-relationships. Product decisions are represented using a generic ontology of entities and links derived from substantial previous work in system engineering (Blanchard 1981) and AI models of design and planning (Tong 1987), (Klein 1991a), (Stefik 1981). This set of links and entities can be extended by creating new subclasses of the existing set.

The entity types used in iDCSS include modules with characteristic attributes and interfaces. Attribute values are represented using a constraint language (Stefik 1981). The links in this case describe decomposition and specialization relationships among components, linkages between module interfaces and so on. Figure 2.3 below shows the subset of the iDCSS language used to represent product design decisions:

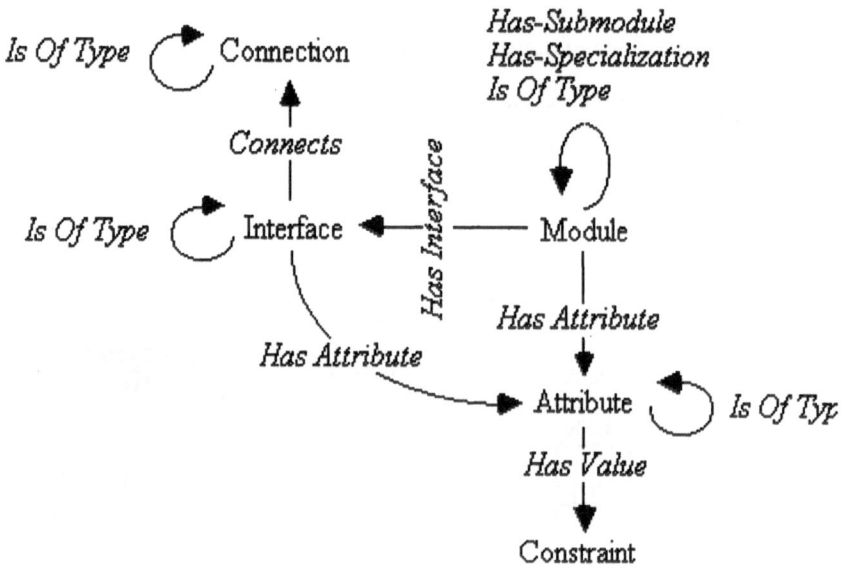

Fig 2.3. Link and Entity Types Used to Represent Product Decisions.

Dependency links can be *prescriptive* or *descriptive*. Prescriptive dependencies, typically used by conflict management systems to infer the consequences of decision changes on other decision parameters, are represented as mathematical constraint expressions. Descriptive dependencies, used to represent the rationale for decisions that have already been made, can refer to qualitative argumentation links such as "supports" or "denies" in addition to mathematical expressions. When a prescriptive constraint leads to the inference of some design parameter value, it becomes part of the rationale (descriptive dependency structure) for that decision.

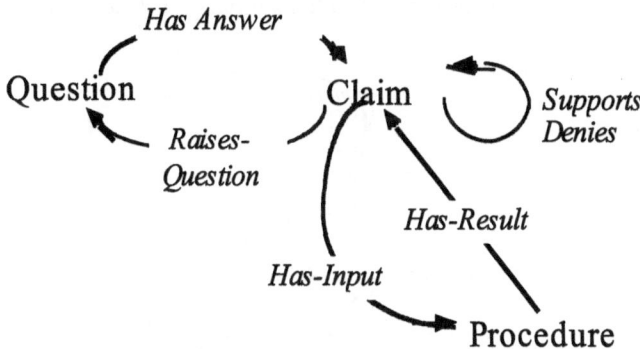

Fig 2.4. An Illustrative Subset of the iDCSS Dependency Language.

The following figure gives an example of how the iDCSS language can represent decisions and dependencies involved in the selection of the material for an airplane wing (Figure 2.5):

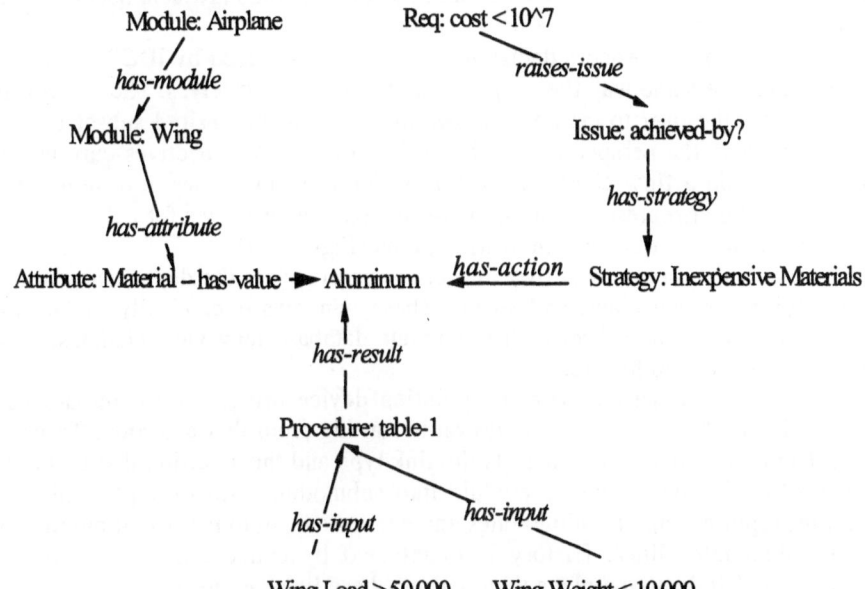

Fig 2.5. An Example Dependency Network for Wing Design.

This dependency network indicates that an airplane has a wing component, and that aluminum was selected as the wing material in order to meet strength and cost requirements.

Process decisions can be represented similarly (Figure 2.6):

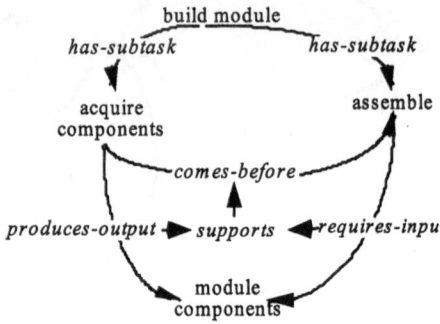

Fig 2.6. An Example Dependency Network for Process Decisions.

Here, the sequencing between two tasks in the plan to build a module is supported by the fact that one task produces as output some artifacts needed as input for the next task.

The product and process decision capture tools provided by iDCSS capture dependencies the same way they capture the decisions themselves. The iDCSS interface allows the user to create windows that present the desired subset of the repository using the perspective of choice (Figure 2.7). Perspectives currently supported include a flow chart representation for work processes, a design versions lattice, a tabular representation of the design parameter values for a design module and a graphical module decomposition graph (Figure 2.7).

One can also create windows that allow one to view the dependency structure underlying a given claim and so on. These windows dynamically update themselves whenever the subset of the rationale database they view changes, so they are continuously up to date.

Selecting an assertion with the pointing device brings up a context-sensitive menu listing the types of links allowable starting from that assertion. To create a link from there, one simply selects the link type and the assertion that is the target of the link. To decompose a module into submodules, for example, one creates entities representing the submodules and connects them to the parent module using "has-submodule" links. History is maintained by connecting all assertions via "has-action" links to the plans they realize (these links are generated automatically when a plan is marked as being currently active).

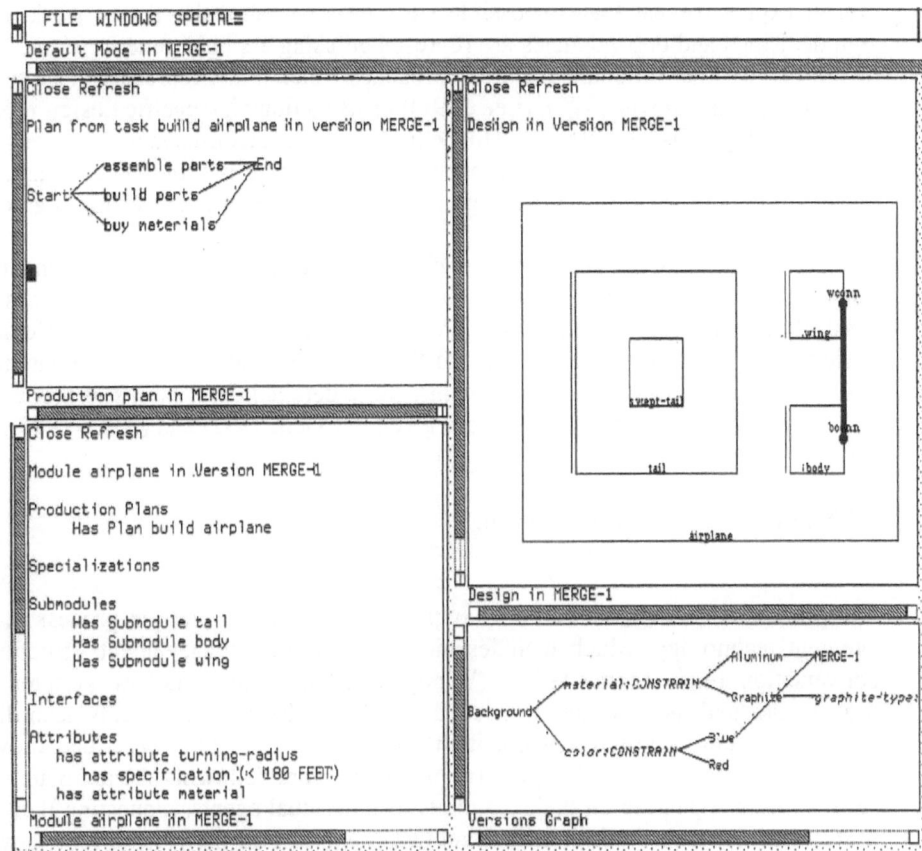

Fig 2.7. Example of the iDCSS Interface in Use.

This kind of direct manipulation graphical interface has proven simple and intuitive to use. iDCSS can, however, work with any decision capture (CAD, CAPP, etc.) systems one wishes as long as they can represent both decisions and their interdependencies in the iDCSS language. Modelling toolkits such as nDim (Subrahmanian 1993) could also be used to develop interfaces for capturing such information using the iDCSS language.

The dependency capture service included in iDCSS differs in several important ways from previous work on rationale capture. The iDCSS language combines into one coherent framework the argumentation and intent information of conventional rationale languages, the constraint expressions used in conflict management technology and the history captured by process management technology. This allows greater expressiveness than is possible with previous rationale capture work. Design decisions and dependencies are represented using a single generic formalism, in contrast to other rationale capture approaches which either represent these separately (e.g. (Yakemovic 1990), (Lee 1991)) or use a domain-specific design representation (e.g. (Fischer 1991)). This eliminates the inconsistency between the decision and rationale data that can occur when a user is required to manually make coordinated changes to two separate data sets whenever one changes a decision.

I believe the iDCSS language is sufficiently expressive to represent the full range of design decisions in a wide variety of domains; it has been applied successfully to the Local Area Network, Avionics, Architecture and Electric Vehicle design domains. Direct predecessors of this work developed by other researchers have been applied to many other domains. More detailed descriptions of this work and its relationship to other systems are given in (Klein 1992) and (Klein 1993).

2.3 The Process Enactment Service

The process enactment service is a simple generalization of current process management technology, which includes messaging, project management, structured conversation (e.g. (Smith 1980), (Winograd 1986)) and workflow systems. It routes tasks and the information needed to achieve them among agents according to a process template represented using the dependency language described above.

Enacting this template (i.e. performing design work following the template) results in tasks appearing on the ToDo lists of individual agents, requesting them to perform some work. Both domain-level tasks (e.g. to find the voltage for a power supply) and meta-level tasks (e.g. decide how to resolve a design conflict) can appear on this list (Figure 2.8.)

ToDo List for Bill C. Engineer

Define mfg process for part 123-23-123
Design pump for hydraulics system 4545-12
Design pump for hydraulics system 4545-12
Resolve design conflict #283
Resolve process error #856

Fig 2.8. A ToDo List for an Agent.

An agent works to perform a task using whatever tools are appropriate, and when finished notifies the process enactment service. The service then removes the task from the ToDo list for the current agent and routes the appropriate tasks to the next agent(s) as given by the current workflow process. As with any process management system, the iDCSS service allows one to track current goal status as well as record process history.

Note that the current process may be defined ahead of time, as it is enacted, or some combination of these two. This allows us to support all of the different kinds of process management technology. The next step in an "ad hoc" process, for example, is defined during the previous step's execution. In structured conversation approaches the next step is selected from a limited palette of options during the previous step. For workflows the process is typically defined in detail before enactment begins. Process templates can be modified as they are being enacted, a feature which, as we will see below, is critical.

The iDCSS process management service (described in more detail in (Faragher-Horwell 1992)) differs from standard process management tools mainly in how is integrated with the exception handling service. The key limitation of current technology is that the structure it enforces is related indirectly at best to the underlying realities that shape these processes (i.e. the task requirements, available resources and current policies for the particular problem and organization) (Klein 1995). Process management systems ensure that some pre-defined process model is adhered to and tracked properly. The problem is that any such model represents a „frozen" or „compiled" picture of what an appropriate process was for a set of constraints that applied at some time in the past. This model can become inefficient or even harmful should these change, i.e. should an *exception* occur and not be addressed properly ((Suchman 1983), (Grudin 1994), (Mi 1991), (Karbe 1990)). The iDCSS service for meeting this challenge is described next.

2.4 The Exception Management Service

The iDCSS exception management service anticipates/detects exceptions that occur during process enactment, and then suggests strategies for resolving them, making extensive use of the information collected by the dependency capture service.

Exceptions can occur in may ways (see Figure 2.9 for a partial taxonomy). They can be caused by changes (in the task requirements, organizational policies or resources) that contradict the assumptions underlying the currently enacting process template. They can result from errors made during process enactment, including completing tasks incorrectly or too late, routing tasks and/or information incorrectly, or making conflicting process or product decisions. Missed opportunities represent another kind of exception, since failing to capitalize on an unexpected opportunity represents suboptimal process performance as well.

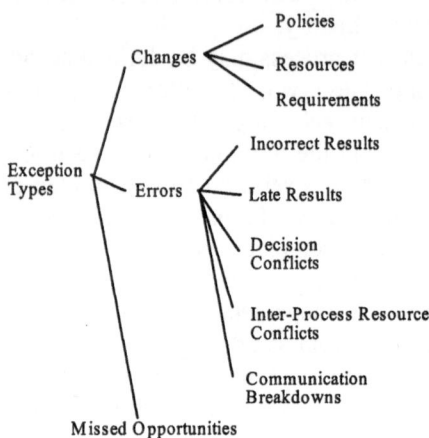

Fig 2.9. A Partial Taxonomy of Exception Types.

The complete set of possible exception types can be derived by performing a failure mode analysis on an abstract model of collaborative work processes; the results of such an analysis are too lengthy to present here and will be described in full in a forthcoming chapter. The subset of exception types known as design decision conflicts are detailed in (Klein 1991a).

Since the range of exception types is so diverse, exception detection requires a suite of technologies rather than a single approach. Exceptions resulting from changes can be handled via truth maintenance systems that use logical dependency information to determine when a change results in invalidating the currently enacting process. Decision conflicts can be detected using such systems as constraint propagation tools (e.g. (Lu 1991), (Smith 1991), (Bowen 1993)), geometric modelers or project management tools, depending on the domain. Missed opportunities can be detected using truth maintenance techniques in some cases (see for example (Petrie 1992)) or more generally by expert systems that encode critiquing rules. For any given domain, only a subset of these exception types may be relevant or important. Some kinds of errors can be detected by the agents themselves, e.g. a human agent may realize that he or she performed a task incorrectly after marking it as complete, and notify the system manually. iDCSS currently incorporates exception detection based on truth maintenance, constraint propagation and manually flagged techniques.

Let us consider some specific examples of common exception types. One can anticipate a possible exception when the number of hours available for the resource allocated to a task is less than the estimated number of resource hours needed to complete the task. An exception can also be detected when a process assumed that a rare and highly capable resource (e.g. a numerically control machine tool) was going to be available to perform a task but it has become unavailable (e.g. due to a breakdown). A third example is when two designers conflict over how a product should be designed; in the architecture domain for example one agent may specify a large south-facing window for a house to maximize the view, while another agent may critique that on the basis that this will produce excessive cooling costs due to increased summer insolation. We can see that if exceptions such as these are not addressed promptly and effectively there can be severe impacts on the efficiency of the overall collaborative work processes. One late task can cause an entire schedule to slide, or require high cost last-minute solutions.

When an exception is detected, the exception management service creates the task of resolving that exception, which appears on a ToDo list just like any other task. Agents may of course define their own process template for resolving the exception, but can also call on the exception management service to suggest one or more plans for doing so.

These plans are defined automatically by instantiating generic and thereby reusable exception handling strategies stored in a "coordination knowledge base". People appear to have a wide variety of rules of thumb that they invoke again and again in different situations when faced with coordination problems (Klein 1991b). iDCSS includes a knowledge base of several hundred of these generic strategies associated with the kinds of exceptions for which they are typically most useful. One example of such a strategy is:

IF: one must reduce the flow time for a task (e.g. to avoid it becoming late)
AND IF: the process for that task includes upcoming sequential steps
AND IF: the rationale for serializing these steps is relaxable (e.g. the steps involve serial approvals that could be done in parallel)
THEN: modify the process so the steps are performed concurrently

Another example for the "missing high-capability resource" exception mentioned above is:

IF: a high-capability resource assumed for a task is now unavailable
THEN: replace the task by a process of simpler tasks that can be performed by currently available resources

A possible strategy for the architecture design conflict is:

IF: there is a negative critique of propagation of some substance (e.g. solar heating) through a conduit (e.g. a window) designed to propagate something else (e.g. a view)

THEN: add a filter to the conduit that stops the unwanted substance but not the desired one (e.g. an overhang over the window for the high summer sun)

Exception handling strategies thus can work by modifying both process and product decisions, including assignment decisions, task sequencing, design components and so on. Selecting and instantiating these strategies almost invariably requires being able to understand the rationale for the decisions leading to the exception.

Exception handling strategies are represented as work processes just like other, the only difference being that their actions have a different intent (that of resolving an exception rather than designing a process or product). The strategies are executed using the regular process enactment service, and the dependency structures underlying exception resolution decisions are captured using the regular dependency capture service. Details of the computational approach used to instantiate generic strategies into exception handling processes are given in (Klein, 1991a).

iDCSS's current knowledge base of exception handling strategies is by no means complete; the system is designed rather to allow one to add new strategies as needed over time. The area of design conflicts is particularly rich with examples of constraint relaxation (Easterbrook 1994), game-theoretic (Zlotkin 1990) and knowledge-based (Marcus 1989) conflict resolution mechanisms that would be appropriate for inclusion in the iDCSS knowledge base. The current contents of the iDCSS knowledge base and further detail on exception detection approaches will appear in a forthcoming chapter.

3. Conclusions

The central claim of this chapter is that conflict management technology can be made more robust if viewed as the exception handling component of an integrated set of collaborative design coordination services. The iDCSS exception handling service differs from current conflict management technology in a number of important ways. iDCSS is unique in that it treats all exception resolution processes just like any other work process. Conflict management benefits as a result from the use of full-fledged versions of dependency capture and process enactment services. iDCSS also handles process and product decision conflicts uniformly. Conflicts between conflict resolution processes, as a result, can be resolved recursively by the exception management service to produce a coordinated solution for multiple simultaneous conflicts. Existing conflict management systems used special purpose representations for conflict resolution strategies and thus lack this attribute. The iDCSS dependency capture service provides a representation of the prescriptive and descriptive dependencies between design decisions that is more expressive than that used by other conflict management technologies. Finally, the process management service allows us to define process templates that delimit how much conflict detection effort is needed at given steps of the collaborative design process. This helps improve the tractability of the conflict detection process.

Integration of coordination services does more than this, however; it is also synergistic in that all the component coordination technologies benefit (Klein, 1995). We can summarize some of the more important synergisms as follows (Figure 3.1):

Each arc represents a way in which one coordination technology adds value to another. We have already discussed the benefits conflict management derives from integration. Rationale capture technology provides argumentation and intent information for process (and product) decisions. This can be used to support process redesign (e.g. allowing us to avoid process changes that violate important goals). Rationale capture derives increased expressiveness from the notions of process execution history and prescriptive constraints. We can also use process templates to delimit what and how much rationale information needs to be captured for given decisions (e.g. by specifying for which sub-goals we need to justify the way the goal was achieved), helping to reduce the potential rationale capture burden. Process management technology benefits from the exception handling capabilities made possible by generalizing conflict management technology. While the need for exception handling in computer-supported collaborative work technology has been widely recognized (e.g. (Suchman 1983), (Grudin 1994)), very little technology for this purpose has been developed, and it has been limited to a small subset of exception types and/or domains (e.g. (Mi 1991), (Karbe 1990)). Conflict management technology addresses an important subset of exception types, of course, but iDCSS is the first system that utilizes a similar knowledge-based approach to cover non-conflict types of exceptions.

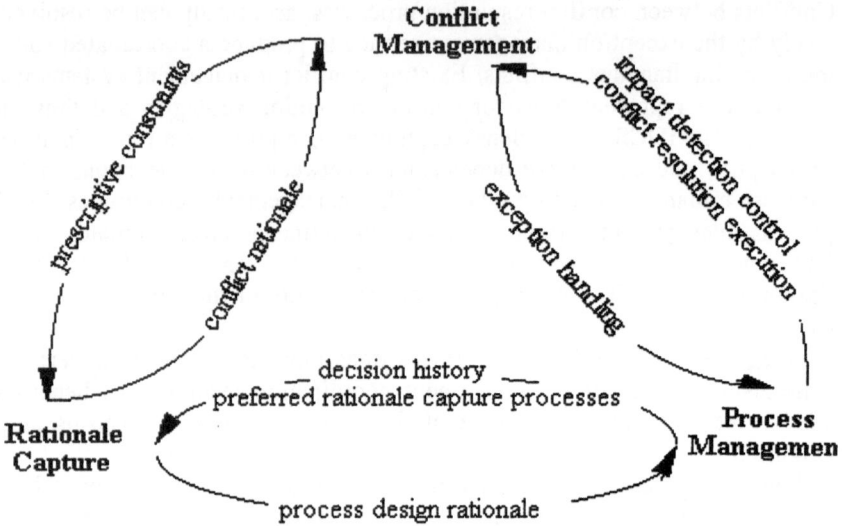

Fig 3.1. Synergism among iDCSS Component Technologies.

The integrated approach explored by iDCSS does, however, present some new challenges. Our view of the component coordination technologies must be broadened somewhat from their current definitions. Rationale capture must be able to capture product, process and organizational inter-dependencies in a way that is integrated with the tools used to capture the decisions themselves. Computer tools for product and process decision capture must thus both be augmented to capture dependencies between decisions both within and between different design decision capture tools. Process management needs to support exception handling; in particular, one must be able to modify processes as they are being enacted. Finally, it must be recognized that conflict management is just a special case of exception handling and thus must be applied to a wider range of exceptions types than has previously been considered.

The idea presented in this chapter relate to the other chapters of this book as follows:

- This chapter addresses how we can best address conflicts *as they arise at runtime*. This is in contrast to efforts to detect (see Ekenberg et al) or resolve (see Spanoudakis et al) such conflicts *ahead of time* (e.g. when the system is being developed), and consistent in focus with the chapters by Brown, Matta, Frohlich, Rollinger, and de Rosis et al.

- This chapter, like Brown's and Matta's, deals with *synthesis* tasks. Synthesis and diagnosis have been identified (Clancey 1992) as constituting two key and distinct forms of inference; work on diagnosis conflicts (see Frohlich et al) is thus complimentary to the work described herein. Synthesis and diagnosis are, in turn, different from the consensual world model building described in the chapters by Rollinger and by de Rosis et al.
- The approach described in this chapter is *knowledge-based*, in the sense that it attempt to collect in a usable form a wide range of techniques for conflict management. It thus depends upon, and extends, ontologies of conflict and resolution types such as those described in the chapters by Castelfranchi and Matta. Brown's chapter, by contrast, deals only the subset of conflicts involving design parameter inconsistencies that can be resolved by negotiation. Delahaye et al's chapter, similarly, describes a single algorithm for a different, but also limited range of conflict types.

The other chapters, in short, describe work that can be used to extend or complement the knowledge-based design conflict management approach described herein.

CHAPTER 10

Conflict Resolution in Distributed Assessment Situations

O. Hollmann[1], K.C. Ranze[1], H.J. Müller[2], and O. Herzog[1]

[1] Center for Computing Technologies, University of Bremen, Germany
[2] Deutsche Telekom, Technologiezentrum Darmstadt, Germany

The following text summarizes the technical basis for the DECIDE system (DECi-sion support In Distributed Environments). DECIDE is an agent-based approach to support a group of experts in order to find a common evaluation for several assessment objects. The approach is based on a legacy system designed for the modelling and processing of assessment tasks. The experts within the DECIDE framework might be human or computer, with different types of assessment criteria. Different types of conflicts between the experts may be resolved through mediated negotiation. Different problem-solving methods are defined within task/method-slots with clear interfaces. The chapter presents the main aspects of our approach focussing on the communication, the negotiation, and the solution of weak and hard conflicts.

1. Introduction

Complex decisions are based on the evaluation of heterogeneous data. If the decisions are important, a team of experts has to come to a mutually accepted evaluation result, which then leads to the decision. In order to come to that point, the experts usually evaluate the data according to their special view of the problem and then negotiate their results by taking into account the potential conflicts between their colleagues.

In summer 1997 the German Ministry of Education and Research started a business foundation initiative. Entrepreneurs were to submit their business plans for evaluation by experts from politics, finance, ecology, marketing, industry and research. Eventually the experts should agree on the five best proposals out of about 2000. Obviously the experts rate the proposals on the basis of their special interests, i.e. high return-of-invest for bankers, easy-to-sell features for marketing experts, ecologically beneficial for ecologists, etc. Moreover, they usually have their own evaluation scale. The politicians may have the fuzzy values: good.for.me, marginal, bad.for.me as results, whereas the researchers may rate from 1 to 6 according to school marks, and bankers might get a real number as a result by correlating the return-of-invest rate and the number of employees after three years. After rating the special aspects of the proposals by the respective experts, the experts have to come to a mutually accepted rate of the whole proposal on a common scale. There is a high potential for conflicts in the result-finding phase, because the goals the experts try to reach with their evaluation may be highly contrary. In the example bankers might prefer proposals with high investments and low financial risk, while ecologists are primarily interested in projects that are positive for the environment. E.g., building an atomic reactor would be interesting for a bank, but it is unacceptable to the ecologist. On the other hand the same goals may not be at all contradictory if the project would be the construction of a solar energy parc.

The DECIDE methodology uses a formal model for evaluation tasks which is based on the multiple experts metaphor. It is a five-phase strategy for distributed evaluation and decision-finding using negotiation principles and conflict resolution strategies as discussed in Distributed Artificial Intelligence. Following Kahle (Kahle 1990) there are five principal relations between the different goal variables of the experts:

- Goal identity: Goals are identical while the goal variables are different.

- Goal complementary: Goals are different, however the goal variables are positively correlated, i.e. increasing one variable will increase the other, and vice versa.

- Goal neutrality: Goals are different and the variables are not correlated.

- Goal concurrency: Goals are different, the goal variables are negatively correlated. Increasing one goal variable would decrease the second and vice versa.

- Goal antinomy: Goals are different and excluding one another. Reaching one goal (i.e. maximizing the goal variable) would exclude the other (i.e. minimizing the goal variable).

With the DECIDE methodology we propose an approach to support an expert group in their evaluation efforts by

- standardizing evaluation tasks
- automatization of summarizing focussed evaluations
- analyzing and resolving goal conflicts (if possible)

The main advantages of our approach are:

- automatization of the evaluation of information in huge data bases, needed for Data Mining tasks and effective Data Warehousing.
- fairness in evaluating all alternatives with the same measurement, needed in official judgements at courts.
- transparency of evaluation efforts, needed in certification activities.

2. A Short Discussion on Conflicts

Coombs and Avrunin ((Coombs and Avrunin 1988)) tried to structure the different conflict approaches and to develop a mathematical theory for conflicts. Their perspective is defined by the key phrase:

> "The essence of social conflict is interaction."

which is refined through the definition of Schellenberg (ref. (Coombs and Avrunin 1988) p.3) stating that a conflict is

> "... a conflict of interest between individuals, motivated by self-interest and bounded by moral and ethical limits."

On this general basis they define three types of conflict:

- Type I is a conflict within an individual because he or she is torn between incompatible goals.
- Type II is conflict between individuals because they want different things and must settle for the same thing.
- Type III is conflict between individuals because they want the same thing and must settle for different things.

The mathematical setting for modeling the three types of conflict is based on Single Peak Functions expressing the preferences and options in the choices the parties (the individual resp.) have. Though we will not use the peak function theory for conflict resolution, it is possible to classify our conflicts as type II. The experts have different preferences, although they have to come to a mutually agreed selection.[1]

The broadest, but most pleasing definition was given by Putnam and Poole (Putnam and Poole 1987):

> "Conflict is the interaction of interdependent people who perceive oppositions of goals, aims, and values, and who see the other party as potentially interfering with the realization of these goals."

Though the definition is not very concrete, it is pleasing because it describes the main characteristics of conflicts, namely interaction between parties, their interdependence, and their incompatible goals, which will be essential to conflict situations in our multiple expert assessment scenario.

Beside the discussion about the semantics of conflicts the conflict theme was taken by the people in the field of Computer Supported Cooperative Work (CSCW). Steve Easterbrook came up with a respectable selection of

---

[1] Just an aside at that point. If the mutual agreement to be found would be just a selection of different choices, then voting might be a simple mechanism for conflict resolution. However, in our scenario the experts may modify the objects which have to be evaluated in order to find a commonly accepted one (see the case study).

related works commencing with an excellent survey of empirical studies of conflicts (Easterbrook(Ed.) 1993). He basically agreed with the definition of Putnam and Pool and he clustered assertions about conflict into six categories:

1. **occurrence**, the factors that affect whether conflict will arise
2. **causes**, the specific causes of conflict
3. **utility**, the role that conflict may play in group interactions
4. **development**, the processes involved in an individual conflict episode
5. **management**, approaches to handling conflicts, including resolution techniques
6. **results**, the outcomes and long-term effects of conflicts

Obviously our work at hand deals with the management of conflicts. It meets the workshop theme (see utility in the above list) in that it shows that through negotiation a new solution may emerge out of a conflict. Negotiation as a conflict resolution principle in multi-agent systems has been studied under different contexts and views (Bussmann and Müller 1992) (Chu-Carroll and Carberry 1995) (Müller 1996) (Parsons and Jennings 1997) (Parsons, Sierra, and Jennings 1998).
However, conflicts that stem from different preferences of different types and which have to be resolved not by adapting the preferences (that would be persuasion and argumentation) but the goals in such a way that all the different preferences match the goal, is new to our knowledge.

3. Basic Formal Framework

In the initial stage of a distributed assessment process the alternative objects to be evaluated have to be defined. In our framework these objects x_i are defined in terms of a set of indicators $I = \{I_1, ..., I_n\}$. D_{I_i} denotes the domain of an indicator, thus $b_x = (d_1, ..., d_n)$, $d_1 \in D_{I_1}, ..., d_n \in D_{I_n}$ specifies the configuration of the indicator set representing an alternative object x.

Definition (ASSESSMENT): The assessment of an expert E_i is a total function f_{E_i} so that

$$f_{E_i} : (D_{I_1} \times ... \times D_{I_m}) \mapsto D_{E_i}$$

where the I_j are indicators with domain D_{I_j} and D_{E_i} is the assessment domain of expert E_i.

We assume that D_{E_i} contains an *ordered* set of rating statements. Each expert E_i uses a subset of the indicator set I for his assessment.

Definition (CONTENTMENT): Let Φ denote a threshold value within an assessment domain. An expert E_i is content with a configuration of a set of indicators, if

$$f_{E_i}(d_1, \ldots, d_m) \geq_{D_{E_i}} \Phi_{E_i} \in D_{E_i}$$

holds. The set of all contented indicator configurations of an expert E_i is denoted as

$$G_{E_i} = \{(D_{I_1} \times \ldots \times D_{I_m}) \mid f_{E_i}(D_{I_1}, \ldots, D_{I_m}) \geq_{D_{E_i}} \Phi_{E_i}\}$$

$\hat{G} = \bigcap_i G_{E_i}$ denotes the consensus set of all experts E_i.

A set of indicator configurations is contentable for a set of experts iff $\hat{G}$ is $|\hat{G}| > 0$

Definition (DISTRIBUTED ASSESSMENT PROBLEM, DAP): Let $B \subseteq D_{I_1} \times \ldots \times D_{I_n}$ be a set of indicator configurations and $E = \{E_1, E_2, \ldots, E_k\}$ a set of experts. A **DAP** is defined by:

Given: B, nonempty
Find: Some $b \in B$, so that all experts are content.

The result of the analysis of a distributed assessment problem can be one of the following situations:

1. **Definition (DAP-SOLUTION):** There is exactly one indicator configuration, so that all experts are contented:
   $\exists b \in B : (b \in \hat{G} \wedge (\forall b' \in B : b' \neq b \Rightarrow b' \notin \hat{G})) \equiv \mid B \cap \hat{G} \mid = 1$

2. **Definition (Weak Conflict):** There is more than one contentable indicator configuration:
   $B' \subseteq B, |B'| > 1 : (\forall b' \in B' : b' \in \hat{G}) \equiv \mid B \cap \hat{G} \mid > 1$

3. **Definition (Hard Conflict):** There is no contentable indicator configuration:
   $\forall b \in B : b \notin \hat{G} \equiv \mid B \cap \hat{G} \mid = 0$

If the result is a weak conflict, then the experts have to negotiate in order to select "the most acceptable" indicator configuration. If the result is a hard conflict, then the experts have to find a compromise, i.e. they have to negotiate about modifying B "moderately" in order to find a consensus set.

Definition (MINIMAL CONSENSUS): Let ω be a similarity function between two indicator configurations:
$\omega : (b_i, b_j) \mapsto [0..1]$ mit $b_i, b_j \in D_{I_1} \times \ldots \times D_{I_n}$
A set of indicator configurations $B_m in$ is a minimal consensus set iff
$\{(g, b) \mid \forall g \in \hat{G}, \forall b \in B_m in : \nexists (g', b') \in \hat{G} \times B : \omega(g', b') > \omega(g, b)\}$ is not empty.

It is now easy to define an algorithm for solving hard conflicts if the conflict is solvable at all. After constructing the set of all possible indicator configurations the set can be sorted along a similarity function and then the minimal consensus set may be found by inspection. However, it is obvious that this procedure is exponential in time and space.

4. Solving Conflicts through Negotiation

The general idea for a more efficient solution is to model the experts explicitly and to use negotiation principles (Müller 1996) in order to find a consensus set. The decentralization of the problem solving process does not only help to break down the complexity but is also more natural than the centralized approach. In reality it depends very much on the expert whether to accept an alternative indicator configuration or not. It is very difficult to find a mutually accepted similarity function. Not only that the rating of a certain indicator is different with each expert, the interdependencies between the indicators are different, too. Moreover, the rationale for the decisions of experts lies in their private knowledge and usually would not be made public.

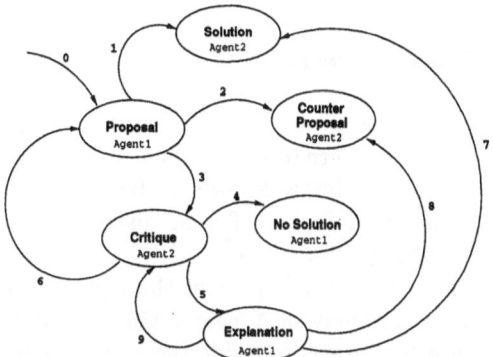

Fig. 4.1. Solving Conflicts through Negotiation

The communication architecture is a mediated negotiation scenario where the communication primitives follow the KQML principles and the negotiation protocol is based on Parsons and Jennings "Mediated Negotiation" method:

> "This process of negotiation starts when an agent generates a proposal. Other agents then either accept it, critique it or make counterproposals. Following this, the original agent then either sends clarifying information that may resolve the problem, critiques a counterproposal, or indicates its acceptance of the counter-proposal. This process continues until all the agents involved are, in some sense, happy with a proposal or it is felt that no agreement can be reached.

By 'happy' it is not meant that this is the optimum proposal from the point of view of the agent, but that it represents an acceptable compromise. " (Parsons and Jennings 1997)

While the extended formal approach of Parsons et al. (Parsons, Sierra, and Jennings 1998) which is based on a labeled deductive mechanism is difficult to handle, their pragmatic approach which is based on a simple negotiation protocol fits well in our context. Table 1 shows that the performatives used in Parsons protocol (i.e. `proposal, critique, accept, withdraw`) were respected. While Parsons et al. had to parametrisize their performatives (they called it "meta-information") in order to finally end up with their formal description, we preferred to introduce new performatives with the intended semantics. E.g. proposal(a, b, ϕ) and proposal(b, a, ϕ) became `proposal` and `counter-proposal` in our context. The message content ϕ is part of the message body. The `critique` performative is replace by the more constructive `modify`. However, in the basic sense the experts in our scenario follow essentially the protocol as proposed in ((Parsons, Sierra, and Jennings 1998), pp 6).

Figure 4.1 outlines the negotiation process between two evaluation agents. In the following the basic elements of the DECIDE approach realizing this negotiation process will be presented.

4.1 Communication Architecture

The DECIDE testbed is based on the legacy system *exupro*[2]. Within this system one is able to define alternative objects as indicator configurations in a database and assessment models as knowledge bases. Our approach extends the existing architecture by defining different distributed evaluation agents instead of a single knowledge base.

Beside the experts a mediator is part of the agent society. In DECIDE these experts are called "Evaluation Agents". The mediator is called "Negotiation Agent" because his task is to guide the negotiation. Human experts may be connected to the system via a "User Evaluation Agent". Furthermore, there are four system components which support the user in defining and maintaining the evaluation agents, the setup of the problem, and the database for the objects to be evaluated. Agents and system components are connected via a CORBA based communication platform. The interface to the platform is uniquely realized by KQML communication primitives. Figure 4.2 shows the whole architecture.

Abstracting from the general architecture with its system components and the interface for human experts we will now concentrate on the Evaluation Agents and the Negotiation Agent. They are the kernel of our multi-agent

---

[2] exupro is an expert system developed by TZI, University of Bremen. It is implemented as a JAVA C/S-application (see http://www.tzi.de/is/exupro).

system.

The *Evaluation Agents* have the following tasks:

- Assessment of a set of assessment objects (AO)
- Computation of an ordered list of AOs concerning its local contentment
- Generating and assessing of alternative indicator configurations for the resolution of hard conflicts

The *Negotiation Agent* has the following tasks:

- Delegating assessment orders to the evaluation agents
- Analyzing assessment results of the evaluation agents
- Finding solutions for weak conflicts
- Initiating the negotiation process in case of hard conflicts

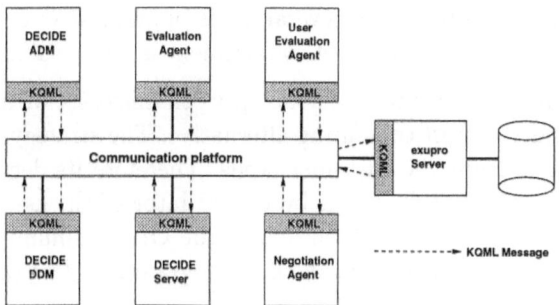

Fig. 4.2. DECIDE Architecture

The question at that point is whether it is necessary to introduce the Negotiation Agent or not. The first reason is based on the natural modeling attempt of the approach. In the real world there is always a customer who ordered the assessment, so there is a central initiator who has to be satisfied. Further, in cases of hard conflicts it has been shown that a mediator is very helpful, e.g. think of divorcement conflicts. The second reason is that it is always possible that one agent may take the *role* of the mediator (cf. (Kreifelts and v. Martial 1990)). However, the third reason is that it is easier to model a mediator explicitly than cloning the mediator abilities and behavior in each agent. Another pragmatic argument is that the communication overhead in the system is obviously reduced.

4.2 Task/Method Slots

Based on the tasks of the Evaluating Agents (EA) and the Negotiation Agents (NA) mentioned in the previous section we have defined several method slots within our architecture. These slots allow for the definition of domain specific methods for the following subtasks:

- Contentment regarding an indicator configuration (EA)
- Solving weak conflicts (NA)
- Optimization by 'minimal' manipulation of indicator configurations (EA)
- Modelling dependencies between indicators (EA)

The concrete realization of these methods depends on the actual application domain and is therefore encapsulated within the agents bodies. Clearly defined interfaces guarantee for the facile adaption of elaborated subsystems. In the first stage of the DECIDE project we only developed simple methods to show the general applicability of our approach.

Contentment regarding an indicator configuration:. In order to compare different assessment results the assessment domain D_{Ei} of an expert E_i should be an ordinal or cardinal value set. Within an ordered set of possible assessment results the definition of several kinds of qualitative or quantitative threshold values for the modeling of contentment is conceivable.

Solving weak conflicts:. In case of a nonempty consensus set we have to define a strategy to find the most contenting alternative. The strategy to be chosen has to take into account the customer needs. Therefore its definition highly depends on the overall goal defined by the initiator of the assessment task. We have inspected several approaches from the OR community, e.g. vector maximum model, utility functions, and goal programming (see (Zimmermann 1992)).

Optimization/Manipulation:. Two major subtasks arise for EAs to manipulate indicator configurations during a hard conflict. On one hand a non-centented EA has to initiate an indicator manipulation which leads to the contentment of all EAs. This denotes a search task for the non-contented EA and a simulation task for the other EAs. On the other hand the EAs have to determine a 'minimal' manipulation.

Modeling dependencies:. In order to manipulate indicator configurations we have to take into account the (physical) dependencies between the particular indicators. These dependencies qualify the possible manipulations and influence the determination of a 'minimal' manipulation. For this purpose we have defined an elementary model in our case study, stating the dependencies qualitatively (*independent, dependent, invariant*). Further investigations should take into account a conceptual model of the application domain.

4.3 Communication Primitives

The whole communication between the agents is realized through KQML
message types.

Table 1 shows the set of performatives which have been found during an
extensive transaction analysis. Since almost all of them are self-explaining
we will skip the full description.

Number	Performative	Sender	Receiver	Content
1	ask evaluation models	ADM	exupro-Server	Content
2	tell evaluation models	exupro-Server	ADM	LinkedList(ModelInfo)
3	register	Evaluation Agent User Evaluation Agent	DECIDE-Server	Registration
4	unregister	Evaluation Agent User Evaluation Agent	DECIDE-Server	Registration
5	ask evaluation subjects	DDM	exupro-Server	
6	tell evaluation subjects	exupro-Server	DDM	LinkedList(SubjectInfo
7	ask registrations	DDM	DECIDE-Server	
8	tell registrations	DECIDE-Server	DDM	LinkedList(Registration
9	define evaluation problem	DDM	DECIDE-Server	DecisionDefinition
10	tell evaluation problem	Negotiation Agent	Evaluation Agent User Evaluation Agent	DecisionDefinition
11	change status	Negotiation Agent	DECIDE-Server	Status
12	ask assessment	Evaluation Agent User Evaluation Agent	exupro-Server	Project
13	tell assessment	exupro-Server	Evaluation Agent User Evaluation Agent	Project
14	tell expertise	Evaluation Agent User Evaluation Agent	Negotiation Agent	Expertise
15	tell result	Negotiation Agent	DECIDE-Server Evaluation Agent User Evaluation Agent	Result
16	modify subject	Negotiation Agent	Evaluation Agent User Evaluation Agent	SubjectInfo
17	sorry	Evaluation Agent User Evaluation Agent	Negotiation Agent	SubjectInfo
18	propose subject	Negotiation Agent Evaluation Agent User Evaluation Agent	Negotiation Agent Evaluation Agent User Evaluation Agent	Project
19	accept proposal	Negotiation Agent Evaluation Agent User Evaluation Agent	Negotiation Agent Evaluation Agent User Evaluation Agent	Expertise
20	submit counter-proposal	Negotiation Agent Evaluation Agent User Evaluation Agent	Negotiation Agent Evaluation Agent User Evaluation Agent	Project
21	reject proposal	Negotiation Agent Evaluation Agent User Evaluation Agent	Negotiation Agent Evaluation Agent User Evaluation Agent	Expertise

Table 1: Communication Primitives

4.4 The Conflict Resolution Process

In the following the resolution process for hard conflicts will be presented
along the activities in the multi-agent system. The general idea is that the
evaluation agents try to (locally) modify the current indicator configuration
and post the result to the negotiation agent who tries to mediate by resolving
local conflicts.

Let $(b \xrightarrow{modify} b')$ be a irreflexive and stable transformation of indicator configurations.

Given: A set of conflicting indicator configurations B

Find: One modified indicator configuration b' $(b \xrightarrow{modify} b', b \in B)$, such that b' is minimal with respect to the number of modified indicators and all experts are contented with b' ($b' \in \hat{G}$).

(I)   **Actor:** *Negotiation Agent*

1. Select an indicator configuration $b \in B$
2. Select the most uncontentable evaluation agent EA_j with respect to b

$$EA_j \mid f_{EA_j}(b) = max\{\Phi_{EA_i} - f_{EA_i}(b) \mid \forall i : f_{EA_i}(b) < \Phi_{EA_i}\}$$

3. Ask EA_j for a complete set of alternatives P_{EA_j} to be generated by modifying b.

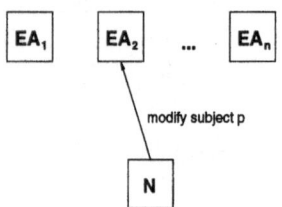

Fig. 4.3. Modification Request

(II)   **Actor:** *Evaluation Agent*

1. Generate $P_{EA_j}(b)$.

$$P_{EA_j} = \{b' \mid b \xrightarrow{modify} b' \wedge f_{EA_j}(b') \geq \Phi_{EA_j}\}$$

2. Mark each indicator used in EA_j.
3. Sort P_{EA_j} with respect to:
   - Minimal number of evaluation agents affected by the modification of the modifications
   - Minimal number of modified indicators
   - Minimal contentness on the modified indicator set
     $min(f_{EA_j}(b'))$
4. Send the sorted proposal to P_{EA_j} the negotiation agent.

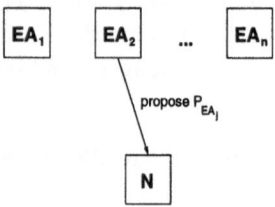

Fig. 4.4. Propose Alternatives

(III)   **Actor:** *Negotiation Agent*

1. Select a proposal $p \in P_{EA_j}$.
2. Generate the set *Asked* of evaluation agents who are not contented with b and who are affected by the modification $(b \overset{modify}{\longrightarrow} p)$

$$Asked = \{EA_x \mid f_{EA_x}(b) < \Phi_{EA_x} \vee$$
$$involved(EA_x, (b \overset{modify}{\longrightarrow} p))\}$$

where $involved : EA \times (B \overset{modify}{\longrightarrow} B') \mapsto boolean$
3. Send p to all evaluation agents in $EA_{involved} \in Asked$.

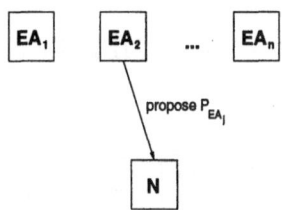

Fig. 4.5. Check Alternatives

(IV)   **Actor(s):** *Evaluation Agent*

1. Assess p.
2. CASE:
   a) Evaluation agent EA_i is contented with p: $f_{EA_i}(p) \geq \Phi_{EA_i}$
      $\Rightarrow$ Send message **accept proposal** p to Negotiation Agent.
   b) EA_i is not contented with p: $f_{EA_i}(p) < \Phi_{EA_i}$
      i. Generate counter proposal CP_{EA_i}.
      $$CP_{EA_i} = \{p' \mid p \overset{modify}{\longrightarrow} p' \wedge f_{EA_i}(p') \geq \Phi_{EA_i}\}$$
      ii. Mark each indicator used in EA_i.
      iii. Sort CP_{EA_i} with respect to:
         – Minimal number of evaluation agents affected by the modi-
           fication of the modifications
         – Minimal number of modified indicators
         – Minimal contentness on the modified indicator set

      iv. CASE:
         A. $CP_{EA_i} = \emptyset$
            $\Rightarrow$ Send message **reject proposal** p to Negotiation Agent.
         B. $CP_{EA_i} \neq \emptyset$
            $\Rightarrow$ Send message **submit counter-proposal** CP_{EA_i} to Ne-
            gotiation Agent.

(V)   **Actor:** *Negotiation Agent*

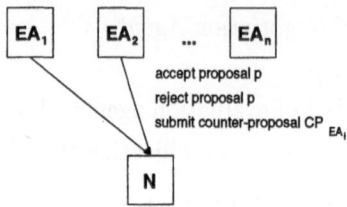

Fig. 4.6. Critique

1. CASE:
   a) All evaluation agents are contented with respect to p
   $$\forall EA_x \in Asked : f_{EA_x}(p) \geq \Phi_{EA_x}$$
   $\Rightarrow p$ is a DAP-solution
   Send **tell result** p to *DECIDE-Server* and to all *Evaluation Agents*

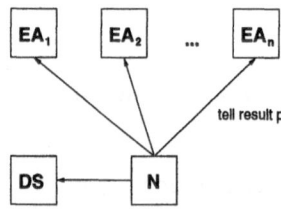

Fig. 4.7. Tell Result

   b) At least one evaluation agent is not contented with p
   $$\exists EA_x \in Asked : (f_{EA_x}(p) < \Phi_{EA_x}$$
   $$\wedge (\not\exists p' : f_{EA_x}(p') \geq \Phi_{EA_x} \wedge p \overset{modify}{\longrightarrow} p'))$$
   $\Rightarrow$ CASE:
   i. If $P_{EA_j} \neq \emptyset$: goto **(III)**
   ii. If $B \neq \emptyset$: goto **(I)**
   iii. Else there is no DAP-Solution:
   Send **tell result** *zero* to *DECIDE-Server* and all *Evaluation Agents*
   c) At least one evaluation agent is only contented with a modification p' of p.
   $$\exists E_x \in Asked : f_{E_x}(p') \geq \Phi_{E_x} \wedge p \overset{modify}{\longrightarrow} p'$$
   i. Select one of the uncontented evaluation agents EA_x.
   ii. Select a counter-proposal $p' \in CP_{EA_x}$.
   iii. Generate the set *Asked* of evaluation agents who are not contented with b and who are affected by the modification ($b \overset{modify}{\longrightarrow} p$)

$$Asked = \{EA_x \mid f_{EA_x}(b) < \Phi_{EA_x} \vee$$
$$involved(EA_x, (b \overset{modify}{\longrightarrow} p'))\}$$

where $involved : EA \times (B \overset{modify}{\longrightarrow} B') \mapsto boolean$

iv. Send p' to all evaluation agents $EA_{involved} \in Asked$.

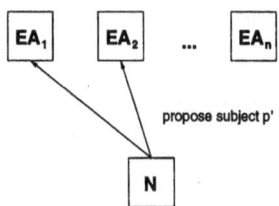

Fig. 4.8. Counter Proposal

(VI)   **Actor(s):** *Evaluation Agent*

1. Assess p'.
2. CASE:
   a) Evaluation agent EA_i is contented with p': $f_{EA_i}(p') \geq \Phi_{EA_i}$
      $\Rightarrow$ Send message **accept proposal** p' to *Negotiation Agent*.
   b) EA_i is not contented with p': $f_{EA_i}(p') < \Phi_{EA_i}$
      i. Generate counter proposal CP_{EA_i}.
      $$CP_{EA_i} = \{p'' \mid p' \overset{modify}{\longrightarrow} p'' \wedge f_{EA_i}(p'') \geq \Phi_{EA_i}\}$$
      ii. Mark each indicator used in CP_{EA_i}.
      iii. Sort CP_{EA_i} with respect to:
        – Minimal number of evaluation agents affected by the modification of the modifications
        – Minimal number of modified indicators
        – Minimal contentness on the modified indicator set

      iv. CASE:
        A. $CP_{EA_i} = \emptyset$
           $\Rightarrow$ Send message **reject proposal** p' to *Negotiation Agent*.
        B. $CP_{EA_i} \neq \emptyset$
           $\Rightarrow$ Send message **submit counter-proposal** CP_{EA_i} to *Negotiation Agent*.

(VII)   **Actor:** *Negotiation Agent*

1. CASE:
   a) All evaluation agents are contented with p'
      $$\forall EA_x \in Asked : f_{EA_x}(p') \geq \Phi_{EA_x}$$
      $\Rightarrow$ The DAP-Solution is p'
      Send **tell result** p' to *DECIDE-Server* and all *Evaluation Agents*

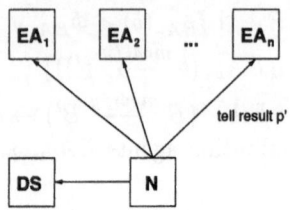

Fig. 4.9. Tell Result

b) At least one evaluation agent is not contented with p'
$$\exists EA_x \in Asked : (f_{EA_x}(p') < \Phi_{EA_x} \wedge$$
$$(\not\exists p'' : f_{EA_x}(p'') \geq \Phi_{EA_x} \wedge p' \overset{modify}{\longrightarrow} p''))$$
$\Rightarrow$ CASE:
  i. If $CP_{EA_x} \neq \emptyset$:
    A. Select counter-proposal $p' \in CP_{EA_x}$.

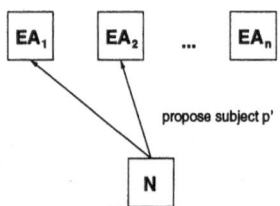

Fig. 4.10. Counter Proposal

    B. Generate the set *Asked* of evaluation agents who are not contented with b and who are affected by the modification $(b \overset{modify}{\longrightarrow} p')$.
    C. Send p' to all evaluation agents $EA_{involved} \in Asked$.
    D. goto **(VI)**.
  ii. If $P_{EA_j} \neq \emptyset$: goto **(III)**
  iii. If $B \neq \emptyset$: goto **(I)**
  iv. Else: There is no DAP-Solution
    Send **tell result** *zero* to *DECIDE-Server* and all *Evaluation Agents*
c) At least one evaluation agent is not contented with only one modification of p'
$$\forall EA_x \in Asked : f_{EA_x}(p') \geq \Phi_{EA_x}$$
  i. Select such an evaluation agent EA_x.
  ii. Select a counter-proposal $p'' \in CP_{EA_x}$.
  iii. Generate the set *Asked* of evaluation agents who are not contented with b and who are affected by the modification $(b \overset{modify}{\longrightarrow} p'')$.

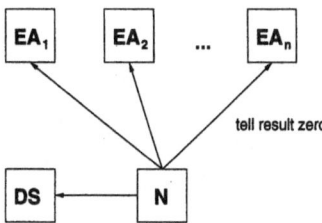

Fig. 4.11. Tell Failure

iv. Send p'' to all evaluation agents $EA_{involved} \in Asked.$. .
v. Goto **(VI)** (p'' instead of p').

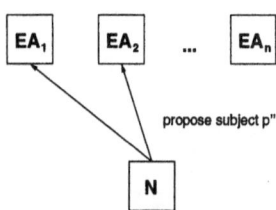

Fig. 4.12. Reproposal

5. Implementation

The DECIDE framework is prototypical realized as a distributed JAVA application. The system requirements for the current version are JDK1.1.x and Swing1.1-final. On top of the middleware technology JAVA RMI, we have developed a KQML framework for our agent communication.

Human experts can define DECIDE evaluation agents with the *Agent Definition Module (ADM)*. The evaluation knowledge is represented as an exupro evaluation model. An evaluation agent has the ability to evaluate subjects. If the agent is not satisfied with an evaluation subject, he is able to use optimization strategies to generate proposals for satisfying subjects. All defined evaluation agents of a DECIDE network are registered at the DECIDE server of the domain.

A human decision maker can define a distributed evaluation problem with the *Decision Definition Module (DDM)*. Therefore he has to select the alternative subjects, which should be considered by the different evaluation agents. In figure 5.1 you can see the subject selection and the definition of the method for the negotiation process. In the example we have chosen the 2/3 majority for decision making.

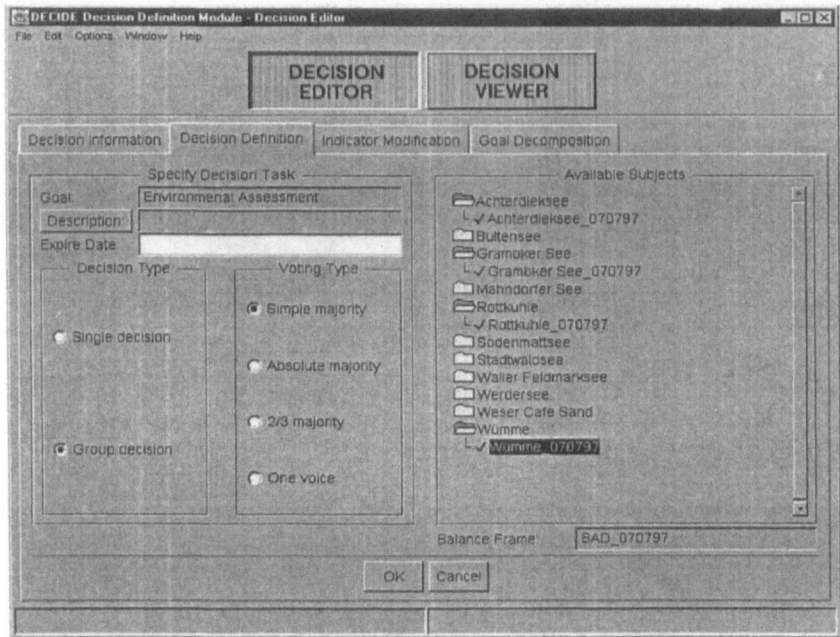

Fig 5.1 Subject selection

The decison maker can chose the different aspects and the corresponding eva-luation agents for the evaluation problem (see figure 6.1). He has the possibility to weight the evaluation agents, if they have a different impotance for the decision. After defining the distributed evaluation problem, the DECIDE framework starts working. First the evaluation agents evaluate the defined subjects and make ran-kings of the satisfied and non-satisfied subjects. They tell the evaluation results to a DECIDE negotiation agent. The negotiation agent analyses the results and finds possible conflicts. For the conflict resolution process he has implemented strate-gies for a mediated negotiation.

For instance he can ask a non-satisfied evaluation agent to optimize the most satisfied subject. Then the other agents have to evaluate the proposal and so on. If there exists a solution for the distributed evaluation problem, the DECIDE frame-work will find it.

6. Case Study

In the following a case study will demonstrate how the concepts may be used in practice. Let's consider three EAs named ECO, COST, and QUALITY, responsi-ble for assessing the ecological aspects, the economical aspects, and the quality aspects of a given product. Table 2 shows the set of indicators with corresponding type, domain, and unit information.

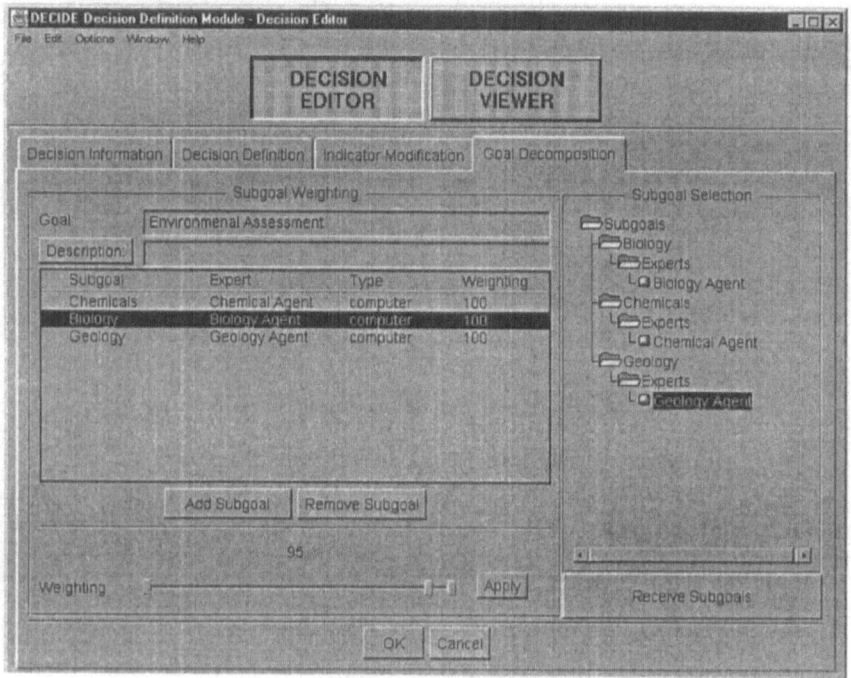

Indicator	type	poss. values	unit
SO$_2$ emission	discrete numeric	10, 50, 75, 100	mg/l
CO$_2$ emission	discrete numeric	10, 100, 200, 500, 1000	mg/l
Noise	discrete numeric	10, 30, 50, 70, 100	dB
Waste management	discrete	recycling, reconstruction disposal, deposition	
Materials	discrete	aluminium, plastics, steel	
Energy consumption	discrete	little, moderate, medium, high	
Surface finish	discrete	plain, coarse, solid, soft	
Tolerance	discrete	$0.0 \leq x < 0.5$ $0.5 \leq x < 2.0$ $2.0 \leq x < 5.0$ $5.0 \leq x < \infty$	mm
Delivery interval	discrete numeric	1, 7, 14, 28	days
Staff	discrete numeric	1, 2, 3, 4, 5	man
Storage	discrete	dry, humid, cool, warm	

Table 2: Indicators

Fig 6.1 Subgoal_selection

Each agent has a special assessment model which reflects the possible indicator configuration possibilities of the expert plus the information how the indicator configurations were combined to the aggregated assessment result. Those assessment models where defined using the *exupro* system. As an example the structure of the quality assessment model for QUALITY is shown in fig. 6.2. Due to their special tasks the experts only use a subtask of the

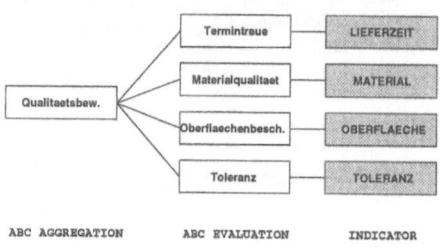

Fig. 5.1. The Quality Model

indicator set for their assessments. The assignment of indicators to agents may be found in table 3.

The following two exemplary assessment objects (alternatives) A and B of a test database have to be assessed by the EAs:

1. **product A** b_A = (75, 100, 100, 'recycling', 'aluminium', 'high', 'soft', '0.5 < x ≤ 2.0', 7, 5, 'humid')

2. **product B** b_B = (10, 500, 10, 'reconstruction', 'steel', 'moderate', 'coarse', '2.0 < x ≤ 5.0', 1, 5, 'cool')

Defining the thresholds of the experts by

$$\Phi_{QUALITY Agent} = 40,$$
$$\Phi_{ECOAgent} = 100,$$
$$\Phi_{COSTAgent} = 110$$

will lead to a weak conflict which could be resolved by using a utility function. Defining the thresholds of the experts by

$$\Phi_{QUALITY Agent} = 25,$$
$$\Phi_{ECOAgent} = 120,$$
$$\Phi_{COSTAgent} = 150$$

will lead to a hard conflict. After the mediated negotiation process the modified indicator configurations are:

b^* =(5, 500, 10, 'reconstruction', 'steel', 'moderate', 'coarse', '2.0 < x ≤ 5.0', 1, 4, 'cool')

Indicator name	ECO	COST	QUALITY
SO$_2$ emission	x	x	
CO$_2$ emission	x	x	
Noise	x	x	
Waste management	x	x	
Materials	x	x	x
Energy consumption	x	x	
Surface finish			x
Tolerance		x	x
Delivery interval		x	x
Staff		x	
Storage	x	x	

Table 3 : Regarded indicators

The negotiation process leads to a selection of a modified product B as the best alternative. During negotiation, the indicator CO_2 emission of product B was reduced from 10 to 5 and staff was decreased by one.

6. Concluding Remarks

The framework of DECIDE allows the definition and processing of distributed assessment and decision tasks. Within the case study referred we mainly focussed on the transaction analysis of assessment processes and the treatment of different kinds of conflicts. From our point of view the achieved results are transferable to other domains of assessment and decision support.

The concrete definition of domain-specific methods within the task/method slots remains an open problem which is beyond the scope of our chapter. Nevertheless our approach introduces a testbed for these methods since we defined clear interfaces to encapsulate them into the agent bodies. For further investigations our elementary methods may be replaced by elaborated models of the specific communities.

As stated above the resolution of possible hard conflicts highly depends on the cooperation strategies for indicator manipulation. In case of the suggested product assessment therefore the actors have to suggest minimal modifications of the physical world. Eventually this leads to a greater satisfaction of the participated stakeholders.

CHAPTER 11

The Iterated Lift Dilemma

How to Establish Meta-Cooperation with your Opponent

J.P. Delahaye, P. Mathieu, and B. Beaufils

Laboratoire d'Informatique Fondamentale de Lille

A very small change in the Iterated Prisoner's Dilemma (IPD) payoff matrix leads to an iterated game called the Iterated Lift Dilemma[1] the properties of which are very different from those of the classical IPD (CIPD). We show that the following ideas are to be noted: (i) two levels of cooperation are now possible, the best one needs a difficult coordination between considered strategies; (ii) only probabilistic strategies can make a high score when they play against themselves; (iii) complex dynamics can appear (at the *edge of chaos*) as soon as three strategies are confronted. Our idea, already argued in the case of the CIPD, is that, in spite of the model simplicity you can obtain many complex phenomena: it is not true that to be good, a strategy must be simple. Building good strategies for the Iterated Lift Dilemma is then much more difficult than for the CIPD.

1. Introduction

Conflicting situations are not only a driving force in nature and society, they are also the entry points for many investigations in Artificial Intelligence especially in Distributed Artificial Intelligence, Multi Agents Systems, formal model of rational action, CSCW, concurrent engineering and HCI.

The Iterated Prisoner's Dilemma is a model for studying cooperation and conflicts. It's an iterated game.

An *iterated game* is a game with two players A and B (also called *strategies*) who play an unknown finite number of rounds. On each round, each player chooses between two actions C (for *Cooperation*), and D (for *Defection*). A round where the player A plays C and the player B plays C is noted [C,C]; a round where the player A plays C and the player B plays D is noted [C,D]; a round where the player A plays D and the player B plays C is noted [D,C]; and finally a round where both players play D is noted [D,D].

When the players play the round number n they play simultaneously taking into account the game history (that is all the preceding choices they both have made at all rounds i with $i < n$).

---

[1] The term *Lift* comes from the French expression *renvoi d'ascenceur* which means *I help you this time, you will help me next time*

A player can also play a round randomly; in such a case we say that it is a probabilistic strategy. The average length of each game must be long enough (> 10) to allow interesting phenomena and to obtain robust results.

The results of the player's choices are quantified by a payoff matrix, which is shown in table 1.1. The parameter R is the reward for mutual cooperation (round [C,C]), T is the temptation to defect against an opponent cooperation, who then gets the sucker's payoff S (round [D,C]). In case of mutual defection both get the punishment P (round [D,D]).

As players can now choose a way of playing before the game begins, or during the game, they can be said having a *strategy*.

Several interesting confrontations can be studied:

- There are *single confrontations* (one strategy against another one). At the end of the confrontation (for example after 100 rounds), the points obtained by each player are cumuled. The winner is the player who has the greatest score.
- There are *round-robin tournaments*. We take k strategies, each one playing against all the others (including itself) in single confrontations. Points of confrontations are cumuled, the winner is the player who has the greatest score.
- There are *ecological evolutions*. For example we consider only 3 strategies A, B, C; we start with a population of one hundred players choosing the A strategies, one hundred playing B strategies and one hundred playing C strategies, that is 300 entities (this defines the first generation); a round-robin tournament is computed (as if each entity plays against the 299 other entities); scores are computed for each strategy (sum of all scores from entities of the same kind); a new population is then computed for each strategy which is proportional to the score obtained. To simplify we consider that the total population is constant (here 300). This defines the second generation. This computation is repeated until populations become stable.

We could let the total population increase but this is not really significant since we are interested in relative strategies range. Thus our choice is to maintain the global population stable.

In *ecological evolutions*, nice[2] strategies proliferate and replace bad ones. To be a good strategy in an *ecological evolution* a strategy needs not only to be good in the round-robin competition but also during all the time and especially when bad ones disappear. Persistent strategies in *ecological evolution* are really robust ones.

In the CIPD the following parameters values are generally used:

$$S = 0 \qquad P = 1 \qquad R = 3 \qquad T = 5$$

---

[2] *nice* strategies, as opposed to *bad* or *naughty* ones, are the strategies which never defect prior to its opponents.

Table 1.1. Iterated Lift Dilemma payoff matrix. Row player scores are given first.

	Cooperate	Defect
Cooperate	$R = 3, R = 3$ *Reward* for mutual cooperation	$S = 0, T = 8$ *Sucker's* payoff *Temptation* to defect
Defect	$T = 8, S = 0$ *Temptation* to defect *Sucker's* payoff	$P = 1, P = 1$ *Punishment* for mutual defection

which obey to the next two fundamental inequations:

$$S < P < R < T$$

and

$$S + T < 2R$$

The first one says that the one shot game is a dilemma, whereas the second is used to favor cooperation in the iterated version.

This game has been found to be a very good way of studying cooperation and evolution of cooperation. A theory of cooperation based upon reciprocity has been set in a wide literature, such as in (Axelrod 1984; Axelrod and Dion 1988; Axelrod and Hamilton 1981).

Experimental studies of the IPD and its strategies need a lot of computation time. Thanks to the progress of computer science and computers, a lot of scientists have studied it as they have been able to use specific methods, like genetic and evolutionary algorithms, see (Axelrod 1987; Bankes 1994; Boyd and Loberbaum 1987; Lindgren 1992; Martino 1995; Nowak and Sigmund 1992; Nowak and Sigmund 1993; Smucker, Stanley, and Ashlock 1994; Yao and Darwen 1994).

As cooperation is a topic of continuing interest for the social, zoological and biological sciences, a lot of works in those different fields have been made on the IPD: (Batali and Kitcher 1994; Bendor 1987; Frean 1994; Godfray 1992; Joshi 1987; May 1987; Molander 1985; Nowak and Sigmund 1990; Pool 1995; Nowak 1990).

In this chapter we study the consequences of the second equality inversion:

$$S + T > 2R$$

For instance we will study the following parameters, which are shown on table 1.1:

$$S = 0 \qquad P = 1 \qquad R = 3 \qquad T = 8$$

This small change on the classical game entails many surprising consequences. It becomes now more interesting to agree with its rival for playing

[C,D] then [D,C] then [C,D] then [D,C] etc. (which gives an average payoff of $(S + T)/2$, 4 points each round for each player) than playing [C,C] then [C,C] then [C,C] etc. (which only gives an average payoff of R, 3 points each round for each player).

It is still a dilemma: due to the first classical inequality that has not been changed, the collective interest contradicts the individual one. To maximize reward needs a subtle agreement.

As for the CIPD it is easy:

- to find cycles (A wins against B, B wins against C, C wins against A);
- to find infinite hierarchical classification (A1 wins against A0, A2 wins against A1, etc.);
- to show that there is no strategy which plays optimally (that is obtains the best possible score) against every other opponent;
- to show that all_d (which always defects) never looses against any other strategy but scores very few points each time (it wins against its opponents but each game its moves costs a lot for it);
- to show that tit_for_tat (which cooperates on the first move and then plays what its opponent played on the previous move) never looses more than T, 8 points, against any other strategy.

With our new parameters the classical game analysis must be revisited. There are now two cooperation levels:

- the basic level (which looks like a *non aggression pact*): to play always [C,C], which gives an average reward of R (3) points by round for each player;
- the upper level (or *meta-cooperation* level): to find a way of agreeing with the opponent to win and loose alternatively, that is to play [C,D] [D,C] then [C,D] then [D,C] etc., which gives an average reward of $(T + S)/2$ (4) points by round for each player.

To have success in meta-cooperation each player must play in *opposite phase* [C,D] then [D,C] then [C,D] then [D,C] etc. which is difficult because it needs some *coordination* and a great risk of loss for the player who plays C first (it could wait reciprocity for a long time !)

Other high-level cooperations are also possible: for example, playing [C,D] [C,D] [D,C] [D,C] [C,D] [C,D] [D,C] [D,C] etc. (periodicity 4). Such meta-cooperations need much more *coordination* and *confidence*.

More complex synchronization schemes are now possible but they are much more difficult to establish and to maintain.

Note that you cannot have any kind of preliminary agreement with your opponent since choices are simultaneous. Other models are possible in which players make their choices alternatively. We do not study these models here (Frean 1994).

The *lift dilemma* does not take into account all the synchronization and meta-cooperation problems, but it is a simple and clean model, and thus allows us to increase our general understanding of cooperation and reciprocity. As we will see, this model is in fact astonishingly more subtle than the CIPD.

Numerous situations with humans or artificial agents can be represented by this game. In particular, every situation where an object is periodically given to the two players, with the possibility that one (and only one) of them takes it, or that no one takes it.

Even if it seems that this new dilemma is very similar to the CIPD, we show that this is not the case and that this game has new surprising properties.

2. Real examples of Iterated Lift Dilemma

Here are some examples of situations which are better described with the Iterated Lift Dilemma than with the IPD.

2.1 Elections with two candidates of the same party

Two members of the same political party X want to be candidate to the next local election. Of course there are also other candidates from other parties. Here are the different possible situations:

- [C,C]. The two candidates of party X take place in the elections but stay fair-play (that is, they will not mutually discredit themselves or trying to injure their respective reputations).
  Chances to be elected are equally shared among them. The party does not loose any votes. The chances of each candidate to be elected are evaluated to 30%.
- [D,D]. The two candidates take place in an aggressive competition which damages their reputations. Their fight scares some electors and the party globally looses votes. Now each candidate has 10% chances to be elected.
- [D,C]. Only one of them is aggressive while the other stays quiet (or even does not really want to win or calls electors to vote for his colleague). Electors are not afraid (amused ?)
  Due to the fact that all votes for the party X are now concentrated on the same candidate. He has now 80% chances to be elected while the kind one does not have any chances to be elected (0%).

In such a case, if there are many elections, it is obvious that the two candidates have to alternatively give way to their colleague (*meta-cooperation*). This is clearly the best global behavior.

Of course in real life, the candidate who gives way to the other hopping to have a feedback takes a great risk (political change, new candidates, defection of the other).

The number of rounds in such a game seems to be rather limited, but the feedback between A and B can already be realized in a different form in future elections, then the total number of rounds can easily increases up to 5 or 10.

2.2 Collaborator's recruitment session

During collaborator's recruitment session (in research centers, universities, or private companies) explicit or implicit agreements between two different teams or sectors against the others are common. They often work in this way: *"This time I will not defend too much my candidate and I will help you to support yours. Next time you will support my future candidate"*.

A round [C,C] is a session where each team kindly defends its candidate, a round [D,D] is a session where the two teams roughly fight for the recruitment of its candidate (with a great risk to see the candidate of a third team be chosen), a round [D,C] is a session where one of the two teams leaves its chances to the other hopping a feedback the next time.

2.3 Sale by auction for art objects

If two collectors are in the same room where the objects they want are presented, it is better for them to agree to buy alternatively the objects, instead of out-bidding mutually which leads to a great global increase of each price. Their agreement is the following one: *"I stay quiet during the auction of this object but please stay quiet for the next one, by this way we will save our money"*.

A round [C,C] is an auction where they try quietly to buy the art object. A round [D,D] is an auction where they wildly out-bid to have the object. A round [D,C] is an auction where one of the two buyers abstain from saying anything hoping a feedback next time.

2.4 The two music amateur neighbors

The music amateur neighbours have also to alternate their listening periods if they want to ear their music in good conditions.

- [C,D]   I can ear my music and I am not disturbed by yours. I obtain a satisfaction of 8 "pleasure points".
- [D,C]   You can ear your music and I can't ear mine. It counts for 0 "pleasure points" for me.
- [D,D]   I am trying to ear my music but I can simultaneously ear yours. I just obtain 1 "pleasure point" but you too !
- [C,C]   We both renounce to listen to music today. This silence counts for 3 "pleasure points".

2.5 The access to an indivisible thing which is periodically available

This case is a generalization of the previous cases.

C   Trying to catch this thing in respect to fairness or non aggression pact.

D   Trying to catch this thing without restraint, defecting any implicit or explicit agreement defining fight rules.

A round [D,C] corresponds then to a case where one of the players submits to the other player's authority. This avoids the fight to degenerate violently.

In the animal world, you can frequently see some fights not really violent taking place between two animals of the same specy, until one of the opponents gives up and shows its defection with a conventional sign. This shows clearly that such a situation is a kind of *Lift Dilemma*.

A round [C,C] corresponds to a fight not really violent (for example between two males which desire the same female). A round [D,D] corresponds to a violent fight which can result in severe wounds.

In animal fight, we can rarely see a meta-cooperation level, but more frequently we see a hierarchical situation with the consequence that the first winner always wins in the following confrontations.

We will see in the studies on homogeneous populations that this situation corresponds to the choice of a *collectively rational* strategy (defined as a strategy which is able to obtain a maximum score against itself even if the rewards are not equally distributed between its representatives).

3. What would a good strategy be ?

Before giving mathematical results and reporting computer experiments, it is interesting to elaborate an *a priori* analysis of the game. The following points have to be quoted:

- As for the CIPD, this game is a non-zero sum game (the total score distributed among the players depends on the actions chosen). Solidarity between the players comes from the game rules. This means that to be successful the players must be able to establish cooperation (or meta-cooperation) to obtain the maximum global score.
- It is a real dilemma: in the Game Theory meaning, the only *Nash* equilibrium (if one of the player changes its position in any way, it will loose points) is a round [D,D]. Of course, the only non-dominated strategy is all_d (which always defects). By construction, the game is more difficult than the CIPD due to the existence of two levels of cooperation and also to the high quality of coordination needed to obtain a maximum global score (that is meta-cooperation).

- There is a kind of paradox in that to reach the meta-cooperation level one of the two players must defect first: by this way there is a risk to scare an anxious opponent which will think that you don't want to cooperate. For example the spiteful strategy (which cooperates while you cooperate and which always defects as soon as you defect once) will never be able to establish *meta-cooperation*. Here, playing D has two significations: (i) refusing to cooperate; (ii) trying to *meta-cooperate*. To avoid this ambiguity must be the aim of all the strategies trying to reach a real success.
- It seems obvious that a good strategy must be able to accept only a first level of cooperation if it cannot establish the second one.
- Reactivity, as in the classical game, seems necessary: you have to adjust yourself by taking into account the rival's reactions.
- A good strategy should also be able to adjust itself to an opponent which plays (CDCDCD) or (CCDDCCDDCCDD) or any other scheme corresponding to an equitable reward's distribution. Taking into account all meta-cooperation schemes seems to be very difficult and needs longer risk periods.
- In an ecological evolution, it is important to play as well as possible against oneself (this problem will be addressed in details later).

About simplicity, graduality, memory, randomness, nothing seems *a priori* obvious.

4. Ecological evolutions in homogeneous environment

In this section we look for strategies which obtain the best possible score in homogeneous environments, that is which are able to collect the best possible score when they play against themselves. Our conclusions are rather surprising.

Definition 4.1. *We call* rational strategy *(resp.: asymptotically rational strategy) a strategy which when it plays against itself obtains the best possible score for every game length n (resp. asymptotically best possible score).*

Let us note $V_n(A)$ the score obtained by a strategy A when it plays against itself during n rounds (when the strategy is probabilistic $V_n(A)$ is the expectation of the A score on n rounds).

By definition, a strategy is said to be *rational* if:

$$\forall n : V_n(A) = \max\{V_n(X); X \text{ is a strategy}\}$$

By definition, a strategy is said *asymptotically rational* if:

$$\lim_{n \to \infty} \left[\frac{V_n(A)}{\max\{V_n(X); X \text{ is a strategy}\}} \right] = 1$$

A rational strategy in an ecological evolution with an homogeneous environment obtains the maximum possible reward. Such a strategy will have a score advantage when it will meet the others (especially in an ecological evolution starting from a sufficiently large amount of copies of itself).

To be efficient when you meet other strategies, the total score does not have to be equally distributed between sister strategies. This is why we will define the notions of *collectively rational* strategies and *asymptotically collectively rational* strategies.

Definition 4.2. *We call* collectively rational *strategy (resp.* asymptotically collectively rational *strategy) a strategy which collects the maximum possible total score for every game length n (resp. asymptotically the best total score) when two copies of itself play together.*

Formally we note $V'_n(A)$ the score obtained by two copies of the strategy A when they play together during n rounds (when the strategy is probabilist $V'_n(A)$ is the expectation of the score on n rounds).

By definition, a strategy is said to be *collectively rational* if:

$$\forall n : V'_n(A) = \max\{V'_n(X); X \text{ is a strategy}\}$$

By definition, a strategy is said *asymptotically collectively rational* if:

$$\lim_{n \to \infty} \left[\frac{V'_n(A)}{\max\{V'_n(X); X \text{ is a strategy}\}} \right] = 1$$

4.1 The CIPD case

In the CIPD (parameters $S = 0$, $P \stackrel{.}{=} 1$, $C = 3$, $T = 5$) rational strategies are exactly those which never defect first (called nice strategies). Indeed to obtain the maximum possible score in a given set each strategy must always play C (round [C,C]) which scores collectively $2R$ (6) points each round (every change in this C sequence will reduce the collective score).

That explains that, in ecological evolutions involving a large variety of strategies, only nice strategies stay alive (if all strategies have nearly the same number of representatives, of course).

Asymptotically rational strategies are those which are able to obtain an average of R (3) points by round when they play against themselves. They can defect sometimes, deterministically or probabilistically, but the defection number must tend from the infinity to 0 (for example, at the round n, defect with the $1/n$ probability).

In the CIPD the *collectively rational* (or *asymptotically collectively rational*) notion does not have any interest because to obtain the best possible score you need to play only [C,C] rounds which assure similar scores, thus *collectively rational* strategies are *rational* and *asymptotically rational* strategies are *collectively asymptotically rational*.

In the Lift Dilemma the situation is different because a strategy will have sometimes to sacrifice for the other. Some *collectively rational* strategies are not *rational*.

4.2 The Lift Dilemma case

In this section we present some mathematical results about the Lift Dilemma:

Theorem 4.1. *If the two following equalities are satisfied: $S < P < R < T$ and $S + T > 2R$, a* deterministic *strategy is* never *rational* nor *asymptotically rational* nor *collectively rational* nor *asymptotically collectively rational.*

Proof. When a *deterministic* strategy plays against itself there is never a round [C,D] or [D,C], thus it will always score R (3) points each round in the best case. We will see that there exist *probabilistic* strategies which score an average of 4 points by round.

We will call *phased round* a round [C,C] or [D,D] , and *unphased round* a round [C,D] or [D,C].

Theorem 4.2. *(Rationality characterization)*
A strategy is rational if and only if:

- *at the first round and while the previous round is not unphased, it plays* C *with a opti $= 0.56696$ probability and* D *with $1 - opti$ probability;*
- *After the first unphased round, it uses a rule such that, for every possible history against itself, the one who played* D *at the first unphased round will play the opposite than the one who played* C *at the first unphased round (thus such a strategy when it plays against itself is deterministic after the first unphased round).*

Proof. The former point will be established later with the justification and computation of the 0.56696 probability, while the latter one is clearly obvious.

4.2.1 First examples. In this section periodic repetitions will be noted with a star. Let us note, for example, the moves (CDDCDDCDD)... as (CDD)*.

Here is the simplest rational strategy called: **reason** (the 0.56696 parameter is explained below).

| **reason** |

- I play C with a 0.56696 probability and D with a 0.43304 probability at the first round and while the previous round is phased;
- then
  - if the first unphased round is [C,D], I play (DC)*
  - if the first unphased round is [D,C], I play (CD)*

The following strategy called **naive-reason** is *collectively rational* but is not *rational*. An homogeneous **naive-reason** population will globally obtain the best possible score for an homogeneous population. Rewards will however not be equally distributed between the entities.

> **naive-reason**
>
> – I play (C : 0.56696; D : 0.43304) at the first round and while the previous round is phased;
> – then
>   – if the first unphased round is [C,D], I play (C)∗
>   – if the first unphased round is [D,C], I play (D)∗

This strategy can be explained by this way: "if at the first disagreement I have been exploited, I consider that I am a looser, and I accept to always be exploited. If at the first disagreement I win, I want to win every time".

Such a rule, used by individuals of the same species could be a mechanism able to create hierarchies. This kind of agreement respects the collective interest even if there is no equality between individuals. This strategy is more simple than the **reason** strategy to obtain collective maximum score. Perhaps we could see here an explanation to the fact that democratical societies appeared more recently than despotic ones.

The following strategies try to improve **reason** by being nicer. The idea is not to annoy easily offended strategies by trying first to cooperate.

> **gentle-reason**
>
> I play like **reason** excepted that the D probability during the first 3 rounds is equal to 0

> **reason-[a,1-a]**
>
> (a is a parameter between 0 and 1)
> I play like **reason** excepted that I play C with probability a when I am waiting for an unphased round.

The two previous strategies are *asymptotically rational* because they only lose few points at the beginning of the game compared to what they can best expect. With a near 1 (for example 9/10) **reason-[a,1-a]**, like **gentle-reason**, will avoid to annoy easily offended strategies.

While similar to **reason**, the following strategy is neither *rational* nor *collectively rational* nor *asymptotically rational* nor *collectively asymptotically rational* because it satisfies itself too easily to obtain an average of 3 points each round. Of course we cannot expect this strategy to be a very good one.

> **coop-reason**
>
> I play all_c (always C) until the first defection of my opponent, then start playing **reason**.

4.2.2 Justification of the 0.56696 parameter. At first sight, the 0.56696 parameter seems strange. We explain here where it comes from. This number is the root of a polynomial equation obtained when trying to minimize the cost of *the period of search of an unphased round* (when the strategy plays randomly C or D) when a strategy plays against itself.

The fastest way to obtain an unphased round in this case is to play C and D with an equal probability of 1/2 (the average number of phased round is then 1).

But with this probability, we lose more points on average in each round than if we play (for example) C with a 3/4 probability and D with one of 1/4 D because [C,C] rounds which give 3 points to each player are more frequent than [D,D] rounds which pay only 1 point.

Thus it is not obvious that the best way to find an unphased round is to play C and D with a 1/2 probability. The mathematical study of this problem shows that the minimal unphased round searching cost is obtained for 0.56696.

The computation of this cost leads to the following equation:

$$-(1 - 2p + 2p^2)(p(R - P) + P - (T + S)/2)/[2p(1 - p)]$$

which gives with our parameters $R = 3$, $P = 1$, $T = 8$, $S = 0$:

$$-(2p - 3)(1 - 2p + 2p^2)/2p(1 - p)$$

We note that the gain obtained by 0.56696 instead of 0.5 is very small (less than 1/10 of a point). Thus for simplicity we can avoid it and make our searching period with a 1/2 probability.

4.2.3 Computation of the parameter 0.56696. Search for an unphased round when two strategies play C with probability p and D with probability $1 - p$.

When we are in the period of search of an unphased round, [D,D] rounds score P points and the rounds [C,C] score R points. Thus during this period, on average we score by round

$$Rp + P(1 - p) = p(R - P) + P$$

Computation of the average length of this period:

length	moves	probability
0	[D,C] or [C,D]	$2p(1 - p)$
1	([D,D] or [C,C]) followed by ([D,C] or [C,D])	$2p(1 - p)(p^2 + (1 - p)^2)$
2	([D,D] or [C,C]) two times followed by ([D,C] or [C,D])	$2p(1 - p)(p^2 + (1 - p)^2)^2$
⋮	⋮	⋮

Thus the expectation of length EL is:

$$\begin{aligned} \text{EL} \quad = \quad & 2p(1 - p)\left[(p^2 + (1 - p)^2) + 2(p^2 + (1 - p)^2)^2\right. \\ & \left. + 3(p^2 + (1 - p)^2)^3 + 4(p^2 + (1 - p)^2)^4 + \cdots\right] \end{aligned}$$

Computation of the sum $X + 2X^2 + 3X^3 + 4X^4 + \cdots$

$$X + 2X^2 + 3X^3 + 4X^4 + \cdots =$$
$$= \; X[1 + 2X + 3X^2 + 4X^3 + \cdots]$$
$$= \; X[1 + X + X^2 + X^3 + \cdots]'$$
$$= \; X\left[\frac{1}{(1-X)}\right]'$$
$$= \; \frac{X}{(1-X)^2}$$

Hence, EL
$$= \frac{2p(1-p)\left(p^2 + (1-p)^2\right)}{[1 - (p^2 + (1-p)^2)]^2}$$
$$= \frac{2p(1-p)\left(p^2 + (1-p)^2\right)}{(2p(1-p))^2}$$
$$= \frac{\left(p^2 + (1-p)^2\right)}{(2p(1-p))}$$
$$= \frac{1 - 2p + 2p^2}{2p(1-p)}$$

The loss L (compared to an immediate unphased round) is:

$$L = \left[\frac{(1 - 2p + 2p^2)}{2p(1-p)}\right]\left[\frac{(T+S)}{2} - [p(R-P) + P]\right]$$
$$= \frac{T+S}{2} - \frac{[p(R-P) + P](1 - 2p + 2p^2)}{2p(1-p)}$$

With our parameters, we obtain:

$$L = \frac{(2p-3)(1 - 2p + 2p^2)}{2p(1-p)}$$

For $p = 0.5$ we find $L = 2$; for $p = 0.7$ we find $L = 2.209$; for $p = 0.9$ we find $L = 5.46$; for $p = 0.4$ we find $L = 2.38$; for $p = 0.6$ we find $L = 1.95$; for $p = 0.55$ we find $L = 1.938$; for $p = 0.65$ we find $L = 2.03$

Minimum loss is obtained for $p = 0.5669640801\ldots$ The cheapest unphased round period searching is obtained when we play C with $p = 0.5669640801\ldots$ probability and D with $1 - p$ probability.

4.2.4 Notes about determinism. We say in theorem 4.2 "for every possible past *against itself*" because it does not matter to play in opposite phase with other strategies when we are looking for *rational* strategies. It is only important for it to play in opposite phase *against itself*.

For example, consider the following strategy:

---

reason-careful

- I play (C : 0.56696; D : 0.43304) at the first round and while the previous round is phased.
- then
  - if the first unphased round is [C,D] I play (DC)* excepted if the opponent has played consecutively 3 D since the first unphased round; in this case I play (D)*
  - if the first unphased round is [D,C] I play (CD)* excepted if the opponent has played consecutively 3 D since the first unphased round; in this case I play (D)*

The excepted actions are never used when the strategy plays against itself and thus it is rational (theorem 2). The following strategy is also a rational one.

---

reason-tit_for_tat

- I play (C : 0.56696; D : 0.43304) at the first round and while the previous round is phased;
- then I play tit_for_tat (I play what my opponent played on the previous move).

There is a generalization of the previous strategy. With a nearly 1 it will be less aggressive at the beginning of the game.

---

reason-[a,1-a]-tit_for_tat

- I play (C : a; D : $1 - a$) at the first round and while the previous round is phased;
- then I play tit_for_tat

4.2.5 Remarks concerning the search of an unphased round. The $a = 0.56696$ parameter has been computed with an homogeneous population hypothesis (all the strategies are identical). Is this value always an optimal one in an heterogeneous population? The answer is no, we now explain why.

In an heterogeneous panel a new factor which favors a value less than 0.5 for a must be taken into account. It is in fact clear that a strategy takes advantage to be the one which defects at the first unphased round, because if the rest of the game lasts an odd number of rounds it will never get back the gain scored at the first unphased round. We can estimate to 4 points this kind of advantage (sometimes it will be played an odd number of rounds thus it will score 8 points, sometimes it will last an even number of rounds thus it will earn 0 points). This is really important in case of short games because the global payoff is small.

Of course no optimal value of the parameter a can be mathematically determined because everything depends of the starting panel. The simulations we have realized by confrontations between various **reason-[a,1-a]** have shown the following results:

- in an ecological evolution with 2 kinds of strategies: $a = 0.5$ wins against $a = 0.567$
- in an ecological competition with 5 kinds of strategies the order is: $a = 0.5$; $a = 0.433$; $a = 0.567$; $a = 0.1$; $a = 0.9$.
- in an ecological competition with 5 kinds of strategies the order is: $a = 0.567$; $a = 0.433$; $a = 0.5$; $a = 0.6$; $a = 0.7$; $a = 0.4$; $a = 0.3$; $a = 0.2$; $a = 0.1$; $a = 0.8$; $a = 0.9$

These results do not allow general conclusions except that choices of a near 0 or 1 are bad choices. Of course these results are very sensible to the random generator and in fact can change according to how experimentations are made (we have made an average of 1000 tournaments).

To obtain a good strategy you can of course watch the behavior of the other player. For example, if your opponent has consecutively defected many times, it is certainly trying to exploit you. In such a case your interest is to search again for a new unphased round. The following strategy is based on this idea with a test of 3 consecutive defections.

`iterated-reason`

- I play (C : 0.56696; D : 0.43304) at the first round and while the previous round is phased.
- then
    - if the first unphased round is [C,D], I play (DC)∗ excepted if my opponent has defected consecutively 3 times; in this case I forget the last phased round and I start again a search of unphased round,
    - if the first unphased round is [D,C], I play (CD)∗ excepted if my opponent has defected consecutively 3 times; in this case I forget the last phased round and I start again a search of unphased round.

4.2.6 Remarks about memory and complexity of strategies. The use of the first unphased round in the formulation of theorem 2 implies that rational strategies keep in memory the first unphased round. Thus rational strategies must not only be probabilistic but must also have a memory (they must remember the number and what they have played at the first unphased round).

To play well against oneself (that is to be rational) implies necessarily a certain level of complexity.

Then to obtain a robust strategy, the complexity of the strategy will be increased. Similar conclusions about the necessity of complexity have already been obtained concerning the CIPD (Beaufils, Delahaye, and Mathieu 1996; Delahaye and Mathieu 1995; Delahaye and Mathieu 1993).

The following experiments confirm the abstract analysis just described about the Lift Dilemma.

5. Practical study of confrontations

5.1 all_d against reason

The reason strategy plays well against itself, but is not reactive (it does not take into account the behavior of the opponent) after the first unphased round. Thus this strategy can be exploited for example by all_d strategy which always defect (D)*. Let us show this result.

all_d against reason gives

$[D,D][D,D]\cdots[D,D][D,C] + [D,D][D,C][D,D][D,C][D,D]\cdots$

After an unphased search period of reason (before the +) which does not take a long time (one round on average), the confrontation continues with the reason exploitation (reason scores an average of 1 point each 2 rounds, while all_d scores 9 points each two rounds).

In a length game of 1000 rounds, globally, all_d against itself scores 1000 points, reason against itself scores 4000, all_d against reason scores 4500 while reason scores 500. See figure 5.1.

5.2 all_d against reason-tit_for_tat

The following experiment shows that the improvement added to reason to obtain reason-tit_for_tat leads to a strategy which now beats all_d. See figure 5.2.

5.3 tit_for_tat against reason

Once again, see (Beaufils, Delahaye, and Mathieu 1996) for previous questions, tit_for_tat reputation have to be reconsidered. In the Lift Dilemma, deterministic strategies cannot be good, and this is the case for tit_for_tat. Nevertheless it is able to favor meta-cooperation with a period of two rounds. In fact it plays well against reason (average of 4 points), unfortunately it is satisfied by 3 points against itself. In an ecological computation it is fatal for it.

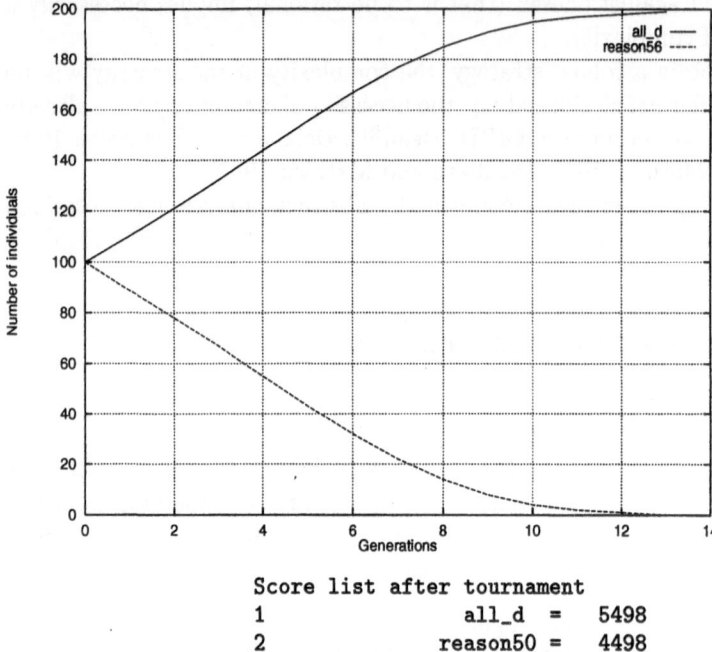

```
Score list after tournament
1              all_d   =   5498
2              reason50 =   4498
```

Fig. 5.1. all_d vs. reason

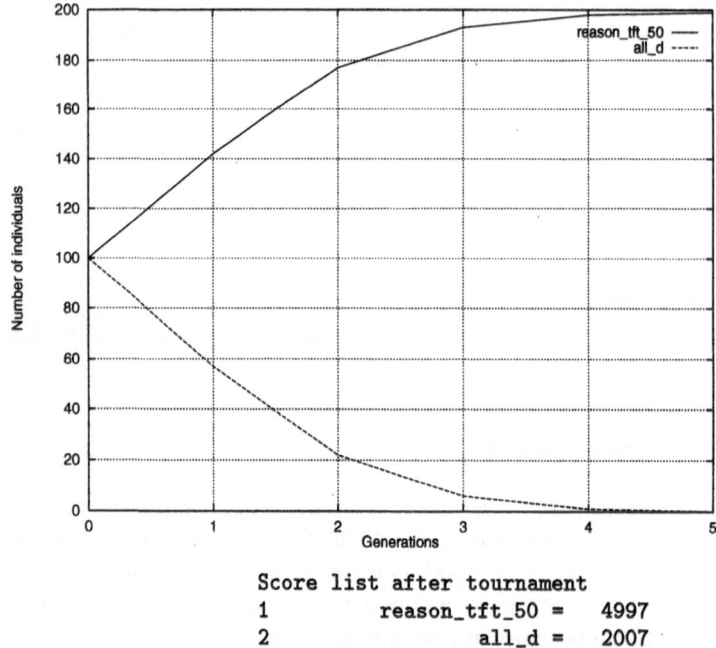

```
Score list after tournament
1         reason_tft_50 =   4997
2               all_d =   2007
```

Fig. 5.2. all_d vs. reason-tit_for_tat

tit_for_tat against reason gives
$$[C,C][C,C]\cdots[C,C][C,D]+[C,D][D,C][C,D][D,C][C,D]\cdots$$

In a length game of 1000 rounds, tit_for_tat against itself scores 3000 points, reason against itself scores 4000 points, tit_for_tat against reason scores 4000 points like reason. See figure 5.3.

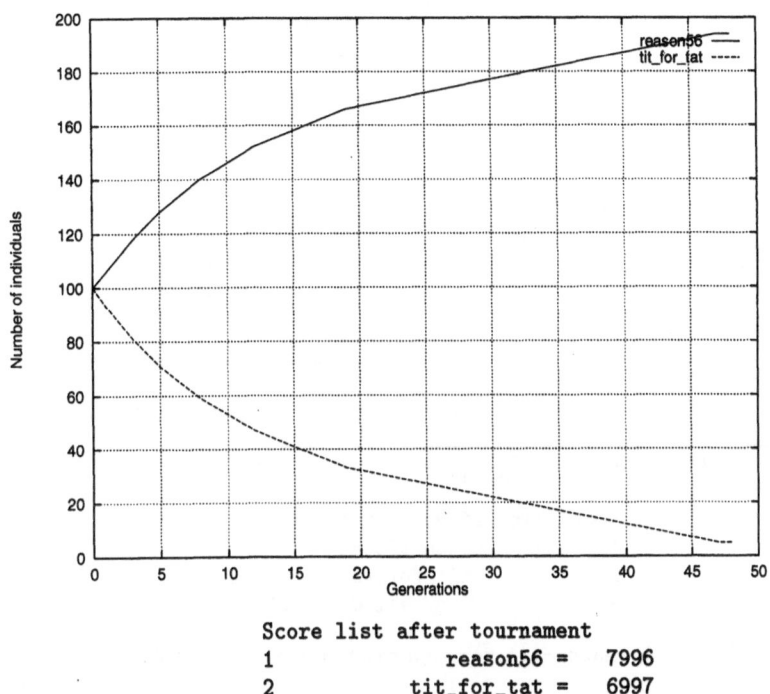

```
Score list after tournament
1              reason56 =     7996
2             tit_for_tat =   6997
```

Fig. 5.3. tit_for_tat vs. reason

5.4 reason-tit_for_tat with tit_for_tat and all_d

– reason-tit_for_tat against tit_for_tat gives :
  $[C,C][C,C]\cdots[C,C][C,D]+[D,C][C,D][D,C]\cdots$ that is an average of 4 points each round.
– reason-tit_for_tat against all_d gives
  $[D,D][D,D]\cdots[D,D][C,D]+[D,D][D,D][D,D][D,D]\cdots$ that is an average of 1 point each round together.
– tit_for_tat against all_d gives $[C,D][D,D][D,D][D,D]\cdots$ that is 1 point each round together in average
– all_d against itself scores 1 point each round
– tit_for_tat against itself scores 3 points each round

– reason-tit_for_tat against itself scores 4 points each round in average.

In an ecological evolution involving these 3 strategies, all_d disappears quickly, then tit_for_tat disappears.

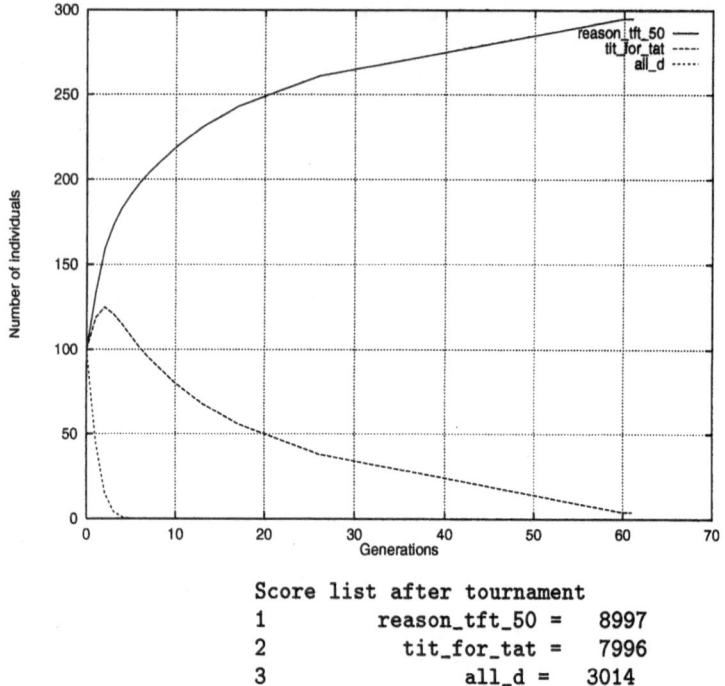

Score list after tournament
```
1          reason_tft_50 =    8997
2            tit_for_tat =    7996
3                  all_d =    3014
```

Fig. 5.4. reason–tit_for_tat, tit_for_tat, and all_d

Note, as shown on figure 5.4, that tit_for_tat until the 5th first generations takes advantage of all_d's population decrease, but it can't do that a long time.

5.5 reason-tit_for_tat against 10 basic strategies

In order to determine if reason-tit_for_tat is a good strategy, let us compare it in an ecological evolution with 10 basic strategies. We first describe the 10 considered strategies:

all_c always cooperates
all_d always defects
ipd_random cooperates with a probability of 0.5
tit_for_tat cooperates on the first move and then plays what its opponent played on the previous move
spiteful cooperates until the opponent defects, then defects all the time

per_ccd plays periodically [cooperate, cooperate, defect]

per_ddc plays periodically [defect, defect, cooperate]

soft_majo plays the opponent's most used move and cooperates in case of equality (first move considered as equality)

mistrust has the same behavior as tit_for_tat but defects on the first move

prober begins by playing [cooperate, defect, defect], then if the opponent cooperates on the second and the third move continues to defect, else plays tit_for_tat

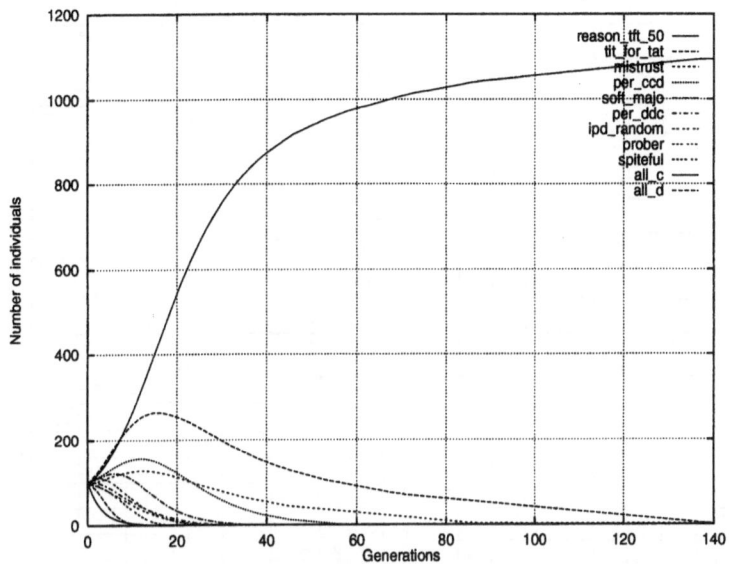

Fig. 5.5. reason-tit_for_tat against 10 basic strategies

As shown on the figure 5.5, during first generations, tit_for_tat beats reason-tit_for_tat, but once again, not for a long time.

6. Parameters sensibility

Graphics on figure 6.1 shows the influence of the T (temptation) parameter in ecological evolutions.

To illustrate this influence let us, in a first time, take 4 basic strategies without **reason** and, in a second time, the same 4 strategies with **reason** added to them.

In each case we change the T parameter from $T = 5$ (CIPD) to $T = 6$, $T = 7$ and finally $T = 8$ (ILD).

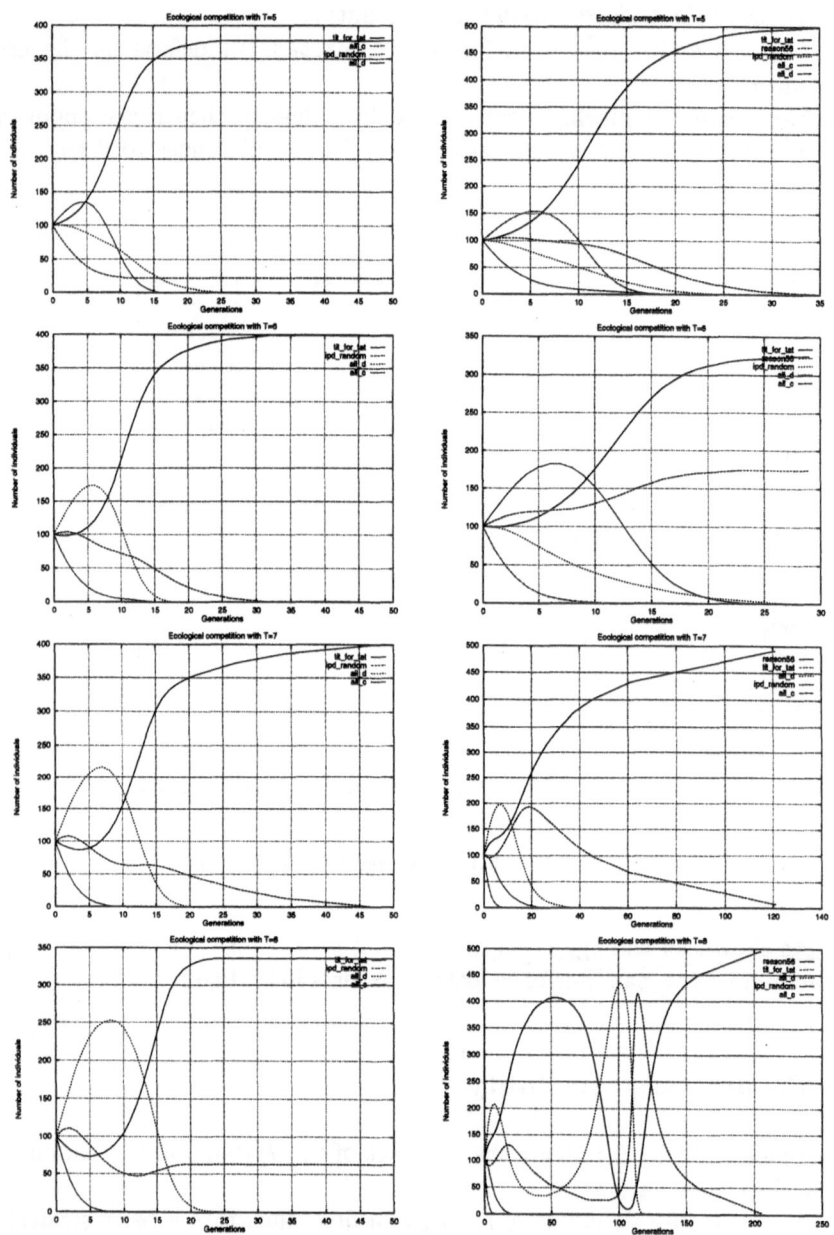

Fig. 6.1. Sensibility to the T parameter

We can see that to be probabilistic is not sufficient to be good in the cases where $2R < S + T$ (see `ipd_random`).

It is also to be quoted that such phenomena could also be seen with the classical Iterated Prisoner's Dilemma.

7. Conclusion

In this chapter we have shown that a very small change in Iterated Prisoner's Dilemma payoff matrix leads to an iterated game which properties are very different than those of the CIPD. Two levels of cooperation are possible in this game. This creates an iterated game much more difficult to analyze than the classical IPD Nevertheless very concrete situations of social life are simulated with it. One of our conclusions, mathematically proved, is that only probabilistic strategies can make a high score when they play against themselves. We have then found interesting characteristics allowing us to define good strategies like `reason` or `reason-tit_for_tat`. Building good strategies for the Lift Dilemma is now much more interesting and complex than for the classical game.

The simulation software we use for the experiments, is already available, with many strategies, for Unix, DOS or Windows computer system architectures on the World Wide Web at `http://www.lifl.fr/IPD` or by anonymous ftp on the following site `ftp.lifl.fr` in `pub/projects/IPD`.

References

Abiteboul, S., R. Hull, and V. Vianu (1995). *Foundations of Databases*. Addison-Wesley.

Abiteboul, S. and V. Vianu (1988). Equivalence and optimization of relational transactions. *Journal of ACM 35*, 130–145.

Adler, M., B. Alvah, R. Weihmayer, and R. Worrest (1989). Conflict-resolution strategies for nonhierarchical distributed agents. In L. Gasser and M. N. Huhns (Eds.), *Distributed Artificial Intelligence*, Volume 2, pp. 139–161. Pitman Publishing.

Assenova, P. and P. Johannesson (1996). First order action logic - an approach for modelling the communication process between agents. In E. V. J. D. F. Dignum and L. H. Weigand (Eds.), *First International Workshop on Communications Modelling - The Language/Action Perspective*. Springer Verlag.

Attardi, G. and M. Simi (1994). Proofs in context. In L. Firbourg and F. Turini (Eds.), *Logic Program Synthesis and Transformation-Meta-Programming in Logic, Proc. of the Fourth International Workshop on Meta-Programming in Logic, META'94*, Volume 883 of *Lecture Notes in Computer Science*. Springer Verlag.

Axelrod, R. (1984). *The Evolution of Cooperation*. New York, USA: Basic Books.

Axelrod, R. (1987). The Evolution of Strategies in the Iterated Prisoner's Dilemma. In L. Davis (Ed.), *Genetic Algorithms and the Simulated Annealing*, Chapter 3, pp. 32–41. London, UK: Pitman.

Axelrod, R. and D. Dion (1988). The Further Evolution of Cooperation. *Science 242*, 1385–1390.

Axelrod, R. and W. D. Hamilton (1981). The Evolution of Cooperation. *Science 211*, 1390–1396.

Bahler, D., C. Dupont, and J. Bowen (1994). Mediating conflict in concurrent engineering with a protocol based on utility. *Concurrent Engineering Research and Applications: Special Issue on Conflict Management in Concurrent Engineering II*(3), 197–208.

Bankes, S. (1994). Exploring the Foundations of Artificial Societies. See Brooks and Maes (1994), pp. 337–342. Artificial Life 4, Cambridge, MA, USA, July 6-8 1994.

Barrouil, C., C. Castel, P. Fabiani, R. Mampey, P. Secchi, and C. Tessier (1998). A perception strategy for a surveillance system. In *ECAI98*, pp. 627–631.

Batali, J. and P. Kitcher (1994). Evolutionary Dynamics of Altruistic Behavior in Optional and Compulsory Versions of the Iterated Prisoner's Dilemma. See Brooks and Maes (1994), pp. 344–348. Artificial Life 4, Cambridge, MA, USA, July 6-8 1994.

Batini, C., M. Lenzerini, and S. B. Navathe (1986). A comparative analysis of methodologies for database schema integration. *ACM Computing Surveys 18*, 323–364.

Beaufils, B., J. Delahaye, and P. Mathieu (1996). Our Meeting with Gradual, A Good Strategy for the Iterated Prisoner's Dilemma. In C. G. Langton and K. Shimohara (Eds.), *Proceedings of the Fifth International Workshop on the Synthesis and Simulation of Living Systems*, Cambridge, MA, USA, pp. 202–209. The MIT Press/Bradford Books. Artificial Life 5, Nara, Japan, May 16-18 1996.

Bell, J. (1995). Changing attitudes. In M. Woolridge and N. Jennings (Eds.), *Intelligent Agents: Theories, Architectures and Languages*. LNAI,Springer.

Bendor, J. (1987). In Good Times and Bad: Reciprocity in an Uncertain World. *American J. of Political Science 31*, 531–558.

Benjamins, R. (1993). *Problem Solving Methods of Diagnosis*. Ph. D. thesis, Universiteit van Amsterdam.

Benthem, J. and J. Bergstra (1995). Logic of transition systems. *Journal of Logic, Language and Information 3*, 247–283.

Berker, I. and D. Brown (1996). Conflicts and negotiations in single function agents. *CERA*. Special Issue on Multi-agent Systems in Concurrent Engineering.

Berry, D., I. Michas, and F. de Rosis (1998). Evaluating Explanations About Drug Prescriptions: effects of varying the nature of information about side effects and its relative position in explanations. *Psychology and Health 13*, 767–784.

Berry, D., I. Michas, M. Forster, and T. Gillie (1997). What Do Patients Want To Know About Their Medicines and What Do Doctors Want To Tell Them?: A Comparative Study. *Psychology and Health 12*, 467–480.

Birkhoff, G. (1940). *Lattice Theory*. ACM.

Biskup, J. and B. Convent (1986). A formal view integration method. In *Proceedings of International Conference on the Management of Data*.

Blanchard, B. and W. Fabrycky (1981). *Industrial and Systems Engineering*. Prentice-Hall.

Boman, M. and al (1997). *Conceptual Modelling*. Prentice Hall.

Bond, A. (1990). Computational model for organizations of cooperating intelligent agents. In *Proceedings of the Conference on Office Information Systems*, Cambridge.

Bowen, J. and D. Bahler (1993). Constraint-based software for concurrent engineering. *IEEE Computer 26*(1), 66–68.

Boyd, R. and J. P. Loberbaum (1987). No Pure Strategy is Evolutionarily Stable in the Repeated Prisoner's Dilemma Game. *Nature 327*, 58–59.

Brazier, F., B. Dunin-Keplicz, J. Treur, and L. Verbrugge (1999). Modelling internal dynamic behaviour of bdi agents. In A. C. . P. Schobbes (Ed.), *Proceedings of the Third International Workshop on Formal Models of Agents, MODELAGE'97*, Lecture Notes in AI. Springer Verlag.

Brazier, F., C. Jonker, and J. Treur (1996). Modelling project coordination in a multi-agent framework. In *Proceedings of the Fifth Workshop on Enabling Technologies: Infrastructure for Collaborative Enterprises, WETICE'96*, I, Los Alamitos, pp. 148–155. IEEE Computer Society Press.

Brazier, F., C. Jonker, and J. Treur (1997). Formalization of a cooperation model based on joint intentions. In J. Mueller, M. Wooldridge, and N. Jennings (Eds.), *Proceedings of the Third International Workshop on Agent Theories, Architectures and Languages, ATAL'96*, Volume 1193 of *Lecture Notes in AI*, pp. 141–155. Springer Verlag.

Brazier, F., B. D. Keplicz, N. Jennings, and J. Treur (1995). Formal specification of mulit-agent systems: a real world case. In V. Lesser (Ed.), *Proc. of the first intern. conf. on Multi-Agent Systems, ICMAS'95*, pp. 25–32. AAAI: MIT Press.

Brazier, F., P. V. Langen, and J. Treur (1995). Modelling conflict management in design: An explicit approach. *Artificial Intelligence for Engineering Design, Analysis and Manufacturing 9*(4), 353–366. Cambridge University Press.

Brazier, F. and J. Treur (1999). Compositional modelling of reflective agents. *IJHCS 50*, 407–431.

Breuker, J. (1994). *A Suite for Problem Types*, Chapter 4 of CommonKADS Library for Expertise Modeling. IOS Press. J. Breuker and W. VandeVelde, eds.

Breuker, J. and W. V. de Velde (1994). *Common-KADS Library for expertise modelling Reusable problem solving components Frontiers n Artificial Intelligence and Applications*. Amsterdam: IOS.Press.

Brooks, R. A. and P. Maes (Eds.) (1994). *Artificial Life IV: Proceedings of the Fourth International Workshop on the Synthesis and Simulation of Living Systems.* Cambridge, MA, USA: A Bradford Book The MIT Press. Artificial Life 4, Cambridge, MA, USA, July 6-8 1994.

Brown, D. (1996). Modelling conflicts between agents in a design context. In *Proc. ECAI'96 Workshop on Modelling Conflicts in AI.*

Brown, D. (1999). Modelling conflicts between agents in a design context. In H. Mueller and R. Dieng (Eds.), *Computational Conflicts: Conflict Modeling as a Primary Design Technique for Distributed Intelligent Systems.* Springer Verlag.

Brown, D. and B. Chandrasekaran (1989). *Design Problem Solving: Knowledge Structures and Control Strategies.* Morgan Kaufmann.

Brown, D., B. Dunskus, and D. Grecu (1994). Using single function agents to investigate negotiation. In *Proc. Workshop on Models of Conflict Management in Cooperative Problem Solving.* AAAI: MIT Press.

Bussmann, S. and H. Müller (1992). A negotiation framework for cooperating agents. In *Proceedings of the CKBS-SIG Conference*, pp. 1–17.

Cañamero, D. (Ed.) (1998). *Emotional and Intelligent: The Tangled Knot of Cognition. Papers from the 1998 AAAI Fall Symposium.* Menlo Park, CA: AAAI Press.

Carbonell, J. (1980). Towards a Process Model of Human Personality Traits. *Artificial Intelligence 15*, 49–74.

Carletta, J., A. Isard, S. Isard, J. Kowtko, G. Doherty Sneddon, and A. Anderson (1997). The Reliability of a Dialogue Structure Coding Scheme. *Computational Linguistics 23*(1), 13–31.

Castelfranchi, C. (1992). No More Cooperation, Please! In search of the social structure of verbal interaction. In A. Ortony, J. Slack, and O. Stock (Eds.), *Communication from an Artificial Intelligence Perspective*, Computer and Systems Sciences. Springer-Verlag.

Castelfranchi, C. (1995a). Guaranties for autonomy in cognitive agent architecture. In N. Jennings and M. Wooldridge (Eds.), *Agent Theories, Architectures, and Languages.* Heidelberg: Springer.

Castelfranchi, C. (1995b). Self-awareness: notes for a computational theory of intrapsychic social interaction. In G. Trautteur (Ed.), *Consiousness: Distincion and Reflection*, pp. 55–80. Bibliopolis.

Castelfranchi, C. (1996a). Conflict ontology. In H. Muller and R. Dieng (Eds.), *Proceedings of ECAI'96 Workshop on Modelling conflicts in AI*, Budapest.

Castelfranchi, C. (1996b). Reasons: Belief support and goal dynamics. *Mathware and Soft Computing* (3).

Castelfranchi, C. (1997). Principles of individual social action. In R. T. R. and G. Hintikka (Eds.), *Contemporary Action Theory.* Kluwer.

Castelfranchi, C. (1999). Conflict ontology. In H. Mueller and R. Dieng (Eds.), *Computational Conflicts: Conflict Modeling as a Primary Design Technique for Distributed Intelligent Systems.* Springer Verlag.

Castelfranchi, C., F. de Rosis, R. Falcone, and S. Pizzutilo (1998). Personality Traits and Social Attitudes in Multi-Agent Cooperation. *Applied Artificial Intelligence 12*(7-8), 649–675.

Castelfranchi, C., R. Falcone, and F. de Rosis (1998). Deceiving in GOLEM: How to Strategically Pilfer Help. In *Proceedings of the Autonomous Agents 98 Workshop on "Deception, Fraud and Trust in Agent Societies".*

Chaudron, L., C. Cossart, N. Maille, and C. Tessier (1997). A purely symbolic model for dynamic scene interpretation. *International Journal on Artificial Intelligence Tools 6*(4), 635–664.

Cholvy, L. (1993). Proving theorems in a multi-source environment. In *IJCAI'93*, Volume 1, Chambéry, France, pp. 66-71.

Chu-Carroll, J. and S. Carberry (1995). Communication for conflict resolution in multi-agent collaborative planning. In *Proceedings of the First International Conference on Multi Agent Systems*, pp. 49-56. AAAI-Press.

Cimatti, A. and L. Serafini (1995). Multi-agent reasoning with belief contexts ii: Elaboration tolerance. In V. Lesser (Ed.), *Proc. of the first intern. conf. on Multi-Agent Systems, ICMAS'95*, pp. 57-64. AAAI: MIT Press.

Clancey, W. (1992). Model construction operators. *Artificial Intelligence 53*, 1-115.

Cohen, P. and H. Levesque (1990). Rational Interaction as the Basis for Communication. In P. Cohen, J. Morgan, and M. Pollack (Eds.), *Intentions in Communication*, Chapter 12, pp. 221-255. MIT Press, Cambridge (Mass.).

Cointe, C. (1997). Guide to manage conflicts in concurrent engineering: A multi-agent architecture. In K. Reger (Ed.), *Proceedings of CEE'97, Building Tomorrow's Virtual Enterprise*, Germany. SCS.

Conklin, J. (1987). Hypertext: an introduction and survey. *IEEE Computer 20*(9), 17-41.

Conry, S., K. Kuwabara, V. Lesser, and R. Meyer (1991). Multistage negotiation for distributed constraint satisfaction. *IEEE Transactions on SMC 21*(6), 1462-1477.

Conte, R. and C. Castelfranchi (1995). *Cognitive and Social Action*. London: UCL Press.

Coombs, C. and G. Avrunin (1988). *The Structure of Conflict*. Lawrence Erlenbaum Assoc..

Corby, O. and R. Dieng (1996). Cokace: A centaur-based environment for commonkads conceptual modelling language. In *Proceedings of ECAI'96*, Budapest, pp. 418-422.

Corby, O. and R. Dieng (1997). A commonkads expertise model web server. In *Proceedings of ISMICK'97, Management of Industrial and Corporate Knowledge*, Compiegne.

de Kleer, J. (1986). An Assumption-Based Truth Maintenance System. *Artificial Intelligence 28*, 127-162.

de Rosis, F. (Ed.) (1999). *UM99 Workshop on Attitude, Personality and Emotions in User-Adapted Interaction, Banff, Canada*.

de Rosis, F., F. Grasso, D. Berry, and T. Gillie (1995). Mediating Hearer's and Speaker's Views in the Generation of Adaptive Explanations. *Expert Systems With Applications 8*(4), 429-443.

de Rosis, F., F. Grasso, C. Castelfranchi, and I. Poggi (1996). Modeling conflict resolution dialogs. *ECAI'96 - Workshop on Conflicts, Budapest*.

Delahaye, J. and P. Mathieu (1993). L'altruisme perfectionné. *Pour La Science (French Edition of Scientific American) 187*, 102-107.

Delahaye, J. and P. Mathieu (1995). Complex Strategies in the Iterated Prisoner's Dilemma. In A. Albert (Ed.), *Chaos and Society*, Volume 29 of *Frontiers in Artificial Intelligence and Applications*, Amsterdam, Netherlands, pp. 283-292. Université du Québec à Hull, Canada: IOS Press/Presses de l'Université du Québec. Chaos & Society 1994, Trois Rivières, Canada, June 1-2 1994.

Descotte, Y. and J. Latombe (1985). Making compromises among antagonist constraints in a planner. *Artificial Intelligence 27*, 183-217.

Deutsch, M. (1973). *The Resolution of Conflict*. New Haven, CT: Yale University Press.

Dieng, R. (1995). Conflict management in knowledge acquistion. *AIEDAM, Special Issue on Conflict Management in Design*, 337-351.

Dieng, R. and S. Hug (1998a). Comparison of "personal ontologies" represented through conceptual graphs. In Prade (Ed.), *Proc. of the 13th European Conference on Artifical Intelligence (ECAI'98*, Brighton, UK, pp. 341–345. Wiley Sons Ltd.

Dieng, R. and S. Hug (1998b). Multikat, a tool for comparing knowledge from multiple experts. In M.-L. Mugnier and M. Chein (Eds.), *Conceptual Structures: Theory, Tools and Application. Proc. of the 6th Int. Conference on Conceptual Structures (ICCS'98)*, pp. 94–108. Springer-Verlag LNAI 1453.

Dignum, F. and H. Weigand (1995). Modelling communication between cooperative systems. In *CAiSE*.

Douglas, R. E., D. Brown, and D. Zenger (1993). A concurrent engineering demonstration and training system for engineers and managers. *International Journal of CADCAM and Computer Graphics 8*(3), 263–301. Special issue on "AI and Computer Graphics".

Dreben, B. and W. D. Goldfarb (1979). *The Decision Problem: Solvable Classes of Quantification Formulas.* Addison-Wesley.

Dunskus, B. V., D. L. Grecu, and D. C. B. snd I. Berker (1995). Using single function agents to investigate conflicts. *AI EDAM: Artificial Intelligence in Engineering Design, Analysis and Manufacturing.* Special Issue: Conflict Management in Design.

Durfee, E. H., V. R. Lesser, and D. D. Corkill (1987). Coherent cooperation among communicating problem solvers. *IEEE Transactions on SMC C-36*(11), 1275–1291.

Easterbrook, S. (1991). Handling conflict between domain descriptions with computer-supported negotiation. *Knowledge Acquisition 3*(3), 255–289.

Easterbrook, S. (1994). Coordinating distributed viewpoints: the anatomy of a consistency check. *Concurrent Engineering Research and Applications: Special Issue on Conflict Management in Concurrent Engineering II*(3), 209–222.

Easterbrook, S. M., E. E. Beck, J. S. Goodlet, L. Plowman, M. Sharples, and C. C. Wood (1993). *A Survey of Empirical Studies of Conflict, CSCW: Cooperation or Conflict?* Springer-Verlag.

Easterbrook(Ed.), S. (1993). *CSCW: Cooperation or Conflict?* Springer, London.

Eggen, J., A. M. Lundteigen, and M. Mehus (1990). Integration of Knowledge from Different Knowledge Acquisition Tools. In B. Wielinga, J. Boose, B. Gaines, G. Schreiber, and M. van Someren (Eds.), *Current Trends in Knowledge Acquisition, Proc. of the 4th European Workshop on Knowledge Acquisition for Knowledge-Based Systems (EKAW-90)*, Amsterdam, Netherlands. IOS Press (Frontiers in Artificial Intelligence and Applications).

Ekenberg, L. and P. Johannesson (1995). Conflictfreeness as a basis for schema integration. In *CISMOD-95*, pp. 1–13. Springer-Verlag.

Ekenberg, L. and P. Johannesson (1996). A formal basis for dynamic schema integration. In *15th International Conference on Conceptual Model-ling ER'96*, pp. 211–226. Lecture Notes in Computer Science.

Elliott, C. and A. Ortony (1992). Point of View: Modeling the Emotions of Others. In *Proceedings of the 14th Annual Meeting of the Cognitive Science Society*, pp. 809–814. Lawrence Erlbaum Associates, Hillsdale, NJ.

Euzenat, J. (1996). Corporate memory through cooperative creation of knowledge bases and hyper-documents. In M. M. B. Gaines and (Ed.), *Proc. of the 11th Banff Workshop on Knowledge Acquisition, Modeling and Management (KAW'98)*, Banff, Canada, pp. 36-1–36-18.

Evrard, F. and N. Maudet (1998). Using implicature to avoid conflicts in dialogue. In *ECAI'98 Workshop "Conflicts among agents: avoid or use them?"*, Brighton, UK.

Faragher-Horwell, R., M. Klein, and D. Zarley (1992). Overview and functional specifications for tcaps task coordination and planning system: A computer-supported workflow management system. Boeing Computer Services Technical Report BCS-G2010-130, The Boeing Company.

Finkelstein, A., J. Kramer, B. Nuseibeh, L. Finkelstein, and M. Goedicke (1992). Viewpoints: a framework for integrating multiple perspectives in system development. *International Journal of Software Engineering and Knowledge Engineering 2*(1), 31–57.

Finkelstein, A. C. W. and H. Fuks (1989). Multi-party specification. In *Proceedings of the 5th IEEE International Workshop on Software Specification and Design*, pp. 185–195. IEEE CS Press.

Finkelstein, A. C. W., M. Goedicke, J. L. Kramer, and C. Niskier (1989). Viewpoint oriented software development: methods and viewpoints in requirements engineering. In *Proceedings of the 2nd Meteor Workshop on Methods for Formal Specifications*. Springer.

Fiorino, H. (1998). *Élaboration de conjectures par des agents coopérants*. Ph. D. thesis, Supaéro, Toulouse, France.

Fiorino, H. and N. Maille (1998). Conflict solving through common belief. In *ECAI'98 Workshop "Conflicts among agents: avoid or use them?"*, Brighton, UK.

Fiorino, H. and C. Tessier (1998). Agent cooperation: a Petri net based model. In *Coop98, Proceedings of the 3rd Intl. Conf. on the Design of Cooperative Systems*, Cannes, France.

Fischer, G., A. Lemke, R. McCall, and A. Morch (1991). Making argumentation serve design. *Journal of Human Computer Interaction 6*(3-4), 393–419.

Foss, C. (1989). Detecting lost users: Empirical studies on browsing hypertext. Report of INRIA N.972, Sophia-Antipolis.

Fox, M. and S. Smith (1984). Isis - a knowledge-based system for factory scheduling. *Expert Systems*.

Frean, M. R. (1994). The Prisoner's Dilemma without Synchrony. *Proc. Royal Society London 257*(B), 75–79.

Gaines, B. R. and M. L. G. Shaw (1989). Comparing the Conceptual Systems of Experts. In N. Sridharan (Ed.), *Proceedings of the 9th IJCAI (IJCAI-89)*, Detroit, Michigan, USA, pp. 633–638. San Mateo, CA : distr. Morgan Kaufmann.

Galliers, J. (1989). A theoretical framework for computer models of cooperative dialogue, acknowledging multi-agent conflict. Technical Report 172, University of Cambridge, Computer Laboratory.

Galliers, J. (1990). The positive role of conflict in cooperative multi-agent systems. In J. Y.Demazeau (Ed.), *Decentralized AI*, pp. 33–49. Elsevier.

Godfray, H. C. J. (1992). The Evolution of Forgiveness. *Nature 355*, 206–207.

Goldstein, I. (1975). Bargaining between goals. In *In Proceedings of the International Joint Conference on Artificial Intelligence*, pp. 175–180.

Grecu, D. and D. Brown (1996). Learning by single function agents during spring design. In J. S. G. . F. Sudweeks (Ed.), *Proc. AI in Design Conference, AID'96*. Kluwer.

Grecu, D. and D. Brown (1998). Dimensions of machine learning in design. *AI EDAM: Artificial Intelligence in Engineering Design, Analysis and Manufacturing*, 117–121. Special issue on Machine Learning in Design.

Grecu, D. and D. Brown (1999). Guiding agent learning in design. In M. M. S. Finger, T. Tomiyama (Ed.), *Knowledge Intensive CAD*, Volume 3. Kluwer Academic Publishers.

Gross, M. (1994). Avoiding conflicts in architectural subsystem layout. *Concurrent Engineering Research and Applications: Special Issue on Conflict Management in Concurrent Engineering II*(3).

Grudin, J. (1994). Groupware and social dynamics: Eight challenges for developers. *Communications of the ACM 37*(1), 93–105.

Hewitt, C. (1986). Offices are open systems. *ACM Transactions on Office Information Systems 4*(3), 271–287.

Hovland, C. and R. Sears (1938). *Experiments on motor conflict- Type of conflict and their moves of resolution.* N.Y.

Jensen, K. (1994). An introduction to the theoretical aspects of coloured Petri nets. In J. de Bakker, W. de Roever, and G. Rozenberg (Eds.), *A Decade of Concurrency*, Volume 803, pp. 230–272. Springer-Verlag.

Johannesson, P. and P. Wohed (1998). Modelling agent communication in a first order logic. *Accounting, Management and Information Technologies 8*, 5–22.

Joshi, N. V. (1987). Evolution of Cooperation by Reciprocation within Structured Demes. *Journal of Genetics 66*(1), 69–84.

Kahle, E. (1990). *Betriebliche Entscheidungen.* München: Oldenbourg-Verlag.

Kannapan, S. and L. Taylor (1994). The interplay of context, process, and conflict in concurrent engineering. *Concurrent Engineering Research and Applications: Special Issue on Conflict Management in Concurrent Engineering II*(3), 183–196.

Karbe, B. and N. Ramsberger (1990). Influence of exception handling on the support of cooperative office work. In S. Gibbs and A. Verrijin-Stuart (Eds.), *In Multi-User Interfaces and Applications*, pp. 355–370. Elsevier Science Publishers.

Katsuno, H. and A. O. Mendelzon (1991). Propositional knowledge base revision and minimal change. *Artificial Intelligence* (52), 263–294.

Katz, M. J. and J. S. Rosenschein (1993). Verifying plans for multiple agents. *Journal of Experimental and Theoretical Artificial Intelligence 5*, 39–56.

Kautz, A. (1987). *A Formal Theory of Plan Recognition.* Ph. D. thesis, University of Rochester.

Khedro, T. and M. Genesereth (1994). Modeling multiagent cooperation as distributed constraint satisfaction problem solving. In *11th ECAI*, pp. 249–253.

Klein, M. (1991a). Supporting conflict resolution in cooperative design systems. *IEEE Systems Man and Cybernetics 21*(6).

Klein, M. (1992). Drcs: An integrated system for capture of designs and their rationale. In *In Proceedings of Second International Conference on Artificial Intelligence in Design*, Pittsburgh, PA.

Klein, M. (1993). Capturing design rationale in concurrent engineering teams. *IEEE Computer.*

Klein, M. (1995a). Conflict management as part of an integrated exception handling approach. *Artificial Intelligence for Engineering Design, Analysis and Manufacturing 9,,* 259–267. Cambridge University Press USA.

Klein, M. (1995b). Integrated coordination in cooperative design. *International Journal of Production Economics Special issue on Integration and Collaboration Systems.*

Klein, M. and A. Baskin (1990). A computational model for conflict resolution in cooperative design systems. In *Proc. Int. Working Conf. on Cooperating Knowledge Based Systems.* Springer.

Klein, M. and S. Lu (1990). Conflict resolution in cooperative design. *International Journal for Artificial Intelligence in Engineering 4*(4), 168–180.

Klein, M. and S. Lu (1991b). Detecting and resolving conflicts among cooperating human and machine-based design agents. *The International Journal For Artificial Intelligence in Engineering*.

Klein, M. and S.-Y. Lu (1989). Conflict resolution in cooperative design. *Artificial Intelligence in Engineering 4*(4), 168–180.

Klein, M. and S.-Y. Lu (1991). Insights into cooperative group design: Experience with the lan designer system. In G. Rzevski and R. A. Adey (Eds.), *Proc. 6th International AI in Engineering Conference*, pp. 143–162. Elsevier.

Kreifelts, T. and F. v. Martial (1990). A negotiation framework for autonomous agents. In *Proceedings of the Second European Workshop on Modeling Autonomous Agents and Multi Agent Worlds*, Paris.

Kuokka, D. and L. Harada (1995). Communication infrastructure for concurrent engineering. *AI EDAM: Artificial Intelligence in Engineering Design, Analysis and Manufacturing*.

Lakatos, I. (1984). *Proofs and refutations*. Cambridge Univ. Press.

Lander, S. (1994). *Distributed Search and Conflict Management Among Reusable Heterogeneous Agents*. Ph. D. thesis, University of Massachusetts Amherst. Computer Science Technical Report 94-32.

Lander, S. and V. Lesser (1988). Negotiation to resolve conflicts among design experts. Technical report, Dept of Computer and Information Science.

Lander, S. and V. Lesser (1991). Customizing distributed search among agents with heterogeneous knowledge. In *Proceedings of the 5th International Symposium on AI Applications in Manufacturing & Robotics*.

Lassez, J.-L., M.-J. Maher, and K. Marriot (1988). *Unification Revisited - Deductive Databases and Logic Programming*. Jack Minker Ed.

Lee, J. (1997). Design rationale systems: Understanding the issues. *IEEE Expert 12*(3), 78–85.

Lee, J. and K. Lai (1991). What's in design rationale? *Human-Computer Interaction 6*(3-4), 251–280.

Lee, R. (1988). Bureaucracies as deontic systems. *ACM Transactions on Office Information Systems 6*(2), 87–108.

Levesque, H. (1984). A logic of implicit and explicit belief. In *Proceedings AAAI-84*.

Lewin, K. (1935). *Dynamic Theory of Personality*. N.Y.

Lindgren, K. (1992). Evolutionary Phenomena in Simple Dynamics. In C. G. Langton, C. Taylor, J. D. Farmer, and S. Rasmussen (Eds.), *Artificial Life II: Proceedings of the Second Interdisciplinary Workshop on the Synthesis and Simulation of Living Systems*, Volume 10 of *Santa Fe Institute Studies in the Sciences of Complexity*, Reading, MA, USA, pp. 295–312. Addisson–Wesley Publishing Company. Artificial Life 2, Santa Fe, USA, February 1990.

Lu, S. (1991). Integrated and cooperative knowledge processing technology for concurrent engineering. In knowledge-based engineering systems research laboratory annual report, University of Illinois.

MacLean, A., R. Young, V. Bellotti, and T. Moran (1991). Questions, options and criteria: Elements of a design rationale for user interfaces. *Journal of Human Computer Interaction: Special Issue on Design Rationale 6*(3-4), 201–250.

Maes, P. and D. Nardi (1988). *Meta-level architectures and reflection*. Elsevier Science Publishers.

Maille, N. (1999). *Les Cubes, un modèle logico-algébrique pour la représentation des connaissances*. Ph. D. thesis, Supaéro. In French.

Marcus, S. and J. McDermott (1989). Salt: A knowledge acquisition language for propose-and-revise systems. *Journal of Artificial Intelligence 39*, 1–37.

Marcus, S., J. Stout, and J. McDermott (1987). Vt: An expert elevator designer. *Artificial Intelligence Magazine 8*(4), 39–58.

Mark, W. and J. Dukes-Schlossberg (1994). Cosmos: A system for supporting engineering negotiation. *Concurrent Engineering Research and Applications: Special Issue on Conflict Management in Concurrent Engineering II*(3), 173–182.

Martino, C. (1995). Emergent Nastiness in Iterated Prisoner's Dilemma Games. 2.725: Design and Automation.

May, R. M. (1987). More Evolution of Cooperation. *Nature 327*, 15–17.

Mazur, D. (1997). Conjecture. *Synthese, an Intl. journal for epistemology, methodology and philosophy of science 111*(2), 197–210.

McCall, R. (1987). Phibis: Procedurally heirarchical issue-based information systems. In *In Proceedings of the Conference on Planning and Design in Architecture*, Boston, MA. ASME.

Meta Software Corporation (1993). *Design/CPN Tutorial for X-Windows*. Cambridge, USA: Meta Software Corporation.

Meyer, J.-J. C. (1988). A different approach to deontic logic: Deontic logic viewed as a variant of dynamic logic. *Notre Dame J. of Formal Logic 29*(1), 109–136.

Mi, P. and W. Scacchi (1991). Modelling articulation work in software engineering processes. In *In Proceedings of the First International Conference on the Software Process*, pp. 188–201. IEEE: IEEE Computer Society Press.

Miceli, M. and C. Castelfranchi (1997). Basic principles of psychic suffering: A preliminary account. *Theory and Psychology 7*, 771–800.

Molander, P. (1985). The Optimal Level of Generosity in a Selfish, Uncertain Environment. *Journal of Conflict Resolution 29*(4), 611–618.

Müller, H. J. (1996). Negotiation principles. In G. M. P. O'Hare and N. R. Jennings (Eds.), *Foundations of Distributed Artificial Intelligence*, pp. 211–229. Wiley Interscience.

Nowak, M. (1990). Stochastic Strategies in the Prisoner's Dilemma. *Theoretical Population Biology 38*, 93–112.

Nowak, M. and K. Sigmund (1990). The Evolution of Stochastic Strategies in the Prisoner's Dilemma. *Acta Applicandæ Mathematicæ 20*, 247–265.

Nowak, M. and K. Sigmund (1992). Tit for tat in heterogeneous populations. *Nature 355*, 250–253.

Nowak, M. and K. Sigmund (1993). A Strategy of Win-Stay, Lose-Shift that Outperforms Tit-for-tat in the Prisoner's Dilemma Game. *Nature 364*, 56–58.

Parsons, S. and N. Jennings (1997). Negotiation through argumentation - a preliminary report. Technical report, Department of Electronic Engineering, Queen Mary and Westfield College, London.

Parsons, S., C. Sierra, and N. Jennings (1998). Agents that reason and negotiate by arguing. *Journal of Logic and Computation 8*(3).

Pawlak, Z. (1984). On conflicts. *Int. Journal of Man-Machine Studies* (21), 127–134.

Perception (1998). Rapport final. Technical Report RF 2/7996.34DCSD-T, Onera-Cert, 2 av. Belin, 31400 Toulouse, France. in French, pages 105–135.

Petrie, C. (1992). A minimalist model for coordination. In *Enterprise Integration Modelling*. MIT Press.

Petrillo, G. (1994). Relazioni Asimmetriche e Strategie di Influenza Sociale: analisi di conversazioni medico-paziente. In F. Orletti (Ed.), *Fra Conversazione e Discorso*, pp. 99–120. La Nuova Italia Scientifica.

Picard, R. (1996). Does HAL Cry Digital Tears?: Emotion and Computers. In D. Stork (Ed.), *HAL's Legacy - 2001's Computer as Dream and Reality*, Chapter 13, pp. 279–303. MIT Press, Cambridge (Mass.).

Pinto and Reiter (1993). Temporal reasoning in logic programming: A case for the situation calculus. In *Tenth International Conference on Logic Progamming, Bucarest.*

Plotkin, G. (1970). *Machine Intelligence 5,* Chapter "A note on inductive generalization". B.Meltzer and D.Michie.

Polat, F., S. Shekar, and H. A. Guvenir (1993). A negotiation platform for cooperating multi-agent systems. *Concurrent Engineering: Research and Applications 1*(3), 179–187.

Pool, R. (1995). Putting Game Theory to the Test. *Science 267,* 1591–1593.

Prevost, S. and E. Churchill (Eds.) (1988). *Proceedings of the First Workshop on Embodied Conversational Characters, Tahoe City, CA.*

Putnam, L. and M. Poole (1987). Conflict and negotiation. In L. Porter (Ed.), *Handbook of Organizational Communication: An Interdisciplinary Perspective,* pp. 549–599. Sage, Beverly Hills.

Ramesha, B. and K. Sengupta (1994). Managing cognitive and mixed-motive conflicts in concurrent engineering. *Concurrent Engineering Research and Applications: Special Issue on Conflict Management in Concurrent Engineering 2*(3), 223–236.

Rao, A. and M. Georgeff (1991). Modeling Rational Agents within a BDI-Architecture. In J. Allen, R. Fikes, and E. Sandewall (Eds.), *Proceedings of the 2nd International Conference on Principles of Knowledge Representation and Reasoning (KR'91),* pp. 473–484. Morgan Kaufmann Publishers, San Francisco, CA.

Rao, A., M. Georgeff, and E. Sonenberg (1992). Social plans: a preliminary report. In E. Y.Demazeau (Ed.), *Decentralized AI-3.* North-Holland.

Reed, C. and D. Long (1997). Collaboration, cooperation and dialogue classification. In *IJCAI'97 workshop on Collaboration, Cooperation and Conflict in Dialogue Systems,* Nagoya, Japan, pp. 73–78.

Reilly, W. and J. Bates (1995). Natural Negotiation for Believable Agents. Technical Report CMU-CS-95-164, Carnegie Mellon University, School of Computer Science.

Reiter, R. (1987). A theory of diagnosis from first principles. *Artificial Intelligence* (32), 57–95.

Ribière, M., N. Matta, and C.Cointe (1998). A proposition for managing project memory in concurrent engineering. In *in International Conference on Computational Intelligence and Multimedia Applications (ICCIMA'98),* Churchill, Australia.

Robinson, W. (1994). Interactive decision support for requirements negotiations. *Concurrent Engineering Research and Applications: Special Issue on Conflict Management in Concurrent Engineering II*(3), 237–251.

Rochowiak, D., J. Rogers, and S. Messimer (1994). Critiquing with multiple criteria:conflict detection and resolution. In M. Klein and S. L. S. (Eds.), *AAAI-94 Workshop on Models of Conflict Management and Cooperative Problem Solving,* Number WS-94-04, pp. 97–106. AAAI-Press.

Ros, C. (1997). Evaluation ergonomique du serveur de connaissances cokace. Report of DESS in Cognitive ergonomics, University of Aix-Marseille-I.

Rosenschein, J. S. and G. Zlotkin (1994). *Rules of encounter. Designing convention for automated negotiation among computers.* Artificial Intelligence. MIT Press.

Russell, S. and R. Norvig (1995). *Artificial Intelligence A Modern Approach.* Prentice Hall.

Sallantin, J., J.-J. Szczeciniarz, M.-S. Barboux, and M. Renaud (1991). Semi-empirical theory: conception and illustration. *Revue d'Intelligence Artificielle 5*(1), 9–67. In French.

Savulescu, J. and R. Momeyer (1997). Should Informed Consent Be Based on Rational Beliefs? *Journal of Medical Ethics 23*, 282–288.

Schlegloff, E. (1988). Pre-Sequences and Indirection: Applying Speech Act Theory to Ordinary Conversations. *Journal of Pragmatics 12*, 55–62.

Schreiber, G., B. Wielinga, W. V. de Velde, and A. Anjewierden (1994). Cml: The commonkads conceptual language. In W. d. V. L.Steels, G. Schreiber (Ed.), *Proceedings of EKAW'94, Lecture Notes in AI*, Number 867, Bonn, pp. 1–25. Springer Verlag.

Shaw, M. and B. Gaines (1989). A methodology for recognizing conflict, correspondence, consensus and contrast in a knowledge acquisition system. *Knowledge Acquisition 1*(4), 341–363.

Shaw, M. and B. Gaines (1994). Knowledge support systems for constructively channeling conflict in group dynamics. In M. Klein and S. Landers (Eds.), *AAAI-94 Workshop on Models of Conflict Management and Cooperative Problem Solving*, Number WS-94-04, pp. 107–116. AAAI-Press.

Shoham, Y. (1993). Agent-Oriented Programming. *Artificial Intelligence 60*(1), 51–92.

Sidner, C. (1994). An Artificial Discourse Language for Collaborative Negotiation. In *Proceedings og the 12th National Conference on Artificial Intelligence (AAAI94)*, pp. 814–819. AAAI press.

Simon, E., J. Kiernan, and C. de Mandreville (1992). Implementing high level active rules on top of a relational dbms. In *International Conference on Very Large Data Base*, pp. 281–290.

Smith, I. (1995). Special issue: Conflict management in design. AI EDAM: Artificial Intelligence in Engineering Design, Analysis and Manufacturing.

Smith, K., H. Karandikar, J. Rinderle, D. Navinchandra, and S. Reddy (1991). Representing and managing constraints for computer-based cooperative product development. In *In Third Annual Symposium on Concurrent Engineering*, pp. 475–490.

Smith, R. (1980). The contract net protocol: High-level communication and control in a distributed problem solver. *IEEE Transactions on Computers C-29*(12), 1104–1113.

Smucker, M. D., E. A. Stanley, and D. Ashlock (1994). Analyzing Social Network Structures in the Iterated Prisoner's Dilemma with Choice and Refusal. RR. CS-TR-94-1259, University of Wisconsin-Madison, Departement of Computer-Sciences.

Sombé, L. (1992). Révision de bases de connaissances. In *Actes des 4èmes Journées Nationales du PRC-IA*, Marseille. Hermès.

Spanoudakis, G. and A. Finkelstein (1991). Reconciliation: Managing interference in software development. In H. Muller and R. Dieng (Eds.), *ECAI'96 Workshop - Modelling Conflicts in AI*.

Stefik, M. (1981). Planning with constraints. *Artificial Intelligence 16*(2), 111–170. (Molgen: Part 1 & 2).

Subrahmanian, E., S. Konda, S. Levy, Y. Reich, A. Westerberg, and I. Monarch (1993). Equations aren't enough: informal modeling in design. *Artificial Intelligence for Engineering Design Analysis and Manufacturing*.

Suchman, L. (1983). Office procedures as practical action: Models of work and system design. *ACM Transactions on Office Information Systems 1*(4), 320–328.

Sussman, G. and G. Steele (1980). Constraints - a language for expressing almost-hierachical descriptions. *Artificial Intelligence 14*, 1–40.

Sycara, K. (1988). Resolving goal conflicts via negotiation. In *Proceedings of the AAAI-88*, Volume 1, pp. 245–250. AAAI: MIT Press.

Sycara, K. (1989). Multiagent compromise via negotiation. In L. Gasser and M. N. Huhns (Eds.), *Distributed Artificial Intelligence*, Volume 2, pp. 119–137. Pitman Publishing.

Sycara, K. (1990). Cooperative negotiation in concurrent engineering design. In *Cooperative Engineering Design*, pp. 269–297. Springer Verlag.

Sycara, K. (1991a). Cooperative negotiation in concurrent engineering design, computer aided cooperative product development. In S. F. D. Sriram, R. Logcher (Ed.), *Proceedings of MIT-JSME workshop*, Cambridge, MA.

Sycara, K. (1991b). Pursuing Persuasive Argumentation. In *AAAI Spring Symposium on Argumentation and Belief, Stanford University*.

Sycara, K. and C. Lewis (1991). Modelling group decision making and negotiation in concurrent product design. *Int. Journal.of Systems Automatisation: Research and Applications* (1), 217–238.

Tennison, J. and N. Shadboldt (1998). Apecks: a tool to support living ontologies. In M. M. B. Gaine and (Ed.), *Proc. of the 11th Banff Workshop on Knowledge Acquisition, Modeling and Management (KAW'98)*, Banff, Canada.

Tessier, C. and L. Chaudron (1996). Constructive difference and disagreement: A suprA-cooperation among agents. *CSCW: The Journal of Collaborative Computing* (5), 323–336.

Thomas, K. (1976). Conflict and conflict management. In D. Dunnette(Ed.) (Ed.), *Handbook of Industrial and Organizational Psychology*, pp. 889–935. Rand Mc Nally Colledge Pubs , Chicago.

Tiwari, S. and H. Franklin (1994). Interactive decision support for requirements negotiations. *Concurrent Engineering Research and Applications: Special Issue on Conflict Management in Concurrent Engineering II*(3), 149–162.

Tjosvold, D. (1997). Cooperative and competitive goal approach to conflict: Accomplishments and challenges. Also in http://www.tetramain.co.uk/coopcon.htm.

Tomiyama, T. (1996). Concurrent engineering: A successful example for engineering design research. In *1st International Engineering Design Debate*, Glasgow.

Tong, C. (1987). Ai in engineering design. *Artificial Intelligence in Engineering* 2(3), 130–166.

van Linder, B., W. van der Hoek, and J. Meyer (1995). How to motivate your agents. In M. W. et al (Ed.), *Intelligent Agents 2: Theories, Architectures and Languages*. LNAI,Springer Verlag.

VanWelkenhuysen, J. (1965). Cooperative design. Technical Report RR-2855, INRIA. Also in http://www.inria.fr/RRRT/RR-2855.html.

VanWelkenhuysen, J. and R. Mizoguchi (1995). Workplace-adapted behaviours: Lessons learned for knowledge reuse. In N. Mars(Ed.) (Ed.), *Towards Very Large Knowledge Bases*, pp. 270–280. IOS Press.

Victor, S. and D. Brown (1994). Designing with negotiation using single function agents. In R. A. A. G. Rzevski and D. W. Russel (Eds.), *Applications of AI in Engineering IX*, pp. 173–179. Computational Mechanics.

Victor, S., D. Brown, J. Bausch, D. Zenger, R. Ludwig, and R. Sisson (1993). Using multiple expert systems with distinct roles in a concurrent engineering system for powder ceramic components. In G. R. J. Pastor and R. Adey (Eds.), *Applications of AI in Engineering VIII. Vol. 1: Design, Methods and Techniques*, pp. 83–96. Elsevier.

Wansing, H. (1996). *Negation: a notion in focus*. Walter de Gruyter.

Watzlawick, P., J. Helmick Beavin, and D. Jackson (1967). *Pragmatics of human communication; a study of interactional patterns, pathologies, and paradoxes*. New York, Norton.

Werkman, K. and M. Barone (1992). Evaluating alternative connection designs through multiagent negotiation. In D. Sriram, R. Logcher, and S. Fukuda (Eds.), *Computer Aided Cooperative Product Development*, Number 492 in Lecture Notes Series, pp. 298–333. Springer Verlag.

Weyrauch, R. (1980). Perspectives for distributed artificial intelligence. *Artificial Intelligence 13*, 133–170.

Wilensky, R. (1983). *Planning And Understanding*. Addison-Wesley.

Winograd, T. (1986). A language/action perspective on the design of cooperative work. In *Proceedings of CSCW '86*.

Wooldridge, M. and N. Jennings (1995). Intelligent agents: Theory and practice. *Knowledge Engineering Review 10*(2), 115–152.

Yakemovic, K. and E. Conklin (1990). Report on a development project use of an issue-based information system. In *CSCW 90 Proceedings*, pp. 105–118.

Yang, Q. (1992). A theory of conflict resolution in planning. *Artifical Intelligence 58*, 361 – 392.

Yao, X. and P. J. Darwen (1994). An Experimental Study of N-Person Iterated Prisoner's Dilemma Game. *Informatica 18*, 435–450.

Zimmermann, H.-J. (1992). *Methoden und Modelle des Operation Research* (second edition ed.). Wiesbaden: Vieweg Verlag.

Zlotkin, G. and J. Rosenschein (1990). Negotiation and conflict resolution in non-cooperative domains. In *In AAAI*, pp. 100–105.

Zlotkin, G. and J. S. Rosenschein (1991). Incomplete information and deception in multi-agent negotiation. In *Proceedings of 12th IJCAI*, pp. 225–231.

List of Contributors

B. BEAUFILS
Laboratoire d'Informatique
Fondamentale de Lille
CNRS
Cité des Sciences et Technologies
de Lille
8022 Villeneuve d'ascq cedex
FRANCE
Email: beaufils@lift.fr
http://www.lifl.fr/~beaufils

I. BERKER
Microsoft Corporation
One Microsoft Way
Redmond, WA 98052
USA
Phone: (425) 882 8080

F.M.T. BRAZIER
Division of Mathematics and
Computer Science
Vrije Universiteit
de Boelelaan 1081a
1081 HV Amsterdam
THE NETHERLANDS
Phone: +31 20 44 47737
Fax: +31 20 44 47653
Email: frances@cs.vu.nl

D.C. BROWN
AI Research Group,
Computer Science Dept.
WPI, Worcester
MA 01609
USA
Phone: (508) 831-5618
Fax: (508) 831-5776
Email: DCB@CS.WPI.EDU
http://www.wpi.edu/~dcb/

C. CASTELFRANCHI
National Research Council
Institute of Psychology
Division of "AI, Cognitive and
Interaction Modelling"
Viale Marx, 15
00137 Roma
ITALY
Phone: +39 06 860 90 518
Fax: +39 06 82 47 37
Email: cris@pscs2.irmkant.rm.cnr.it

L. CHAUDRON
Information Modeling Dept
2 avenue Edouard Belin
31055 Toulouse
FRANCE
Phone: +33 562252655
Email: chaudron@cert.fr

O. CORBY
INRIA (ACACIA)
BP 93
06902 Sophia Antipolis Cedex
FRANCE

G. DAVIES
Department of Information Technology
Mid Sweden University
852 70 Sundsvall
SWEDEN

F. DE ROSIS
Intelligent Interfaces
Department of Informatics
University of Bari
ITALY
Email: derosis@di.uniba.it

P. DELAHAYE
Laboratoire d'Informatique
Fondamentale de Lille
CNRS
Cité des Sciences et Technologies
de Lille
8022 Villeneuve d'ascq cedex
FRANCE
Email: delahaye@lifl.fr
http://www.lifl.fr/~delahaye

R. DIENG
Directeur de Recherche
INRIA – Sophia Antipolis
2004, route des Lucioles
B.P. 93 – 06902 Sophia Antipolis
FRANCE
Phone: +33 49238710
Fax: +33 93657783
Email: Rose.Dieng@sophia.inria.fr

L. EKENBERG
Address DSV: Dept. of Computer
and Systems Sciences, Stockholm
University, Electrum 230,
SE-164 40 Kista, SWEDEN
Address ITE: Dept. of Information
Technology, Mid Sweden
University
SE-851 70 Sundsvall, SWEDEN
Phone : +46 8 16 1679
Email: lovek@dsv.su.se

H. FIORINO
Onera – Cert
Département de Commande des
Systèmes et Dynamique du vol
Unité de Recherche Conduite et
Décision
2, avenue Edouard Belin
BP 4025
31055 Toulouse Cedex 04

Phone: +33 (0)5 62 25 27 83
Fax: +33 (0)5 62 25 25 64
FRANCE
Email: Humbert.Fiorino@cert.fr

F. GRASSO
Department of Computer Science
University of Liverpool
Peach Street
Liverpool L69 7ZF
ENGLAND
Phone: +44 151 794 3706
Fax: +44 151 794 3715
Email: floriana@csc.liv.ac.uk

O. HERZOG
TZI – Center for Computing
Technologies
FB 3 University of Bremen
Universitätsallee 21–23
P.O. Box 33 0440
D-28334 Bremen
Germany
Phone: +49-421-218-7089/7090
Fax: +49-421-218-7196
Email: herzog@informatik.uni-
bremen.de

O. HOLLMANN
Universität Bremen, FB 3 TZI
Postfach 330440
Universitätsallee 21–23
28359 Bremen
GERMANY
Phone: +49-421/218-2234
Fax: +49-421/218-7196
Email: oho@tzi.de
http://www.tzi.de/~oho

P. JOHANNESSON
Department of Computer and
Systems Sciences
Royal Institute of Technology
and Stockholm University
Electrum 230
164 40 KISTA
SWEDEN
Phone: +46 8 16 1671
Email: Pajo@dsv.su.se

M. KLEIN
Center for Coordination Science
Sloan School of Management
Massachusetts Institute
of Technology
One Amherst Street, E40-169
Cambridge MA 02139
USA
Phone: +1 (617) 253-6796
Fax: +1 (617) 253-4424
Email: m_klein@mit.edu
http://ccs.mit.edu/klein/

N. MAILLE
Onera – Cert
FRANCE
Email: Nicolas.Maille@cert.fr

P. MATHIEU
Laboratoire d'Informatique
Fondamentale de Lille
CNRS
Cité des Sciences et Technologies
de Lille
8022 Villeneuve d'ascq cedex
FRANCE
Email: mathieu@lifl.fr
http://www.lifl.fr/~mathieu

N. MATTA
Université de Technologie de Troyes
GSID
12 rue Marie Curie, BP.2060,
10010 Troyes cedex
FRANCE
Phone: +33 3 25 71 58 65
Email: nada.matta@univ.troyes.fr

H. J. MÜLLER (FE14k)
T-Nova Deutsche Telekom
Innovationsgesellschaft mbH
Technologiezentrum Darmstadt
D-64307 Darmstadt
GERMANY
Phone: +49 6151 83 5682
Fax: +49 6151 83 4124
Email: muellerhj@tzd.telekom.de

I. POGGI
Department of Linguistics
University of Roma 3
ITALY
Email: poggi@uniroma3.it

K.C. RANZE
University of Bremen
Center of Computing Technology
Universitätsallee 21–23
Seekamp Studio
P.O. Box 330440
D-28334 Bremen
GERMANY
Phone: +49 421-218-2449
Fax: +49 421-218-7196
Email: krc@tzi.de
http://www.informatik.uni-
bremen.de/~kcr/

C. TESSIER
Systems Control & Flight
Dynamics Department
Control & Decision Research
Group
Onera – Cert
BP 4025
31055 Toulouse Cedex 04
FRANCE
Phone: +33 5 62 25 29 14
Fax: +33 5 62 25 25 64
E-mail: catherine.Tessier@cert.fr
http://www.cert.fr/fr/dcsd/PUB/P
ERCEPTION/cath.html

J. TREUR
Department of Artificial
Intelligence
Faculty of Sciences, Vrije
Universiteit Amsterdam
De Boelelaan 1081a
1081 HV Amsterdam
THE NETHERLANDS
Phone: +31.20.4447763
Fax: +31.20.4447653
Email: treu@cs.vu.nl
http://www.cs.vu.nl/~treur

Index